Praise for *White House Wild Child*

"With verve and vividness, *White House Wild Child* spotlights Alice Roosevelt during her father's presidency from 1901 to 1909. Like a tragedy building to a crisis and cascading to its aftermath, this well-grounded account offers illuminating details even for readers well-acquainted with Theodore Roosevelt's life and times. Shelley Fraser Mickle makes our hearts go out to this exuberant but lost child, Alice Roosevelt."

—Susan M. Stein, author of *On Distant Service*

"Shelley Fraser Mickle chronicles the life of Alice Roosevelt, a lost soul starving for love and recognition and careening from passion to passion to fill the bottomless void within her, while at the same time attracting a devoted following that kept her at the center of the nation's attention throughout her father's presidency and beyond."

—Richard Moskovitz, author of *Lost in the Mirror*

"A fascinating look into the inner workings of a presidential family, with a tragedy at the heart of the story—tragedy shaped the development of this beautiful, willful child's personality, driving her in a constant bid for her father's attention and love. Alice comes across as sensitive, brilliant, often unsure of herself, indulging in her wild antics in order to create havoc in a passive-aggressive bid for her father's love, which she never truly achieves. The story is beautifully researched and told in Fraser Mickle's signature voice—down-to-earth, frank, and often very funny, in a story that is, in the end, terribly sad."

—Sidney Wade, poet, translator, and author of *Deep Gossip*

"Mickle carefully crafts the poignant inner workings of a political family that played an indelible role in American history. *White House Wild Child* reflects the lifelong pain of death, family assistance, love, marriages, divorces—dramas played on the public stages of New York and Washington at the turn of the century."

—Jean Chance, professor emerita, University of Florida
College of Journalism and Communications

White House Wild Child

How Alice Roosevelt Broke All the Rules and Won the Heart of America

Shelley Fraser Mickle

An Imagine Book
Published by Charlesbridge
9 Galen Street
Watertown, MA 02472
(617) 926-0329
www.imaginebooks.net

Library of Congress Cataloging-in-Publication Data
Names: Mickle, Shelley Fraser, author.
Title: White House wild child: how Alice Roosevelt broke all the rules and won the heart of America / by Shelley Fraser Mickle.
Description: Watertown: Charlesbridge Publishing, [2023] | Includes bibliographical references. | Summary: "A biography of American socialite and writer Alice Roosevelt Longworth."—Provided by publisher.
Identifiers: LCCN 2022000883 (print) | LCCN 2022000884 (ebook) | ISBN 9781623545499 (hardcover) | ISBN 9781632899903 (ebook)
Subjects: LCSH: Longworth, Alice Roosevelt, 1884-1980. | Children of presidents—United States—Biography. | Roosevelt, Theodore, 1858-1919—Family. | Politicians' spouses—United States—Biography. | Roosevelt family. | Washington (D.C.)—Biography.
Classification: LCC E757.3 .L585 2023 (print) | LCC E757.3 (ebook) | DDC 973.91092 [B]—dc23/eng/20220112
LC record available at https://lccn.loc.gov/2022000883
LC ebook record available at https://lccn.loc.gov/2022000884

Display type set in Didot by Linotype, Bodoni 72 by Linotype, and Monsieur La Doulaise by Sudtipos
Text type set in Andrade Pro by Dino dos Santos
Printed and bound by Maple Press in York, Pennsylvania
Jacket and photo insert printed by JP Pow in Boston, Massachusetts
Production supervision by Jennifer Most Delaney
Jacket design by Nicole Turner
Interior design by Mira Kennedy

Printed in the United States of America
(hc) 10 9 8 7 6 5 4 3 2 1

For all of us,
in celebration of history's guidance.

"History is a vast early warning system."

—Norman Cousins (1912–1990)

"The use of history is to give value to the present hour and its duty."

—Ralph Waldo Emerson (1803–1882)

Contents

Part III
Paulina and Joanna

A Note to Readers

Dear Readers,

Being a novelist for many years and switching now to writing narrative history, I naturally brought with me a lively curiosity about what goes into the development of character and personality. When I was writing the history of the first successful kidney transplant, published as *Borrowing Life*, the fascinating fact of how many historical figures, as well as characters in novels, suffered from kidney disease captured my attention during the research—one of these being Theodore "T. R." Roosevelt's first wife, Alice Hathaway Lee, mother of his daughter Alice, the subject of this book. Thus began my research and writing.

Drawing on my education in psychiatric social work and as a nursing technician in a hospital ward for emotionally disturbed children, I took on studying the effects of Alice's mother's death coupled with her father's response while she was a child. As indicated in the title, *White House Wild Child*, this book is focused on Alice's childhood. Her adulthood was not lived in the White House, though she always wanted to return through marriage, marrying someone who would take her back.

When I saw that the scenes where she appeared in the political maneuverings of her father's successful presidency would not only give us a look into her personality but also into the art of politics practiced by T. R.—a master and outright genius with sterling character—I thought, Ah! Here is the story that will enlighten us all. The revelations in seeing T. R. and his daughter together, seeing our nation undergoing a thorough bath in trying to cleanse it of corruption, is what has emerged as of significant value in my eyes. The effects of a father on a daughter's development can be seen as a cautionary tale, though one must take in account the Victorian culture that held the reins to a young woman's future.

Discovering the part that racial issues played in T. R.'s presidency was disturbing, especially as they embroiled Alice without her awareness. Simply, seeing how this nation was during her childhood is essential to knowing how in the last years of her life Alice grew to push for a different future. The facts are harsh, but they are essential to a remedy.

Enjoy Alice as tour guide through this fascinating era in America when the nation was emerging from the Civil War, expanding its power across the globe and trying to face its complicated past while a young girl longed for her father's unconditional love.

Shelley Fraser Mickle

Introduction

The young reporter slowly climbed the steps of Alice Roosevelt Longwood's townhouse near Dupont Circle in Washington, DC. It was early afternoon on a bright summer's day in 1979. Alice was ninety-five, the last year of her life. He knocked on the door; the maid answered, and he followed her into the hall. The once-grand townhouse—four stories and twenty rooms—was not in good shape. Old animal skins, left from her father's collection, were tacked to the wall over the staircase. Her father, as president, often called T. R. or Teddy, was such an avid hunter that one of his bear hunts led to Americans calling their beloved toys teddy bears. Alice's oriental carpets worn to streaks of naked thread lay on the hardwood floors. As the maid led the reporter into the sitting room, he saw that the sofas had been clawed by generations of cats. Resting among the sofa cushions was an embroidered denim pillow with the stitched legend: *If you haven't got anything good to say about anyone, come and sit by me.*

Alice was still in her bedroom. It was her custom rarely to get up before two in the afternoon. The maid thumped a gong hanging in a wooden frame, the kind that announced dinner in grand houses many generations ago. A loud clang rang through the house.

A few minutes later Alice appeared, ramrod straight and walking rapidly, despite her nearly century-old bones. She liked to say she'd fought polio as a child and always claimed she did not want to be "labeled a cripple"—an astonishing comment considering how she had often criticized her cousin Franklin's New Deal program by likening it to a case of polio paralyzing the nation. The reporter noted that her "Alice-blue" eyes, so famous they were once mentioned in hundreds of newspapers, were still vibrant. Her hair, white as a china plate and brilliantly arranged, was pulled upward, away from the lace-like wrinkles crisscrossing her face. Though ninety-five years old, she retained the stunning beauty she had inherited from her exquisite mother, as well as the natural air of fierceness from her father.

She gestured to her surroundings. "I used to ring for my servants," she told the reporter. "Now they ring for me." Janey McLaughlin, the maid who had let him in, had worked for Alice for nearly twenty years. Her cook, Harriet, kept the kitchen humming, sending Alice's meals up to her third-floor bedroom in a dumbwaiter. The reporter took notes, aware that the nation still relished the opinion of this woman who had earned political power by who she was and how long she had survived. Being the daughter of one of the presidents whose face is on Mount Rushmore was one distinction, but she was also the cousin of the *other* Roosevelt president, who was so effective and beloved he had been voted into office four times. While she never did completely approve of Franklin and Eleanor, she was one of few living who was related to them and had lived during their time. And the history of her house as a gathering place for power and wit over the decades bore the stamp of another Roosevelt, not as famous as the two presidents but quietly influential in her own way—Theodore's sister Bamie, Alice's "Auntie Bye," who had run the most renowned salon in Washington for many years. The imprint that Teddy and his older sister left on Alice was subtle but detectable, not unlike the presence of a pressed flower in the pages of a book.

Also telling was the silence in her house, signaling that her Roosevelt life has slipped from the crescendo that few of us could have kept up with, much less lived day after day. "What was it like growing up Roosevelt?" the reporter wanted to know. "Something was going on every minute of the day," she told him. She described life at Sagamore Hill, the Long Island home of her father's family from 1885 until Teddy's death in 1919. The family conversations until midnight; the trekking through woods; the picnics; life with her adventurous, energetic father. . . .

But on this day nearly a hundred years later, the reporter was interested in more contemporary thoughts. What did Alice think of the current president, Jimmy Carter? And he had come prepared, with a list of all the things she had said about other presidents and presidential hopefuls, beginning with her skewering of Calvin Coolidge, who, she said, looked like "he'd been weaned on a pickle." Thomas Dewey was "the little man on the wedding cake," an image he never seemed able to erase from voters' minds. Lyndon Johnson was a "rogue elephant" and "Old Slyboots." After LBJ had had his gall bladder removed and lifted his shirt to show off the scar, she quipped, "Thank God it wasn't his prostate." Her cousin Franklin? "Two-thirds mush and one-third Eleanor," she said. Truman seemed incapable of overcoming "that Cincinnati quality, which after wearing it as a persona for so long, it just became him." About Eisenhower, she announced: "You could watch [him] trying to find the right words and arrange them in his head like Scrabble."

Her favorite politician was Bobby Kennedy. She marveled, "There was nothing like the Kennedys since the Bonapartes, and like the Bonapartes, the Kennedys have these extraordinary women. They are all for one and one for all among themselves, which is quite different from our family, who were completely individualistic. What an extraordinary upbringing they had." She admitted she liked to have fun trading insults with Bobby Kennedy, especially teasing him about what her father said about Irish politicians—that they were low, venal, corrupt, unintelligent brutes. He laughed. Robert Kennedy, she added wistfully, "would have been an excellent president. It's sad. Both brothers were first rate."

When Senator Goldwater ran for the 1964 Oval Office, she voted Democrat for the first time. And despite being close to Nixon, spending lots of social time with him, she summed up Watergate as "good unclean fun," adding that "in Ohio they turn out Jerry Fords by the bale." The Roosevelts, she said, were a group of Dutch upstarts who made a couple of bucks. And when the reporter asked where she thought she would fit into the history books, she said thoughtfully, "Perhaps I'll be a footnote."

Finally, she came to Jimmy Carter. "Oh, the one who's always so happy and smiles so much?" she said. "Oh, I couldn't think of giving anyone advice, except to be themselves. Everyone has to learn for himself. Everyone has to do it his or her way."

In 1979, Alice Roosevelt Longworth was a long, long way away from her days as a wild child—in every sense. But a wild child she had been. In her heyday, she could generate more newspaper print than her father, if she cared to. And *this* when her father just happened to be the president of the United States. She tipped off newspapers about where she'd be and what she'd be up to, then pocketed the cash for the info. *Of course* she did it to stick a finger in his eye. *Of course* she did it to get back at him for not loving her the way she needed.

She was born before women could vote, before cars were invented, before electricity lighted homes. She was brilliant before women were allowed to be brilliant. She was beautiful, rich, and privileged. But she was also shy and so learned how to control the media from offstage.

She carried a dagger, a snake, and the Constitution in her purse and became the first woman to drive a car forty-five miles an hour. When her father told her she could not smoke under his roof, she climbed to the top of the White House and smoked there, *on* the roof.

Coming of age when birth control was a matter of rhythm, she said, "Fill what's empty, empty what's full, and scratch where it itches." Which included sex. When she was a teenager, her stepmother, Edith Carow, begged her husband, then the governor of New York, to send his daughter to a boarding school because "she had the habit of running the streets uncontrolled with every boy in town." The wild child straight-out told her father, "If you send me, I will do something that will shame you. I tell you, I will."

But the reasons for her obstinacy were complex. For reasons we will explore, her father refused to call her by her name. Yet, when young women passed her on the street, they stopped and cheered. She was Gloria Steinem before there *was* Gloria Steinem. When she was seventeen, the public was so in love with her, some newspapers said, "She has become one of the most regarded women in the world." Within the first four years of her father's presidency, she became the most photographed woman in the world. Five feet, seven inches tall, she had golden hair and gray-blue eyes that she called "postman color" (after their uniforms), a hue many of the Roosevelts used as Alice did: to help hypnotize listeners. She shared her cousin Franklin's imperious lift of the chin, a gesture that labeled them both *haughty*. When she was photographed she rarely smiled, not wanting to take on the image of her father's cartoon toothy grin.

She wore outrageousness as a badge earned by a wounded and spoiled childhood. In one fifteen-month period, she went to 407 dinners, 350 balls, 300 parties, and 680 teas, and she made 1,706 social calls. She married Nicholas Longworth, the Speaker of the House, and took his name. And when he played around on her, she played around on him. At the age of forty-one, she had a child with another lover, then botched up motherhood and didn't know how to fix it.

After her father's death, she set up a kingdom in Washington, where newcomers to politics went for photo ops hoping she'd not skewer them to light up newspapers. She became known as "the other Washington Monument" and began describing herself as "a combination of Scarlett O'Hara and Whistler's Mother"—an apt comparison, since her father's mother was said to be the model for Margaret Mitchell's beloved bitchy heroine in *Gone with the Wind.*

Over her long life, she was never happy, not as she should have been. She was never loved as she wanted. And over time, she began sending her zingers where they were most needed, shattering social norms as if stomping on glass. When she met Senator Joe McCarthy at a charity event at the height of his Red Scare, he called her by her first name. She told him: "My gardener may call me Alice. The trash man on my block may call me Alice. But you, Senator McCarthy, may call me Mrs. Longworth."

One night, while her African American chauffeur was driving her to a prize fight—her favorite sport—a driver cut in front of her antique Cadillac, causing squealing brakes and a whiplash-inducing halt. The driver of the other car rolled down his window and yelled at Alice's driver. "What do you think you're doin', you"—followed by a racial epithet. Alice rolled down her window and shot back, "He's driving me to my destination, you white son of a bitch." As she aged, she became outspoken about gender discrimination, proudly announcing that she received a letter from a gay liberation group offering to make her their first honorary homosexual. No doubt, she accepted, and in her nineties adopted a famous quote as her own: "I've always been a supporter of people's sexual rights as long they don't do it in the street and frighten the horses."

At the age of eighty, after a double mastectomy, she called herself the only octogenarian in Washington going topless. At eighty-three, she stood by President Johnson as together they unveiled a statue of her father. The president quoted her father's inspiring warning: "Woe to the country where a generation arises which . . . shrinks from doing the rough work of the world." Alice refused the microphone, only later saying about the statue: "I like it enormously. I have a rather mean disposition. I *specialize* in meanness, but I have nothing critical to say about it. I think it is excellent." By then she had attained full peace with her father, at least as he was represented as a statue.

Or had she? In spite of the wildness and the verbal sparkle, there was an essential sadness to Alice throughout her life. Before the days of Freud, before the days of therapeutic lingo sprinkling parents' talk—when no one took their child to a therapist or helicoptered in to make sure needs were met—there was Alice and an American childhood that was catch-as-catch-can. Death from disease was as quick as a fired bullet. Lives changed in a matter of hours. She lived not only with the challenges of a distant father but the challenges of a time when society set rigid rules for women, and woe be to those of the female sex who bucked them.

We know many of her famous quips but little of her inner life or the forces that ate at her in degrees we can barely imagine. This book is an attempt to examine that inner life, formed in her early years, a life that was particularly shaped by the relationship with her famous father. As Toni Morrison asked of every parent: "Does your face light up when your child comes into the room? Because they notice." Alice noticed. And she saw no light. In the days when passive-aggressive was not an everyday term, Alice became a living definition. When the impact of a father upon his daughter was not even of interest, Alice was the embodiment. Her story has much to tell about how a father's crippling grief can affect a child's life. As Shakespeare aptly pointed out, "Everyone can master a grief but he that has it." And certainly Alice could not, even as she tried day after day, year after year, to budge the barricading door of her father's grief.

And then, as if the universe could not resist wanting to go one better, she was sent her own crushing grief when, at the age of seventy-three, she stood at the gravesite of her beloved daughter, who had died from a drug overdose. For five months, Alice dissolved in a quicksand of sorrow from which she eventually retrieved herself, transformed. When she returned to a semblance of ordinary life, she answered a condolence note from her cousin

Eleanor—to whom she had rarely been kind—writing words that would astonish anyone who'd followed Alice's life: "Dear Eleanor, for months . . . whenever I tried to write, I simply crumpled."

Although her barbed wit did not disappear, her heart was different. And it is this change that signals the possibility of radical change within any of us. What Alice did can easily be listed. The *how* and *why* are what these pages seek to unwrap. The hunt for how she changed allows her to dance through these pages, displaying what Faulkner called "the problems of the human heart in conflict with itself."

Late in Alice's life, the writer Lillian Rixey went to her hoping to get Alice's permission to write her biography. Alice, Rixey wrote, "fixed me with a cool compelling blue eye and said, 'Why not do Auntie Bye?'" Who was Auntie Bye? Alice quickly replied, "If Auntie Bye had been a man, *she* would have been president." Yes, the woman Alice knew best, who gave her the only deep experience of unconditional love, who walked in and out of her life as circumstances allowed, played a major role not just in Alice's life but in the life of her own brother, whose career she engineered and whom she advised throughout his presidency.

But Alice's Auntie Bye—Bamie, as she was generally known in the family—extraordinary woman that she was, has more or less evaporated from history. We can see her tracks from when her brother as president began holding cabinet meetings at her house, which became known as "the little White House." Who knew it was this brilliant older sister who would leave so much influence on our current history, like a kite that has lost its tether? And who knew that this brilliant older sister was, in many ways, the rudder to his career? Brilliant, physically challenged, and hypnotic in her influence, Auntie Bye—Bamie Roosevelt—appears here as she appeared in Alice's life, to be awakened from history. To understand why the wild child was so wild, we must understand her family—especially Bamie and the mercurial T. R.

Part I

T. R. and Bamie

"The Aim of My Whole Life Shall Be to Make Her Happy"

Tuesday, February 13, 1884. The weather was abysmal. The *New York Times* said it was "suicide weather." Fog and rain covered most of the northeast United States. Trains were backed up. Rivers overflowed. Boat traffic crawled. Theodore Roosevelt Jr.—"T. R."—was at the New York Assembly in Albany during a legislative session. Married for three years, his adored wife, Alice Hathaway Lee, had become pregnant only after gynecological surgery allowed her and T. R. to begin the large family they planned. And now, for two days, she had been in labor. He knew the household was in a hubbub because Alice had written him earlier. His mother was ill, but they all thought it was just a cold.

He and Alice had rented a house at 55 West Forty-Fifth Street in New York, but as Alice got close to her due date, they moved nearby into T. R.'s mother's house, the grand home built two blocks from Central Park. There, Alice was surrounded by relatives. Her own mother had arrived on Monday, the eleventh, to help with the birth, so T. R. knew Alice was being well taken care of.

Early that foggy morning, T. R. received a telegram from his sister Bamie telling him that at 8:30 the night before, Alice gave birth to an eight-pound, twelve-ounce baby girl. Although the telegram added that Alice was "only fairly well," T. R. felt no real alarm. And since he wanted to hear the vote on one of his bills, he planned to wait for the result and then take the five-hour train ride home. Exuding joy, he rushed around the Capitol, broadcasting his news. That his child was born on Lincoln's birthday made it much more fun to share. He basked in the congratulations from his fellow legislators, savoring the admiration he had won from them over the past two years.

But that afternoon, Bamie sent a second telegram: *Alice has taken a turn for the worst.*

What the first telegram hadn't said was that Alice was unwell soon after she had gone into labor. During her pregnancy, no one suspected anything amiss. Only once, Theodore's mother commented that Alice Hathaway Lee looked "very large." If T. R. himself noticed that "puffy look about her eyes and badly swollen ankles, he did not allow it to worry him." No one considered Alice's "largeness" a sign of fluid retention from nephritis—kidney disease. But during labor, the doctor diagnosed her with Bright's disease. And now, after the baby's delivery, the fatal disease was on full display. Her first comment at the birth of her daughter was "I love a little girl," and she asked to hold her, but the doctor was alarmed at her condition—her kidneys had failed and her vital organs had begun to shut down. As the baby was being swaddled in warm flannel, Alice heard the infant sneeze. She cried out, "Oh, don't let my baby take cold," then quickly slipped into delirium from uremic poisoning.

After T. R. read the second telegram, he rushed to the train. During the five-hour train ride, delayed even more by the hellish fog, his mind, no doubt, kept asking *what might be happening . . . what might not . . . what he could . . . couldn't do.* With these desperate hours of longing to control the outcome, he was likely doing what most of us would: bargaining with the universe.

Marrying Alice Hathaway Lee had not been easy. Arousing her love had been the most passionate goal he had ever undertaken. He was nineteen years old when he first saw her; she was only seventeen. They were both in the midst of becoming who they eventually would be, prone to changing moods, the influence of others, and above all, their biological drive to be loved.

Young T. R. was like an exotic recipe, one for which you had to acquire a taste. He was a compulsive talker, rushing to get words out that were always a step behind the rhythm of his mind. And he tended to be overenthusiastic about everything—in particular bugs and plants. He wasn't tall. He was slight and muscular, but there simply wasn't much of him—he was five feet, eight inches tall and not even 150 pounds. He was barely taller than Alice Hathaway Lee. His face was dominated by bottle-thick glasses that could get him teased as "four-eyes," and when he was in the Dakotas, indulging his love for the West, many cowboys associated spectacles with moral decay. Yet, he could not live the life he wanted without them and explained that as a boy he was "under a hopeless disadvantage in studying nature. I was very near-sighted, so that the only things I could study were those I ran against or stumbled over. When I was about thirteen, I was allowed to take lessons in taxidermy [from] a companion of Audubon. It was this summer that I got my first gun, and it puzzled me . . . that my companions seemed to see things to shoot which I could not see at all. One day they read an advertisement in huge letters . . . and . . . I could not even see the letters. I had no idea how beautiful the world was until I got spectacles."

Even before he could see the world and recognize its splendor, he spent every day living as if devouring a delicious meal while letting it dribble down his chin. Few could keep up with him. Even his mother, whom he called "sweet Motherling," took to her bed in exhaustion from keeping up with her eldest son, whom she called "my little berserker." Her three other energetic children had also inherited their father's vigor for life. Hiking, studying, touring the Nile in a dahabieh, reading voraciously, the family in which T. R. was raised was extraordinary, forging him by nature and household culture, the likes of which have rarely been documented. It was said that T. R. often read three books a day and even years later could recall in detail what he had read.

Now in his third term as a legislator, everyone agreed that the change in him had been extraordinary. He knew more about state politics than nine out of ten assembly members. A fellow legislator remarked that in his first term, "he would leave Albany Friday afternoon . . . come back Monday night and you would see changes that had taken place." Yet he was aware of his weaknesses. After he firmly decided that politics would be his career, he had admitted to his mother, "I do not speak enough from the chest. . . . My voice is not as powerful as it ought to be."

Many thought he had a speech defect of some "odd kind." He would lean over his desk in the assembly, yelling, his voice going from a tenor to a falsetto "Mr. Spee-kar! Mr. Spee-kar!" Since he was a member of the Republican Party because his father had been, following the party's platform from the days of Lincoln, Democrat newspapers considered him fair game. Some described him as a "jane-dandy," a "weakling," "silly," and a "wild little man." He wore a silk top hat, full evening dress, a pince-nez, and English side-whiskers known as "dundrearies." With a mouthful of teeth, flashing in frequent smiles, he kept popping up in the assembly every few minutes to interrupt meetings to ask questions. Newspapers printed that "his trousers were cut so tight that when making his 'gyrations' before an audience he only bent from the joints above the belt." Yet "you could see that here was an uncommon fellow, distinctly different. . . . He worked hard. . . . He saw everything and formed an opinion on everything."

His love for his father influenced everything he did. Theodore Sr., a great bear of a man with a full beard, a lion-like head, and kindness radiating from his deep-set eyes, was nicknamed Greatheart by his family. He wore spectacles but never had a photograph taken with them on, and always had a yellow rose in his buttonhole. His ebullient personality was like overflowing paint, spilling out a highly colored blaze of enthusiasm for everyone he met and for every idea that would benefit humankind. He was the son of one of the wealthiest men in New York, Cornelius Roosevelt, and when younger worked for his father in the business that made their fortune, supplying plate glass in the early days of America's building boom. When he discovered he loved children above everything else, Greatheart found his calling in philanthropy and dedicated his life to serving his community, helping found the Museum of Natural History, the Metropolitan Museum of Art, the Children's Aid Society, and the Newsboys' Lodging House to help New York's homeless.

T. R. said, "I never knew anyone who got a greater joy out of living." But he died at forty-six from stomach cancer. A junior at Harvard, T. R. was unable to make it home in time to be with his father during his last moments, which spawned a gnawing guilt. He collapsed under this first devastating blow, his first acquaintance with searing grief. In his diary five days after Greatheart's death, he wrote: "I feel that if it were not for the certainty that . . . he is not dead but gone before, I should almost perish." A month later, he wrote that whenever he thought of his father's death, it seemed his heart would break, adding that his father "shared all my joys and in sharing, doubled them, and soothed all the few sorrows I ever had." He also wrote to Bamie, "My own sweet sister, you will have to give me a great deal of advice and assistance, now that our dear father is gone, for in many ways, you are more like him than any of the rest of the family."

Clearly Greatheart's death opened a chasm in T. R.'s life that he was longing to fill, as well as pushing him to do something equal to his father's legacy. Later he wrote a portentous diary entry: "No one but my wife, if ever I marry, will ever be able to take his place."

Nine months later, he met Alice.

When Alice Hathaway Lee first saw young T. R., she was an innocent seventeen-year-old. She had not even had her debut, her "coming out," when a young Victorian girl was signaled to be marriageable. Likely, Alice was overwhelmed by T. R.'s thirst for life. He certainly took some getting used to. A friend introduced him to her on October 18, 1879, at her family's home in Chestnut Hill, six miles outside of Boston. T. R. was in his third year at Harvard, and from that moment he was struck helpless.

He even admitted, despite his reluctance to own up to any vulnerability, that he was simply knocked crazy in love with no hope of recovery. Among all the gifts he inherited from his family, both through genetics and privilege, was a magnificent ability to love. Not just to love as a passing fancy but to love deeply, steadfastly. In his lust for life in all its varieties, he was not inclined to consider that a depth of feeling, while enriching, also held the devastating danger of loss. He knew only that after meeting Alice Hathaway Lee, he would never be the same. "See that girl?" he exclaimed to a friend. "I am going to marry her. She won't have me, but I am going to have her." And since it was less than a year after Greatheart's death, the yawning hole in his universe was in need of something to ease his grief. New love was the perfect elixir.

Honey-blonde, fetchingly beautiful, coquettish Alice Hathaway Lee was so cheerful, she sported the nickname "Sunshine." Born in July, the first year of the Civil War, she excelled at archery and tennis—clearly athletic enough to keep up with T. R. In short, she was the total package of what we call *lovely*. And she was also privileged and protected, the second of six children, the daughter of a wealthy banker who thought she was too young to marry, too young to know her own mind. In days when young men and women were not allowed to be alone together, she and T. R., in the presence of a chaperone, displayed enough sidelong looks and honeyed conversations to broadcast that they were up to something. Or at least T. R. was. During a walk with others, they would slip off far enough to manage private moments.

The Victorian etiquette they had to follow set the tone: when first introduced, T. R. had presented a card and lifted his hat, using the hand farthest from her. In return, Alice had not been allowed to take his hand or offer hers but likely only smiled coquettishly. T. R.'s visits had to be always between 2:00 and 4:00 in the winter and 2:00 and 5:00 in summer. If he were on horseback, he had to dismount before talking to her, for it was impolite to force a lady to look up to converse. In any company, Alice was required never to indulge in a long argument, speak of religion, or interrupt a person speaking. She did not gossip or whisper. Instead of jewelry she wore flowers to a ball, although pearls were always acceptable. Dinner started with soup, and she was never to have more than three glasses of wine, although married ladies could have five or six. Morning dress worn in the evening was vulgar. Gloves signaled everything for both men and women—always to be worn out on the street, made only of kid or calfskin. Any other glove was seen as uncouth. These prescribed behaviors immediately signaled class status, and woe be to any who tinkered with them.

Alice's father was concerned that T. R. had no prospects to support her, which seemed odd since everyone knew the Roosevelts were one of the wealthiest families in old New York. His Dutch family had cashed in on the early development of New York City, and he had an annual trust income of $8,000 a year, $3,000 more than the salary of the Harvard president. But T. R. came off as unfocused. He was suspected of having no real purpose, and had turned twenty only a few weeks after meeting Alice Lee. Yet it was clear to everyone that he was unfocused on anything other than Alice Lee.

His senior year at Harvard, he bought a dog cart and a horse named Lightfoot to quickly cover the six miles from Harvard to Alice Hathaway Lee's home in Chestnut Hill. He enhanced his wardrobe with dandy clothes. Prior to his first year at Harvard, Bamie had traveled to Cambridge, concerned that her adored brother would not be free of his frightening asthma attacks in a dormitory. She set him up in an apartment near the campus, had it scoured of dust, decorated, and outfitted with linens—all the necessities of good living. She loved every minute of doing these things for her beloved brother. After he met Alice, she watched this budding romance with intense focus, ready to jump in to help in any way. Bossiness and management were Bamie's specialties.

As T. R.'s courtship of Alice Hathaway Lee took over his every minute and thought, he wrote in his diary: "The aim of my whole life shall be to make her happy, and to shield her and guard her from every trial."

Two

"I Have Been Pretty Nearly Crazy"

A **BRILLIANT STUDENT,** T. R. had already drafted the first two chapters of *The Naval War of 1812*, which would be published after his graduation from Harvard. But after meeting Alice Lee, he set all that aside to concentrate on winning her. Besides, he had already decided not to go after high marks in his studies. He would be satisfied with what was called "a gentleman's C." Most of all, he'd accomplished being liked. Good-natured and fun, he never complained, even when he was not feeling well.

He still suffered from asthma. His childhood battles with the condition were among his first memories, the times his father would gently hold him in his arms, walking the floor all night as young T. R. gasped for breath. Or when Greatheart held him in the family carriage as they rode through the streets of New York, hoping the night air would end the attack. Those times gasping for breath, thinking he would never again breathe without a struggle, taught him that life was a battle. It set his nervous disposition into high gear, always fearing when breath would be taken away.

Fear was a theme of his childhood and his life. He read books about "grizzly bears, mean horses, [and] gun-fighters," hoping to understand how to deal with fear. One day, he read a passage where a warship captain explained to the hero of the story how to become fearless. The idea was to get a grip on himself so as to act as if he were *not* afraid, and therefore to go into action. "After this is kept up long enough, it changes from pretense to reality, and the man does in very fact become fearless by sheer dint of practicing fearlessness when he does not feel it." With that same hope for fearless determination to always pull in enough air to last, T. R. aimed his forces at winning sunny Alice.

His childhood friend Edith Wharton remarked—after T. R. had become who he was in history and she a famous novelist—that he was "so alive at all points and so gifted with the rare faculty of living intensely and entirely in every moment as it passed." He was irresistible and also dangerous. Eventually he would be described as a "locomotive in pants." Living with him would require patience, tolerance, and great energy. As for himself, channeling his intensity would require an iron self-discipline, which eventually he developed.

T. R. had the magical mix of charisma. In early childhood, he reveled in Greatheart's directing him and his three siblings in their homemade theatrical productions, rehearsing for hours. At the dinner table, while plates were being cleared by servants, Greatheart often asked each child to stand up and give an impromptu speech. A family friend said, "These Roosevelts were without inhibitions to an unusual degree." Their gaiety was "unquenchable . . . touched by the flame of the 'divine fire' . . . lovers of books and poetry . . . investing everything they did with their own 'extraordinary vitality.'"

T. R.'s willingness to accept change became his most valued trait, leavening his brilliance. Soon after he entered Harvard with his intention to become a scientist in natural studies, he let go of that dream. Finding his professors more focused on theory, doing indoor laboratory study rather than field studies, he realized that would not be him—no small change considering he had thought of himself as a scientist all during his boyhood after falling obsessively in love with the natural world.

If fear was part of his childhood, so was intellectual curiosity. Teedie, as his family called him, became obsessed with pets, collecting all sorts of living things in his study of biology, which seriously tested his family's patience—such as the night at dinner when a Dutch cheese was passed to Greatheart and a live mouse leapt out. Or the day he was on a streetcar and politely tipped his hat to one of his mother's friends, and frogs landed at her feet. His brother Elliott, three years younger, threatened to give up sharing a room, citing the unbearable stench of the critters Teedie was preserving. The final blow came the night Teedie's collection of snakes passed the line that Elliott had drawn between their beds.

At thirteen, T. R. got his first gun and glasses and began tramping through marshes and woods as an amateur ornithologist to collect specimens. He took lessons in taxidermy from a white-haired old gentleman who had been a companion of Audubon. It was then that he experienced knowing *that's* who he would be. Becoming a scientist in the vein of Audubon would also give him an excuse for often smelling to high heaven from the critters preserved in jars all over his room. In the self-deprecating humor he developed, he described himself as "grubby." But being a scientist was not all he envisioned for himself, and while at Harvard he began his parallel dream of becoming a man of letters and writing significant contributions to American literature.

After meeting Alice Lee, all that changed.

To win her, he began working on himself, always working on himself. He taught Sunday school, refused to smoke, and refused to tolerate "low humor." And since her cousin Richard Saltonstall kept bringing T. R. to the Lees' home, she couldn't avoid him. As soon as he came in, he would throw himself into a chair and launch into stories about wolves and bears that at least enthralled Alice Lee's five-year-old brother.

He looked for ways to impress her. At Harvard, he had joined the boxing team. As a teen he had been harassed by bullies, and he vowed never again to be put in such a helpless position. He started to learn to box, and when his father saw how slow and awkward he was, he brought in an ex-prizefighter to teach him. Despite his health issues and poor eyesight, T. R. developed a powerful right punch which, by the time he was at Harvard, got him into the finals of the college lightweight boxing class. Since he was in the midst of trying to win Alice Lee, he insisted she be there. Sitting in the gymnasium balcony, she watched, a bit repelled but also intrigued. When the referee called "Time," T. R. dropped his hands, and his opponent whacked him a savage blow, bloodying his nose. The spectators cried "Foul!, Foul!," and hissed, but young T. R. cried out, "Hush! He didn't hear." His good sportsmanship and stalwart character won the admiration of the spectators, surely impressing Alice Lee.

Not enough, however, to win her completely.

Whenever she discouraged him, he sank into a deep gloom. He had always suffered from slights that plunged him into feeling that everything was black. But equal to his brooding nature was his persistence. And he was sure she would eventually give in. In a groundbreaking moment, he escorted her across Harvard Yard, giving her a tour of where he spent his life, and, of course, showing her off. At lunchtime, he took her to the Porcellian, the posh club he had been invited to join, which did not allow women. Perhaps the fact he was breaking a tradition did not occur to him; perhaps he meant to break it.

He had unusual regard for the intellect of women, extraordinary in an age when their names appeared in the newspaper only at marriage and death. Growing up with his older sister, Bamie, he was naturally well aware of and respected *her* brilliance. Compared to Bamie, his inner strength was squishy; he was more nervous, more quaking. Bamie was strength personified. She had the family's intellect and will but as a Victorian woman was not allowed its full expression. And T. R. knew it. As an undergraduate, he was writing a thesis on women's rights titled "The Practicability of Equalizing Men and Women before the Law." He even argued that women should keep their birth names upon marrying.

He brought this respect of women to his pursuit of Alice Hathaway Lee. Everything he said and did reflected his adoration of her, his physical desire for her. He could not help but push her to marry him. The lifespans of their time also could have played into their sense of urgency. Men expected to live only forty years; women, forty-eight. And since Greatheart had been only forty-six when he died, young T. R. already carried a scorching lesson in the fragility of life.

So six months after he met her, he proposed. And she turned him down.

Distraught, he wandered night after night through the woods. "I have been pretty nearly crazy," he admitted. In his despair he turned to Bamie, who everyone agreed was most like Greatheart. And since T. R. was the center of Bamie's universe, she welcomed his leaning on her. Besides, she liked nothing better than taking over everything for everyone. She immediately went into action to secure what he most wanted.

Bamie surmised that since it seemed Alice's father was concerned not only that Alice was too young to marry but also that T. R. had no declared profession, she wrote Mr. Lee, saying that upon her brother's marriage to Alice, the couple could live with her in the Roosevelt house that their father had built on the south side of Fifty-Seventh Street, just west of Fifth Avenue and two blocks from Central Park. That was the posh part of town, and the house was one of the grandest in New York. The location, and Bamie herself, would provide stability and social prominence, a fact that would not have been lost on the Lees.

The house was extravagant, with tremendous mirrors, tasseled chandeliers, walls of books behind glass, carved sliding doors, paneling and tiled fireplaces, huge urns, polished silver, and Persian rugs. It had live-in servants; Alice Lee would be well looked after, safe, and secure. Bamie continued to manage the house after their father died, living there with her mother, her younger brother and sister until they married, and any other relatives visiting. The house had been designed by the prominent New York architect Russell Sturgis, with custom-made furniture built in Philadelphia by Frank Furness.

Winning Alice Lee needed more than an act of passion. It had also required this calculated strategy, the first of many Bamie engineered on behalf of her brother. And it worked. Finally, on January 25, 1880, Alice submitted. On the day that she finally accepted T. R.'s proposal, he gushed in his diary: "I am so happy that I dare not trust my own happiness. . . . How she, so pure and sweet and beautiful can think of marrying me I can not understand, but I praise and thank God it is so. Thank heaven I am absolutely pure. I can tell Alice everything I have ever done."

February 2 he bought her a diamond ring. The following day he wrote: "Snowing heavily, but I drove over in my sleigh to Chestnut Hill, the horse plunging to his belly in the great drifts . . . My sweet life was just as lovable and pretty as ever; it seems hardly possible that I can kiss her and hold her in my arms; she is so pure and so innocent, and so very, very pretty. I have never done anything to deserve such good fortune. Coming home I was upset in a great drift, and dragged about 300 yards holding on to the reins, before I could stop the horse. . . . I do not think ever a man loved a woman more than I love her."

As Alice succumbed to his passion, she too was changed, reaching out with an increasing warmth. She wrote to T. R.'s mother that she "felt as if in a dream to have 'such a noble man's love' and it will be my aim both to endear myself to those so dear to him and to retain his love."

They set the date for October.

T. R. wrote his younger sister, Corinne: "She is just the sweetest, prettiest sunniest little darling that ever lived, and with all her laughing, teasing ways, she is as loving and tender as she can be." What he did not tell anyone was that he had gone to the college physician for a routine physical examination and was told he had "heart trouble" and should lead a quiet life. Immediately he declared to himself that he would *never* live like that and would do exactly the opposite. To prove it, he took off on a hunting trip to the West for six weeks. He passed the trip off as his last adventure as a bachelor and took his brother Elliott as a companion. Alice lamented, "I do not know what I will do when you go out West for six weeks. . . . Teddy, I love you with my whole heart and am never happier than I am when I am with you."

At the Red River, as his party approached Dakota Territory, he had an attack of asthma that had him sitting up all night to breathe. The next day he had excruciating pain with colic. Yet he never spoke of these ailments. Helplessness was his greatest fear, a feeling he would never admit. Back home, on October 27, 1880, he and Alice Lee married at the Unitarian church of Brookline just outside of Boston. It was Theodore's twenty-second birthday.

Three

"There Is a Curse on This House"

THE MARRIAGE OF T. R. AND ALICE would begin in bliss and soon turn to tragedy. Their time together would be less than three and a half years, a period that launched T. R. on his political career but ended on those foggy February days when he would lose both his mother and his new wife.

After the wedding, Bamie had arranged for the newlyweds to honeymoon at the family house in Oyster Bay, Long Island. While there, T. R. bought enough acreage to build a house for Alice and him and suggested to Bamie that she buy acreage nearby to build a house for herself. About the honeymoon he confided to his diary a single sentence: "Our intense happiness is too sacred to be written about." Two weeks later, they moved into their own suite, which Bamie prepared for them, on the third floor of the grand Roosevelt house near Central Park.

They lived the early days of their marriage in total contentment. Alice joined a sewing circle, played tennis, and kept up a socially busy life with friends and family, often visiting her parents in Chestnut Hill. T. R. was researching and writing *The Naval War of 1812*, which Alice liked to tease by calling it his book on "little boats." Though he had enrolled in Columbia Law School, he found his writing much more engaging and soon dropped out. Casting about for a useful career, and perhaps influenced by his father's desire to scrub corruption from government, he joined the Twenty-first District Republican Association and attended its meetings regularly.

These meetings were held in a barn-like room over a saloon, furnished with dingy benches, spittoons, and a speaker's area with a table and chair and a pitcher of iced water. He was unlike the other politicos—a rough-and-tumble group of saloon-keepers and draymen and city toughs. He promised himself that he would not quit until he had made the effort to find out whether he really was strong enough to hold his own among them. But Bamie supported him warmly, reminding him that it was his duty as the son of their father to take his place in the community, and in time he saw that, though the men of the association were far different from him socially, he was able to deal with them on their terms. A year after his marriage, he ran for election to the New York State Assembly from the twenty-first district. And won.

He made a name for himself at once, cutting an eccentric figure in the assembly while focusing on Gilded Age financial corruption. He kept his seat in the election of 1883 and caused a ruckus when he took on the wealthy owners of the Manhattan Elevated Railroad and outraged both friends and enemies by giving a speech in which he used the term "the wealthy criminal class." He was accused of being insufferably pious, with a tendency to simplify issues into good and evil. The press coverage was painful: he was called a "weakling," "hoodlum," and "bogus reformer." One newspaper wrote that he was a "tight-trousered snob given to sucking the nob of an ivory cane."

T. R. knew he had overstepped. In despair, he resolved to "pick myself up after learning by bitter experience the lesson that I was not all-important. The things I wanted to do, I was powerless to accomplish." The stress resulted in a bout of asthma so severe that his doctor sent him to a health resort in the Catskill Mountains. Soon after this crisis, Alice became pregnant, something they had been hoping for since their marriage. As she settled into her confinement in New York, T. R. headed west to the Dakotas once again, this time without his brother Elliott, where he breathed the clean air, fell in love with the Dakota countryside, and bought his first ranch.

Returning to New York later in the year, T. R. threw his prodigious energy into his enormous new house on Oyster Bay. Building Leeholm, as it would be called, after Alice Lee, was an elixir for his troubles and an expression of his joyful anxiety over becoming a father. The project became the center of his and Alice Lee's attention: twenty-two rooms, eight fireplaces, a foundation two feet thick. It said everything about their hopes for, and value of, family. As he described it, the house was to be exactly as he liked his food: "Simple but plentiful, heavy on the plate." Here they dreamed to live with a large family of their own children, increased often by the noise and revelry of the extended Roosevelt family.

In the new year he returned to the legislature, and on February 6, only six days before the birth of his daughter, he wrote to Alice from Albany, telling her that he had given one of his best speeches in the assembly. "My own tender true love, I never cease to think fondly of you; and oh how doubly tender I feel towards you now! You have been the truest and tenderest of wives, and you will be the sweetest and happiest of all little mothers."

The following weekend he was back with Alice in New York City as Alice's mother and T. R.'s mother, Mittie, arrived to help with the birth. He returned to Albany and legislative business. But neither Alice nor Mittie was well. After he left, Alice wrote to him: "Darling Thee—I hated so to leave you this afternoon. I don't think you need feel worried about my being sick as the Dr. told me this afternoon that I would not need my nurse before Thursday—and I am feeling well tonight but am very much worried over . . . your mother, her fever is still very high and the Dr. is rather afraid of typhoid. It is not in the least catching. I will write again tomorrow and let you know just how she is—don't say anything about it till then. I do love my dear Thee so much. I wish I could have my little new baby soon. Ever your loving wife, Alice."

That heartfelt letter was followed by days of tragedy. The next day, February 12, Alice Lee gave birth to her daughter, Alice, and fell dangerously ill. Mittie's condition worsened. The morning of February 13, T. R. received Bamie's sober telegram. On February 14, both wife and mother would die within hours of each other.

He had arrived at the Fifty-Seventh Street house just before midnight. His younger sister Corrine was already there. So was their brother Elliott, who stood in the doorway with the light from the hall framing him. There was a horrified look on Elliott's face as he announced to T. R. coming up the walk: "There is a curse on this house. Mother is dying, and Alice is dying too."

Rushing to Alice's bedroom on the third-floor bedroom, T. R. was immediately struck by the gravity of her illness. She was unable to recognize him. Through the night he held her, breaking away only to spend a few minutes with his mother in the ground-floor bedroom, the same room where her husband had passed away six years earlier. Bamie stayed by her mother's side. That Mittie was dying of typhoid was a bitter irony, considering her obsession for cleanliness. But in the days before sanitation became a government responsibility, several hundred New Yorkers died of typhoid every year.

At 3:00 a.m. on February 14, he was called away to his sweet Motherling as she died. At her bedside, T. R. repeated now what his brother Elliott announced earlier, "There is a curse on this house." He then rushed back to Alice. At 2:00 the next afternoon, while she lay in his arms, Alice died. Now to haunt him, along with the sudden loss, were the words he had written in his diary on the day she agreed to marry him: "The aim of my whole life shall be to make her happy, and to shield her and guard her from every trial." A sudden fatal illness was a trial he had not been equal to. He had been rendered helpless. And that feeling sharpened his searing grief to a stabbing agony.

In his diary, he put a large X on the page for February 14, 1884, and beneath wrote: "The light has gone out of my life." Only blank pages would follow.

Whisked up in blankets, baby Alice Lee was turned over to Bamie. Kind, brilliant, and talented beyond her culture's comprehension, twenty-nine-year-old Bamie did what everyone expected of her. She took charge.

As soon as it was clear that Alice Lee was dying, Bamie had sent out word that they needed a wet nurse, who was rushed to the nearby house of Mittie's sister, Aunt Annie Gracie. Baby Alice was sent there. The wet nurse's face, smell, touch, and voice were little Alice's first connection to the world, and yet when Alice was weaned, this first experience of essential human warmth would walk out of her life.

Who was she, this wet nurse? Most likely an Irish immigrant who kept her body producing breast milk as a means of employment. Women who took on wet-nursing had either kept their milk flowing after their own babies died or were weaned, or, in the worst of circumstances, had gotten pregnant on purpose, given away the child, and kept producing milk to secure a job that was well paid. She would move into someone's home to breast-feed a newborn, making more money than her husband could as a laborer. Aristocratic women kept the job market going, since most upper-class women feared breast-feeding would ruin their figures.

The year of Alice's birth was the heart of the Victorian era, with its strict social norms that governed not just courtship but every aspect of life, particularly for the class into which Alice had been born. In this pre-Freudian world, childhood was catch-as-catch-can. Children grew up in the margins of their parents' lives, and if something was missing in their emotional development, there was no prompt to notice it. It was wallpapered over, most often to unravel later. The anonymous wet nurse was one reality of Alice's class and time, but there was also the harsh personal reality of the deaths of her mother and grandmother. Along with arranging for the care of an infant, Bamie next had the terrible ordeal of planning a double funeral.

In Albany, when word of the tragedies reached T. R.'s colleagues in the assembly, one rose to say he had never in all his life been in the presence of such sorrow. Six others rose to speak, including three of T. R.'s most virulent opponents. All were visibly shaken, and they voted to adjourn until the following Monday. When T. R. learned of this, he likely suffered even more distress, for the one thing he most wanted to avoid was the sympathy of his colleagues. He despised being an object of pity, the handmaiden to helplessness.

The following Saturday, two thousand people crowded into the Fifth Avenue Presbyterian church at Fifty-Fifth Street. Two rosewood coffins, covered with roses and lilies of the valley, were carried down the aisle. T. R., Elliott, and Corrine, with Bamie, walked behind. T. R. looked dazed. Six years before, he had been there at the funeral of his beloved Greatheart. Then too, more than two thousand people had crowded into the church, among them the most renowned New York families, such as the Astors and Vanderbilts. Now, as the minister prayed for those grieving the loss of Mittie Roosevelt and Alice Lee Roosevelt, he also, weeping openly, mentioned the four-day old baby. After the service, two horse-drawn hearses clattered off down Fifth Avenue while other carriages carrying the family followed to Greenwood Cemetery, where Mittie and Alice Lee were buried next to Greatheart and Mittie's mother.

The day after the funerals, Baby Lee was christened. Bamie and Aunt Gracie dressed her in the smocked gown that Alice Lee, weeks before, had said was her favorite. They placed a locket around her neck with her mother's golden hair in it. T. R., still dazed, held the baby. Since the name Roosevelt meant in Dutch "field of roses," cascades of roses tumbled down her christening robe. With a rose also in his buttonhole, such as his father wore every day, T. R. held Baby Lee while the vicar poured water over her forehead from a Roosevelt heirloom silver bowl.

T. R. could not say her name, Alice. The sound throbbed with his loss. He could barely look at the baby who symbolized that tragic moment when Alice Lee, "not knowing that she was in the slightest danger, but thinking only that she was falling into a sleep, died in his arms." "You could not talk to him about it," a friend said. "He did not want anybody to sympathize with him."

Immediately, the family decided that the grand house that Greatheart had built and where the deaths occurred, would be sold, and the belongings divided up—tasks that Bamie would take on. On the fourth morning after the funeral, T. R. was back in Albany in seat forty on the floor of the assembly, still overwhelmed by shock and grief, numb to the needs of the squalling little girl he simply called "Baby."

The baby herself would learn in degrees the problem that her father had with her. Every time he saw her, he could not meet her eyes. He could not say her name. He called her "Baby" or "Baby Lee," or referred to her in his letters as "Mousiekins." He threw himself into work as a way of distracting himself from grief, traveling back and forth to Albany by night train. One day in March, he reported fifteen bills out of committee, then six more at a night session. Those close at hand began to wonder how much longer he could maintain a hold on himself. One said, "You could see at once that it was a grief too deep. . . .There was a sadness about his face that he never had before." He poured his sorrow into a manic whirl of activity.

Bamie was the one, who, despite her own grief, made sure that life went on, not just for small Alice, but for all of them. She instructed her uncle to sell the house. She searched for a place for herself and prepared to move there while also answering more than a hundred condolence letters. While T. R. wrote privately in his diary that "the light has gone out of my life," he admitted to Bamie that he was plagued with insomnia and restlessness. He wrote to her that he was "determined to live so as not to dishonor the memory of those I loved who have gone before me." He also wrote her about his mania in Albany: "We are now holding evening sessions and I am glad we are for an evening in an Albany hotel leaves much to be desired; indeed, the more we work the better I like it."

The work was merely an anesthetic. He had lost his zest for politics. He was expected to play his part in the Chicago National Republican Convention of 1884 and could not go back on his promise to his party, but he declared that afterward he would return to the West to live forever at his ranch on the Missouri River and give up politics altogether. Bamie supported his promise to attend the convention, thinking it would help divert his thoughts. She would call the year of 1884 "a perfect nightmare," yet she too was active. Once the grand house was sold, she bought a house of her own at 422 Madison Avenue, hired servants, and began moving in with the wet nurse for small Alice. She intended it to be not just a home for her and Baby Alice but also for Theodore whenever he was in New York. She planned to make it so comfortable it could lure him there. And when he was, she would invite politicians and intellectuals to dinner. Anything to assuage his hovering grief.

Yet T. R. threw a curve. As she was in the midst of moving, furnishing her new home "with my share of the Fifty-seventh Street things," he sent her a telegram. He had invited a new friend, Henry Cabot Lodge, to meet him at the Fifty-Seventh Street house to go together to the Chicago convention. But he'd forgotten to tell Bamie! "Bringing Cabot Lodge for a few days," he warned her. She didn't object, but panic set in. She'd already emptied every room. Having someone to go with T. R. to Chicago would keep his mind busy and stave off his grief. Anything to keep him from drowning in sorrow. She was thrown into a tailspin.

Bamie rushed to put things back. She didn't want the house to look sad and dismantled. When Theodore walked into Greatheart's house, she wanted to protect his fragile emotional state.

She put flowers in the rooms. She returned enough furniture to make it seem its old self. She rehung pictures and sent the servants scurrying to prepare for a guest. This was the house that had welcomed Alice Lee as a newlywed; where Bamie and Theodore, along with Elliott and Corrine, came of age; where Mittie and Greatheart practiced their love for each other and soaked each of their children in that affection. She had managed it since she was sixteen, when it became clear her mother found it all too much. Leaving it was agony, and having to refurnish it compounded the pain. When T. R. and his friend arrived, it would be the last time she would stand in these rooms.

Four

"The World on Her Shoulders"

Barely five feet tall and described by her brother as "a little feminine Atlas with a small world on her shoulders," Bamie was exactly three years and nine months older than T. R. Elliott called her "the Major Generaless." Named Anna Eleanor Roosevelt, the first in a long list of Roosevelt women to be named Anna Eleanor, she was nicknamed Bamie as a variation of "bambino." In time, she would also be called Auntie Bye because she was so often on the go, waving "bye"—which was remarkable since she lived with a spinal deformity bending her a little forward with a slight hump in her back causing a "stooping gait." During the first few years of her life, no one expected she would ever walk.

When she was four, her father found a young physician who believed that special exercises could help her. Greatheart felt that even though the climate was severe, life should be lived in the open air, so he renovated the third-story back bedroom of his house into a piazza with a nine-foot-high railing acting as a wall, otherwise leaving the room open. There, swinging bars and ladders fitted out the piazza. Every day, Bamie swung on the equipment, if not changing what was most likely a congenital malformation, at least gaining strength in what she said "saved her from being helpless [and] distorted."

Some historians have attributed her deformity to Pott disease, tuberculosis of the spine. Others have noted she was "dropped in her bath as a very small baby, and her spine had been injured." Others have suspected her deformity to be scoliosis from a bout with polio. Yet there is no record of a polio epidemic at the time. In any case, she was far from what a normal baby was expected to be, and for the first three years of her life her father carried her each morning from the nursery to spend the entire day on a sofa in the third-floor playroom of the Roosevelt brownstone on East Twentieth Street in New York. She would be harnessed in a "terrible instrument" made of steel and leather. This brace rubbed a sore on her back that a doctor came each morning to wash and bandage, then strapped her in again to lie facedown on the sofa all day, waiting to hear her father's "quick light running up the stairs" to burst in with ice cream or a toy. Then Greatheart would carry her back to the nursery.

Her father's love for her gave her the sense she was someone of value, someone important, someone treasured without question. And yet, while that strong identity piloted her through a remarkable long life, she also lived with the reality of being born a female in 1855, when women were not allowed to vote, could not in most states own property, and in many were even considered to *be* property. This gender discrimination shadowed what she did to the point where her enormous contribution to history has been ignored. Few knew that she engineered her brother's political career or that T. R., as president, held cabinet meetings at *her* house. She managed events like a hidden chess master, employing skills learned through a challenging life. And since she left no written history, what we know of Bamie today has been unearthed from her letters, which some consider her memoir.

Some who knew both Bamie and T. R. said that Bamie was the more accomplished. At parties, her conversation and charisma were unmatched. She was described as having "no good looks . . . really plain. Even her figure was bad . . . dumpy looking. But she . . . projected such a keen interest, such an animated intelligence and curiosity, that people . . . saw only the beauty. When her face was animated it was extraordinary. She gave out a light and an animation . . . very, very rare. It was contagious." Yet when she made her debut, announcing she was marriageable, no one really took it seriously.

There were several reasons that she was never expected to marry. Her disability was considered an impediment. Even her adoring father insisted that she not wear the spectacles she needed, as he thought they made her less attractive. On the other hand, she was thought of as being simply too independent to marry, incapable of assigning her affections to anyone outside her family. During her debut, there was some speculation that she would marry her fourth cousin, the middle-aged widower James Roosevelt, twenty-seven years her senior, known as the "Squire of Hyde Park" and Franklin's eventual father. James's grown son, J. Roosevelt Roosevelt, known as "Rosy," the son of the deceased wife and half-brother to yet unborn Franklin, was also considered a prospect for her.

But Bamie was not in love with either of the Hyde Park Roosevelts, and she was relieved when James married her good friend Sara Delano and Rosy married her friend Helen Astor, one of the richest women in America. Bamie had a secret desire and plans of her own. *She* knew what she wanted for herself, and in time it would be little Alice who would reveal it.

It was said that she "shrugged at life," which, no doubt, came from her private daily physical struggle, coupled with her realization that by being female, she was destined to live with circumstances she could not change. It may seem odd to us that history has ignored her, yet even her contemporary Henry Adams pointed out that "American history mentioned hardly the name of a woman, while English history handled them as timidly as though they were a new and undescribed species." The America into which Bamie was born was small and unsure of itself, rigid and suspicious of change. She was six years old when the nation split apart, violently battling out whether America should be two nations, one slave-free, the other slave-holding, based on a specious reverence for "property" that included the legal ownership of a human being. She began life in the midst of this great American argument, brought up in a home where her Southern mother's family was, as T. R. put it in his autobiography, "entirely 'unreconstructed'"—that is, she remained sympathetic to the Confederate cause.

Yet in time T. R. and Bamie would work toward fulfilling Abraham Lincoln's prophesy that the United States would be a world power. When her adored brother was at the window of their grandfather's house, watching Lincoln's funeral procession move down the street toward Union Square, Bamie may have been there too. Certainly Edith Carow was. Age four, towheaded, curly-haired, nicknamed "Spotless Edie," Edith Carow more than once had remarked that one day she would marry Theodore Roosevelt. And she would. As she became a complicating factor in Alice's life, Bamie would navigate the churning waters of a family not only adjusting to unspeakable tragedy but also charting a political life that would bring America into the twentieth century. Bamie was the embodiment of good sense. She was strength. She was charm. It would eventually be said of her that if she had been born a man, she would have been president. She was the one who would always be the anchor in Alice's life, the one who would hold her together, such that it would be Alice herself who, near the end of her own life, would give history the quote, "If Auntie Bye had been born a man . . ."

By the time Bamie was fourteen, she had outgrown the home school that her mother's sister ran. She had exhausted the stock of history and biography in her father's library. She could dazzle her father's friends with her wit and knowledge. And by the time she was sixteen, she was ready for the European education her wealthy family wanted for her. She attended the famous Les Ruches school at Fontainebleau, on the outskirts of Paris, renowned for educating the daughters of politicians, statesmen, and prominent American and European families. Through their influence, many of the girls educated there became powerful women in global affairs. The school's founder, Marie Souvestre, taught her students to analyze, think independently, and live with a purpose—broadly meaning to make a "commitment to human justice." It was an Enlightenment education that brought politics and history alive, and Marie Souvestre planted the belief in her students that they could wield significant power and influence in spite of society's discrimination against women. The time that Bamie spent there ignited the dedication to world affairs that would come to bear on her brother's career.

When she returned to America, chased from France by the Franco-Prussian War, she arrived home transformed. T. R., now fourteen, saw his beloved sister in stylish Parisian gowns and French high heels. Her hair was wavy, piled in a high chignon. Her manner was softened. She practiced conversation as an art. Her unbounded energy had not been dampened nor her instinct to dominate, but she was definitely revised, ready for a role she had been led to recognize.

Though Bamie would more or less fade from history, we know how she stepped forward after the deaths of her mother and T. R.'s beloved Alice Lee to become "the power behind the scene . . . the driving wheel of destiny." It was she who would support the young Theodore Roosevelt through his devastating grief, who would play a significant part to reconnect him with his life, to play a strong hand in his remarriage, and to become his most trusted insider throughout his presidency. But now, in the midst of the horrifying family tragedy in that winter of 1884, it was Bamie who knew what had to be orchestrated, what had to be set in motion.

Five

"She Would Be Just as Well Off without Me"

When T. R. returned to New York with his friend Henry Cabot Lodge, Alice Lee had been dead not quite four months. The two men were preparing to attend the 1884 National Republican Convention in Chicago, and Bamie quickly understood that by going with Cabot Lodge, T. R. would not have to be alone and could avoid those situations in which he feared losing hold of himself. During their visit, Bamie wanted Cabot Lodge to reawaken her brother to his life and his possibilities in politics. And after they left for Chicago, she continued to send her brother letters and newspaper clippings, encouraging him, hoping to arouse the sense of fight he'd shown throughout his political career so far.

But the convention was a discouraging one for T. R., who ended up on the wrong side of its political infighting, and when it was over he headed to the Badlands, snapping at a newspaper reporter as he left, "I am going cattle-ranching in Dakota. . . . What I shall do after that I cannot tell you."

As soon as he reached his ranch, the Elkhorn, Bamie's chatty letters began arriving. She wrote how she was fixing up a study for him at her new house. She had always insisted that they not live together, that they only visited since that would be a much easier relationship to maintain than had they made a mutual home, but now she wanted to reignite his interest in living. And part of that reignition would be to assure him with a warm place to fall. Her long letters were like tours through future landing spots: her house in New York and the Oyster Bay house, now under her supervision, which held the promise of the summer fun they would have there together. She always laced her letters with a list of the cunning things that little Alice, whom he called Baby Lee, had done that week. She also tucked into each letter clippings from the papers on all the political news of the day, with, of course, her own shrewd comments. T. R. himself would take a rifle, load up a horse, and ride off into the prairie totally alone for days and days, "far off from all mankind."

Bamie hoped his love for writing would sustain him. She knew he needed a new project to engage his restless intellect. And he soon decided on one. Soon after his arrival in the Dakota territory, he took up writing about his western life. His publisher in Boston was encouraging. But sitting at his desk in his rustic cabin, ready to write his western tales, he found himself thinking about Alice Lee and began writing a memorial to her.

He intended his piece for private circulation. He started it in the style in which he wrote history, but sorrow pulled him in the direction of poetry:

> I first saw her on October 18, 1878, and loved her as soon as I saw her sweet, fair young face; we were betrothed on January 25, 1880, and married on October 27th of the same year; we spent three years of happiness such as rarely comes to man or woman; on February 12, 1884, her baby girl was born; she kissed it and seemed perfectly well, some hours afterward she, not knowing that she was in the slightest danger, but thinking only that she was falling into a sleep, became insensible, and died at two o'clock on Thursday afternoon, February 14, 1884, at 6 West 57th Street, in New York; she was buried two days afterward in Greenwood Cemetery.
>
> She was beautiful in face and form and lovelier still in spirit; as a flower she grew, and as a fair young flower she

> died. Her life had been always in the sunshine, and there had never come to her a single great sorrow, and none ever knew her who did not love and revere her for her bright, sunny temper and her saintly unselfishness. Fair, pure, and joyous as a maiden, loving, tender, and happy as a young wife, when she had just become a mother, when her life seemed to be but just begun, and when the years seemed so bright before her—then by a strange and terrible fate, death came to her.
>
> And when my heart's dearest died, the light went out from my life for ever.

"Her baby girl was born"—those words let the painful truth leak out. Not "our baby girl." He saw Baby Lee as only Alice Lee's child. Maybe he believed that by writing of the tragedy, using his extraordinary self-discipline, he could put Alice Lee's death behind him. Already he had put the child that came from his love for Alice Lee out of his present, out of his heart, out of his future, never to be felt as a reminder of the marriage that had brought him so much happiness—and unspeakable pain.

Soon he wrote Bamie reiterating his wish for her to take on finishing the building of Leeholm at Oyster Bay, later to be renamed Sagamore Hill. And he added that she should continue to raise Baby Alice. He would cover all the baby's expenses, but Baby Lee was to stay with her—with Bamie. Bamie agreed and pushed to finish up Leeholm in a grand manner. When she visited the site, she often took Alice with her, and since her aunt Gracie and brother Elliott lived nearby, Alice would often play with Elliott's daughter Eleanor. That summer of 1887, Eleanor and Alice, though each not yet four, became friends, laying the foundation for a relationship that would have many ups and downs over the next seven decades. Bamie felt that when the magnificent house was finished, it might be the only hope to bring her adored brother back east. So she drove the construction crew as only Bamie could. She knew her brother was living out his grief in the western plains like some "ancient, wounded animal."

And he was. Living in a numb state, riding the range after cattle and wild game, his future seemed too empty to contemplate. He turned to the elements, the air, the rough terrain that required all his attention to travel over it. He began to hint in his letters to Cabot Lodge and Bamie of a reawakening. It was the land that did it. It was the requirements of living. In his letters to them he described breathing "sweet fresh air under a crystal sky" and his wild affection for Manitou, his horse who was "perfectly sure-footed, willing and spirited." Riding the forty miles between his two ranches required crossing the Missouri River more than twenty times, and he wrote of the ecstasy of coming "out on the top of the first great plateau," how "the sun flames up over the edge, and in the level red beams the galloping horsemen throw long, fantastic shadows. Black care [depression] rarely sits behind a rider whose pace is fast enough."

He sat down every Sunday night to write to Bamie. He had no heart for politics or for anything or anyone back home, he said, and sent "best love" and "many kisses" to his small "Mousiekins." He also urged Bamie to stay after finishing Leeholm so that she and he would spend their future summers together there. At night, camping with the rough but sympathetic companions who tried to cheer him by reminding him that he must live for the sake of his small daughter, he replied, "Her aunt can take care of her better than I can. She would be just as well off without me."

After writing his memorial to Alice Lee, he had succeeded in walling off his grief. The helplessness that Alice Lee's death made him feel strengthened that wall. He pushed hard against it in his alone hours, in the dark hours, and especially every time he thought of, or looked at, or spoke to, Baby Lee. Like the muscle memory of an athlete who practices a move over and over until it becomes virtually instinctual, he reached the ultimate silence: *Do not speak of her. Do not tell of loving her. Or losing her. Nothing of that shall exist in the present. Or the future.* In the crowded and eventful years that would follow, T. R. never mentioned Alice Lee, not even to their daughter who was named for her. His silence was barricaded behind a wall maintained by "inhumane discipline that some said approached cruelty."

Yet Bamie kept sending letters. He opened them at night to hear her voice coming off her handwriting as he recovered from long hours riding and tending his ranches. She also forwarded correspondence from his political friends. They were all telling him he should speak up about the friction in the party. Bamie told him he should be man enough to at least say publicly and unequivocally exactly where he stood. Reading those letters after a day of herding cattle or hunting affected him like a "match applied to a slow-burning fuse."

She was betting on what she knew of his temperament. He could not much longer ignore the fiery internal call to enter the bear pit, as he called politics. And she intended to keep stoking the flames. Cabot Lodge—who was standing alone in the political party fight while running for reelection to Congress on the Republican ticket—needed him. That need was a mighty prod.

In July T. R. went to Boston to see his publisher and, while there, paid a visit to Alice Lee's parents in Chestnut Hill. It was unlikely they talked of Alice Lee; T. R.'s reluctance could shut down anyone. And anyway, the Lees practiced the same fabricated comfort: that never speaking of a death would keep sorrow a corpse, too. After he returned to the Badlands, he wrote Cabot Lodge, "I do not think we need take any active part in the campaign. Indeed, I may be in Dakota on Election Day."

In a September letter Bamie detected a flicker of change. T. R. was at Fort McKinney in Wyoming, just down from the mountains after killing three grizzly bears and six elk. He told her he intended the animal heads for the hall of "the house on the hill" at Oyster Bay, referring to it that way rather than as Leeholm. The hunting seemed to help him mentally: he called it "good sport" and "enough excitement and fatigue to prevent overmuch thought." He added: "At last I have been able to sleep well at night." The best news of all for her was that after another week at his ranch on the Little Missouri, he "would be on my way home," adding, "I am afraid I should soon get as restless with this life as with the life at home."

On October 9 Bamie found him at the front door of her new home on Madison Avenue. His face was a reddish brown from the western sun, and he looked fit and healthy. As she showed him around, he riffled through the mail stacked high on the desk in the new study she had made for him. Most of the letters were from politicians. Soon, the front door was besieged by reporters who had heard he was in town and rushed to hear his political views. Bamie was delighted. Inviting them in, she watched her brother meet with them, and as he sat talking, she savored watching him reveal flashes of interest in his former life. Most of all, she enjoyed watching him play with Baby Lee.

Alice was thriving under Bamie's care, and several times T. R. promised that he intended for Bamie to keep raising Baby Lee, which touched her deeply. Being a mother to the motherless Alice was the lasting purpose she longed for. The feelings of loving Alice, and feeling her love in return, brought back her experiences with her father. Bamie realized more than anything she could ever know that motherhood was the greatest pleasure, the greatest sense of satisfaction, the best use of her life on earth. Being a mother answered her most ardent longing: to be needed, to be valued, to be the center of someone else's outburst of joy. Whenever two-year-old Alice saw Bamie, she laughed until her sides shook. Golden-haired, with features as exquisite as those of her mother, Alice seemed like a storybook child. Raising her promised a joy-washed future, echoing what Bamie had shared with Greatheart.

By Saturday morning, two days after his arrival, T. R. agreed to a one-on-one interview in Bamie's house with a reporter from the *New York Sun*. Offering the reporter a glass of sherry, T. R. sat down and opened up: "I had no intention of taking any part whatever in the presidential canvass but resolving the matter, it is altogether contrary to my character to occupy a neutral position in so important and exciting a struggle." He stated he intended to support the Republican ticket, admitting he had been against the chosen candidate, James Blaine, at the Chicago convention but felt sure that Blaine, as the candidate, would live up to the Republican Party's platform. He added that he and Lodge were watching for reform within their party and stressed publicly that he had no interest in politics for himself, only for reform within the party.

His heart may have not been in politics, but his head was. That evening he gave a speech to Young Republicans in Brooklyn setting out the reasons he supported the Republican ticket. In the rest of the campaign of 1884, he gave seven speeches, three of them in Massachusetts in support of Cabot Lodge. But soon after that he fled again to the Badlands, where he bought another thousand head of cattle and continued to maintain an ambiguous attitude to politics. In November, both Blaine and Cabot Lodge lost, victims of the split in the Republican Party. T. R. still insisted he had no interest in politics for himself. He wrote Lodge, assuring his friend that despite Lodge's loss, he would come back in time, but as for himself, he would never "be likely to come back into political life."

While T. R. spent long days herding cattle and hunting in the Dakota territory, Bamie made sure her letters were waiting for him at the end of the day. She knew he was still using physical hardships to keep a grip on his emotions. Finally, in June of 1885, he joined her and Baby Lee at the finished house at Oyster Bay. This was their first summer together. And while there, he concentrated on writing *Hunting Trips of a Ranchman*, about his experiences in the West. By now he was calling himself just "a rancher" or "a literary fellow."

One night, however, he found himself sitting at the rear of a hall during a political gathering. And when a reporter discovered him there, he said, "I am only a private in this battle—but I am ready to be commanded for any movement." Little by little, the core of him was reigniting, reminding, indeed commanding that he serve the passion for politics that he had discovered soon after he discovered Alice Lee.

Six

He Was Not a Man to Live Alone

By that summer at Oyster Bay, Baby Lee was weaned. How she reacted when the wet nurse who had been her link to survival walked out of her life, we can only surmise. And while Bamie feared losing Baby Lee if T. R. ever wanted her back, she also took comfort in his writing her several times that she should continue raising the baby. He would meet all of Baby Lee's expenses, but Bamie must keep on as she had been. That was his wish.

Bamie, however, was aware of a danger in her brother's future. He was not a man to live alone. Without the anchor of a marriage, T. R. could flounder. She knew he needed to be married. And Bamie being Bamie might just be the one to engineer it. She even may have worried that he would fall into the lifestyle of their brother Elliott, who by now had descended into alcoholism. Elliott's problems consumed her life as much as her concern for T. R.'s political talents. And clearly, she wanted T. R. to be happy and settled. Just as she had engineered other moments in his life, she now took on this one.

Edith Carow may have been the first solution she thought of. Certainly, she was a fitting one. From the time that Edith was four, she had been in the Roosevelt household part of every day. Their fathers were business friends. Charles Carow's wealth came from his family's shipping company. The Carow family was considered the social equals of the Roosevelts. Edith attended the Roosevelts' home school, and she was almost a member of the family. When T. R. was ten and Edith eight, the Roosevelt family took their first trip to Europe, and the day they sailed, T. R. cried on the way to the docks. That night he wrote in his diary: "It was very hard parting from our friend. In the evening mamma showed me the portrait of Edith Carow and her face stirred up in me homesickness and longing for the past which will come again never, alack never." It was clear that Edith resided in his affection in special ways.

She was private by nature, a stickler for rules, perfect in her dress, perfect in her manners, stoic in brushing aside trivialities. Her father's known alcoholism meant that family's reputation suffered accordingly, reaching a low after he suffered a head injury falling down the hold of one of his ships. He was never totally stable afterward. Her mother was a hypochondriac and her sister was frivolous, so Edith was always surrounded by embarrassment and drama. As she grew, she became even more stoic and private, to the point where she came across as aloof and judgmental. Inwardly, she must have been tortured by a need to overcome her family's lost reputation, and so she sought to create a distinction for herself: to be perfect in all things. And the most perfect thing she saw on earth was Theodore Roosevelt Jr.

As they grew into young adulthood, they became riding, rowing, and dancing partners. They had respect for each other's intellect and shared a love for vigorous conversation, drawing on their knowledge of literature and art. They attended weddings, funerals, city events, and church gatherings together. When they grew into their teens, it seemed natural that T. R. and Edith's relationship would flame into more than a friendship. Everyone expected them to marry.

And probably they would have if it weren't for an argument they had the summer after Greatheart died. No one knew exactly what had happened. Neither Edith nor T. R. would talk about what broke them apart. It was only known that during that summer at Oyster Bay where the families were vacationing, T. R. seemed to want Edith with him all the time: rowing, picking water lilies together, sailing or riding. Then on August 20, after tea, they went into the summerhouse and something happened so that their growing affection exploded into hostility.

T. R. said, "We both of us had tempers that were far from the best."

Edith said, "Theodore had not been nice."

Some think that T. R. proposed to her and she turned him down. Perhaps he was physically forward, touching her without her permission. Members of Edith's family thought he had proposed to her several times, but she felt she was too young to marry and kept turning him down. Furthermore, some in the Carow family believed in a rumor that the Roosevelts "had a history of scrofula," a condition caused by the tuberculosis bacteria. And, of course, after the breakup, while T. R. was at Harvard, he met Alice Lee.

Stoically, Edith had attended their wedding and hosted a party for the newlyweds. They stayed friends. By the time Bamie was arranging for Edith Carow to come back into T. R.'s life, they had known each other for twenty-one years. Edith was twenty-five, T. R. twenty-seven. The rematch seemed predestined.

Since Edith had remained T. R.'s sister Corrine's closest friend, Bamie knew it would be easy to bring the couple together. As teens, Edith and Corrine had organized a reading club called Paradise Ravenous Eaters, which was when Corrine said, "I have a feeling for Edith which I have for no one else, a tender kind of feeling. . . . Every time I see her I notice what a clever girl she is." T. R. always said that Edith had more knowledge of literature than anyone he knew. She recited passages from literary works as often, and as well, as T. R.'s very literary mother.

But Bamie faced a significant hurdle when trying to engineer bringing Edith back into T. R.'s life: he had warned her to alert him whenever Edith was visiting because he wanted to avoid anyone attractive to him so soon after Alice Lee's death. For a while Bamie adhered to his wishes. Then, at the end of that summer of 1885 at Oyster Bay, he stayed on in the East for the Meadow Brook Hunt, a fox hunt and big social occasion. It was an ideal opportunity for Bamie to arrange an impromptu meeting.

On the hunt, T. R. rode a hunter that had been converted from a buggy horse because of its devil-may-care love of jumping, and at one fence the buggy horse somersaulted over, spilling T. R., who found when he remounted that his left arm wouldn't work. He urged the happy-go-lucky horse to catch up, and they finished the hunt, but when they drew up at the end, T. R.'s left hand had slipped out of position, and he saw his arm was broken. So on the pivotal day that October, when T. R. came into Bamie's New York townhouse, he stood at the bottom of the stairs with his arm in a sling and looked up to see Edith coming down the stairs toward him. She had grown more attractive physically; she was "no longer the moody teenage girl" he had known, and beneath her steely composure was a softness.

He too had changed. The last time she had seen him had been at Alice Lee's funeral, when he had been thin, pale, and distraught. Now he was range-hardened, thirty pounds heavier, with his face nut brown and leathery. But underneath, she sensed the old exuberant "Teedie," and when they looked at each other for the first time since Alice Hathaway Lee's death, they instantly, with no hesitation, no questioning or effort, fell back into love.

Had Bamie ignored his warning to tell him if Edith would be at her house? Had she arranged this surprise meeting to jolt him back into his life, to organize his suffering into *Before* and *After*? It seems likely, especially with the knowledge of Bamie's desire to arrange her adored brother's life with his happiness at its center. In any case, T. R. and Edith both knew they would spend the rest of their lives together—which then sent Theodore walking the floor through the night muttering angrily to himself, "I have no constancy—no constancy." The Victorian code of etiquette believed that the consummation of a marriage was an eternal bond between a husband

and wife. Years later, when he wrote his autobiography, he mentioned neither Alice Lee nor his father's avoidance of military service during the Civil War, which young Theodore had mistakenly viewed as cowardice. Clearly, shame caused both omissions.

Choosing happiness over the paralysis of grief was a struggle. In his diary, T. R. referred to Edith as "E." He told Bamie and Corinne that he and Edith were secretly engaged, but no one else was to know. They wanted to wait a year, to give the Victorian code's proper period of respectful mourning for Alice Hathaway Lee.

In the spring, he returned to the West and Edith went with her mother and sister to live in Europe, where their money would go further. After Charles Carow's death, the three women fell into what passed for financial hardship among their class, and living in Italy was their solution. T. R.'s guilt over the marriage was no doubt partly driven by what Corinne privately surmised about the coming marriage. There had been hints that Greatheart had disapproved of the relationship that T. R. and Edith forged in their teens. Edith's father's alcoholism and failure in business troubled Greatheart. But now, after both fathers were gone, those concerns no longer played a significant part. Besides, Edith and T. R. were in love and had been in varying degrees since they were children. Perhaps they knew each other better than most people ever know each other, having shared so much personal history over many years.

That summer, out west, T. R. began writing a life of Thomas Hart Benton, the Democratic senator from Missouri who was the architect of westward expansion known as Manifest Destiny. Benton was the perfect subject for T. R.'s passions, and Cabot Lodge had convinced the editor of the American Statesmen series that Roosevelt was the right person to write that biography. Also, T. R. was beginning to see writing as his profession. This would be the means he chose to support his future with Edith. But Bamie and Cabot Lodge had other plans. They encouraged his writing, but only as preparation for what they believed was his destiny—a return to politics.

After he traveled back to his ranch, a surprise nomination jolted his appetite for what he thought he had lost. He was unexpectedly nominated as head of New York's Twenty-first District Republican Association. Clearly flattered, he declined the office, saying he was at too much distance to do the job well; but writing to Bamie he admitted, "You were very sweet to send me the newspapers cuttings. I was greatly amused to find I had unknowingly won a political victory, but I would much rather not have been made President of the Association. If I am going to do anything at all I like to give my time to it."

Preparing to sail for London to marry Edith, he got another political call. The Republican Party nominated him to run for mayor of New York City, and even though he knew he had no chance to win, he was still delighted and jumped into the campaign. When he realized he'd be out of the country marrying Edith on election day—which would make it seem that he'd been expecting defeat—he secretly booked passage on the ship to London as "Mr. Merrifield," traveling with his sister, "Miss Merrifield," aka Bamie.

Bamie assumed she would continue to have Baby Lee as her own to raise, as she had been assured by her brother so many times. *Go on as before. We will all go on as before.* There was no foreshadowing of what his marriage to Edith would mean. On election night, Bamie even wrote Cabot Lodge's wife, Nanny: "Theodore has insisted on my keeping baby, in fact for the present at least we will go on as we are."

In that election of 1886, Cabot Lodge was reelected to Congress. In the mayoralty election, T. R. came in third. Writing later to Cabot Lodge, T. R. said, "At least I have a better Party standing than ever before." He had indeed shown that from his young maverick legislative days, he now could accept party discipline and act as if he were a regular himself—at least on occasion.

Yes, the T. R. who loved a bear pit was back.

Seven

Orange Gloves

WEDDING DAY. Thursday, December 2, 1886, dawned with a typical London pea-soup fog. Bamie, not wanting Theodore to marry so far away from home without family, had left Baby Lee in New York under the care of Corrine. Then, before sailing, Bamie wrote to all the interesting men she knew in London, telling them she was coming, ready for fine conversation and tea.

T. R. had been so insistent that no one should know of his marrying, shunning newspapers and all other means of spreading the word, that he had asked no one to be his best man. In typical exuberant fashion, he had made a new friend on the passage over, British diplomat Cecil Spring Rice, whom he asked to be best man. Despite having only just met T. R., Rice heartily agreed. "Springy" had a long face, broad forehead, aquiline nose, and pale hair. He was frank and warm. After they docked, he led T. R. around for the two weeks prior to the wedding day, introducing him to British statesmen, including Joseph Chamberlain. They rode horses together and would have gone on a hunting trip but for lack of time.

On the eve of the wedding, Edith arrived, trying not to give off even a hint of insecurity in becoming Theodore's second wife. But its effects were there all the same. No one follows a first wife without throwing off sly comments fishing for comforting comparisons. On occasion, Edith would remark that Alice Lee had been beautiful but lacked depth; that Alice Lee would have bored Theodore to death. During the short period of T. R.'s first marriage, Bamie and Corrine had called Alice Lee "Little Alice" even though she was five feet, seven inches tall. Edith, however, was a different story. Neither Corrine nor Bamie would ever have referred to her, or thought of her, as "little." Indeed, Edith was huge in her effect, constructing an invisible wall to protect her from any slight. Shame-driven by her father's alcoholism and fall from social standing, Edith did not tolerate teasing well. By her sheer judgmental presence, she made everyone mind their p's and q's.

As soon as Edith arrived in London, Bamie realized how the relationship with her childhood friend was about to change. Not always able to check her own tendency to dominate, Bamie saw that Edith could very well become jealous of the influence Bamie had over Theodore. And in typical Bamie fashion, she redirected her energy. She threw all her attention on a new friend "Springy" introduced her to: Robert Ferguson, known as "Fergie." Fourteen years younger than Bamie, he quickly became totally adoring of her, bringing out both her maternal and romantic side. In the months and years of their friendship, Bamie enjoyed fretting over Fergie's weak lungs, reveling in his humor, and rejoicing in his lively conversation. She kept him in her closest circle, which eventually prompted Edith to describe Bamie and Fergie's friendship as "rather eccentric."

As the hour of the wedding grew near and it was time to go to the church from the hotel, Bamie helped Edith put on her lace gown and veil. While the women were busy with their preparations, T. R. and Springy began intensely discussing the population of an island in the South Pacific. Ask T. R. what time it was, people said, and he would give you a lecture on how a clock was made. The fog had not lifted. The mist would slow traffic. They might have trouble getting to the church at Hanover Square. But T. R. was obsessed with the history of a South Pacific island! So Bamie prodded him, letting loose her bossy streak and telling T. R. and Springy to stop talking.

Still talking, T. R. and Springy got into a horse-drawn cab while Edith and Bamie followed in another. Somewhere along the way to the church, Springy told the carriage driver to pull over and dashed into a men's store, where he bought T. R. a pair of bright orange gloves. When Edith came down the aisle, the men enjoyed the look on her face as she noticed T. R.'s gloves with their eye-popping color.

T. R. signed the church registry in his flashy handwriting, calling himself "Rancher." The couple then headed out for a three-month honeymoon in Europe. Soon after, Bamie got a letter post-marked from Dover: "You, dearest sister. I cannot say how much I appreciated your coming over; it has been everything to Edith and myself; I am so very glad you came over as you did and you have been too sweet for anything during the past fortnight. Remember to give a thousand kisses to Baby Lee."

Bamie went home and prepared for Christmas alone with Alice. A tree spread toward the ceiling with candles lit on the branches. In typical Victorian tradition, wrapped candies were hidden among the evergreen needles. And at every table setting lay a wrapped party favor called a "cracker" with trinkets ready to spill out. It was the first Christmas that T. R. had not spent at home. Even when he was at his ranch in the Badlands, he had always made it home for Christmas. Now he wrote Bamie from Paris, Florence, and Rome. He and Edith had met their favorite poet, Robert Browning. Soon, Bamie would begin to absorb how much this second marriage would change her life.

Because Edith had begun thinking about more than poetry. While away, she had started brooding over the state of T. R.'s finances. He paid little attention to money; it bored him. But Edith, terrified after her father's death that the money he had left his wife and two daughters would not be sufficient to support them, started fretting about money all the time. News that a catastrophic blizzard in Dakota had led to severe losses in T. R.'s cattle herd distressed her. T. R. wrote Bamie: "My financial affairs for the past year make such a bad showing that Edith and I think seriously of closing Sagamore Hill and going to the ranch for a year or two."

Bamie was alarmed. She loved Sagamore Hill as much as T. R., but she also couldn't envision Edith roughing it at the ranch for long, even to save money. She also feared losing Baby Alice. What distressed her most was how all this would hurt her brother's political career—especially when he added that he did not "much care whether I change my residence from New York or not. I have not the slightest belief in my having any political future." Bamie believed his letter had been fueled by Edith—her instinctive dislike of life in the public eye. She saw now how she and Edith would be pitted against each other with competing intentions for her brother. In time, she would have to subtly lead Edith to understand that politics was essential to T. R.'s happiness. But for now, she would wait until she had a better sense of this huge shift in her brother's life.

The celebration of Christmas at Madison Avenue revolved around Little Alice. The three-year-old's flaxen curls; her big bright blue eyes, so much like Bamie's; and the sound of her giggle were the house's centerpiece. Bamie was the only one who spoke of her mother, of Alice Lee—of Alice Lee's beauty, of her sunny disposition, of her skill at tennis and archery. Bamie was the one who gave Baby Lee unconditional warmth and love, making her feel special and secure. She told Alice stories of her grandfather Roosevelt, Greatheart, how he drove a four-in-hand and used to bring the children iced peaches, which he would feed to them bite by bite as they all four lay flat on their middles on the edge of the piazza so that the ice would not drip on them. She told how Alice's grandmother was called Mittie and was very dainty and never went to town in the summer without bundling up in veils and dust coats and putting on brown paper cuffs so that not a single speck of dust or smudge could touch her. She told of the difficult times during the Civil War when Grandmother Roosevelt's brothers were fighting on the Southern side. Alice heard stories of Bamie living in

Paris during the Franco-Prussian War and would make Bamie describe over and over the sound of the soldiers marching past, singing, on their way to fighting. Baby Lee was the center of Bamie's universe, and Bamie was the harbor of Baby Lee's world.

That winter, while T. R. and Edith honeymooned in Europe, Bamie worried over the possibility of Alice being taken from her and brought to the ranch in Dakota. In her anxiety she made a tactical error. She wrote Theodore to remind him of his proposal that Alice "stay on with her." As an added reason, she pointed out that the western ranch was no place for a child of three. Soon after, she received a letter from Rome. In her brother's words, Bamie could hear Edith directing his voice. It was clear: T. R. was caught between two equally determined women. As he shamefully wrote: "I hardly know what to say about Baby Lee. Edith feels more strongly about her than I could have imagined possible. However, we can decide it all when we meet. Give my best love to the darling; and many kisses." He also added sheepishly that it was all his fault and please to not blame Edith. It was now clear to Bamie that T. R. and Edith would soon rip Alice from her, tearing away the greatest joy she had known since losing Greatheart.

To Edith, the idea of Theodore visiting Madison Avenue to see his own daughter was repellent. She would not have it. Having a proper family was foremost in her mind. Her own family's financial and social fall was a puncture wound that would not close. Being perfect—or at least being *seen* as perfect—in all things was her only remedy. Her future family would be the measure of her success.

Despite the pain, Bamie knew that she had to endure giving up Alice. It was the right thing to do. Her own experience had taught her the importance of a daughter's relationship with her father. Everything Bamie became, everything she was, came from the unconditional love and special feeling her father gave her. Knowing she would lose her role as Baby Lee's surrogate mother, Bamie did what she always did; she faced a defeat head-on. She moved into a new house farther out on Madison Avenue and settled in with Baby Lee to wait until the newlyweds came to take her. She was prepared. If she was going to be alone, she would make the best of it. She then sent out invitations to friends to call.

At the end of February, T. R. wrote: "I shall be glad to get home. I am an American through to the backbone." He also received a copy from the publisher of his Benton biography, and "although it was rough in places, he was sufficiently encouraged to want to tackle some more ambitious historical work." It was clear he saw his future as a writer, not as a politician.

As the March date of the honeymooners' return approached, Bamie learned they had decided to keep Sagamore Hill. But her relief was tempered by knowing that Alice would not be living with her much longer. T. R. and Edith would go to Sagamore Hill after a short visit with Bamie who now arranged for Cabot Lodge and Springy to be staying with her to greet the couple when they arrived. Having her friends with her would help soften the blow of losing Alice.

Little Alice would soon have a stepmother who, like her father, would never speak her mother's name.

Part II
Alice

Eight

"The Child of Another Marriage"

In the cold New York February of 1887, Alice turned three and a month later welcomed her father and stepmother. Forty-six years later she would say it was "among the first recollections I am sure of . . . an afternoon in the winter of 1887." Perhaps she could even recall the feel of the fabric of her "Sunday best," the rustle of its skirt, its pretty sash around her waist. And the smell of the pink roses that Bamie placed in her arms, saying, "These are for your new mother."

If Alice wore the locket with her mother's hair in it, there is no record. And if not, its absence was yet another reminder that the loved one for whom she had been named was not to be mentioned. She walked down the stairs. Her father and Edith were watching, waiting, their faces, no doubt, alight with their decision to make her part of their new family. The next few days would be the first time they would be alone together with her—the first time to practice being the new family they had decided to be.

It was all for her; everything was all about her. The hour stood still, suspended. And for those stretched-out minutes, in which, no doubt, her papa and this new mother hugged and kissed her, touching her guardedly as in any first meeting with one whose trust had to be earned, she locked away the feeling in her mind. It would always be the first, the deepest, the most confusing and yet the most cherished memory. She was Baby Lee, the center of their attention.

Just back from their three-month honeymoon, Edith was already pregnant. In contrast to the general view at that time, she embraced the sexual part of marriage as the "wonderful silky private part of woman," rather than as "duty." Next September, Alice was to have a brother or a sister, they told her. But how they all fit together was a fog-wrapped puzzle that Alice was never quite able to sort out. Was Edith "papa's sister," just as Bamie was? Her father's other sister, Auntie Corinne, also took care of her, sometimes in Bamie's house, sometimes in her own house nearby. There was also Great-Auntie Gracie, a sister also, even more confusing, who was explained to her as the sister of her grandmother Mittie. And Mittie was dead like her mother was dead. And a grandfather long taken away too, leaving only a portrait on the wall, whose great leonine head spoke of a sweet power. There was Nanny Mary, who bossed her around, and a butler, Chamberlain, whose shoulders as a perch allowed the most amazing sights. And grandparents named Lee who lived in a place called Chestnut Hill that sounded like a fine home for squirrels. Now there was this "new mother," while the dead one's pictures were nailed to the wall over her bed and sat in a frame on a table with her name never mentioned, only as having been "taken away." Every night Alice was prompted to mention in her nightly prayers "my mother who is in heaven."

The three of them now sat together on the floor trying to become acquainted—Alice, her father, and this other one who told her to call her "Mother," playing blocks, building houses, peopling them with imaginary characters who hopped around and had tea. But this was only to be a snatch of time. T. R. wanted to leave right away for the Badlands to assess the severe winter's damage to his herd. Edith wanted to visit relatives for a few weeks, leaving Alice in Bamie's charge a bit longer. In addition, the Lee grandparents wanted Alice with them for six weeks. It was all a jumble: who was who, who was where. That summer, there would be a lot of coming and going, of pulling apart and supposedly joining up. Alice was expected, as she later said, as the child of "another marriage," to cope with it all.

There was much for T. R. and Edith to do to get Sagamore Hill ready for their new family. With a baby coming in the fall, they needed to adapt the Oyster Bay house to a year-round address where T. R. would live the quiet life of a writer. Edith would have a household staff to manage, overseeing the twenty-two rooms, stables, and grounds. It was more than a new family they were putting together; it was a new life. And Edith and T. R. were eager to get started. Before leaving for Sagamore Hill, T. R. pointed out how convenient it would be for Alice Hathaway Lee's parents to pick up Baby Lee at Bamie's, then return her to Sagamore Hill after their time together at Chestnut Hill.

Hearing these plans, Bamie faced the stark reality that she really was about to lose Alice—not just for a weekend or a visit but forever. The loss took on a deeper dimension.

To that point, everyone in the family had called Alice "Bye's Baby Lee." But when the Lees came for her, she could no longer be Bye's. And now this truth was a glass shard ready to pierce her well-being, perhaps forever. Bamie didn't think she could bear to live through the moment of her Baby Lee leaving. To avoid it, she made plans to be away with friends, touring Civil War battlefields. She wrote Grandmother Lee to come for Alice in the middle of May, explaining that she herself would not be there, but that the butler, Chamberlain, and Alice's nanny would be in charge, as well as T. R. when he returned from his ranch. Edith would be in town, too, staying in Bamie's house.

Before Bamie left, she explained to Alice that her grandparents would soon come get her to visit with them in Boston, and that at the end of the summer, she would go to live at Sagamore Hill with her father and new mother. She warmly added a sweet lie, "Remember, Darling, if you are very unhappy you can always come back to me." Weeks later, while Bamie was on her trip, Theodore wrote to her about the day that the Lees came to pick up Alice at Bamie's house. How it must have nearly broken Bamie's heart as she read T. R.'s description of Baby Lee walking toward the grandparents who would take her to their Chestnut Hill home. "She looked just like a little white penguin when she said good-bye."

Bamie took time to absorb the blow, then confided in a letter to a friend that she would never again put herself in the position of loving someone like that—so deeply. Giving up Alice had been the worst pain she had ever felt. She vowed never again to be faced with such loss.

After her travels, Bamie returned to her house on Madison Avenue and soon found an invitation from T. R. to visit Sagamore Hill. Alice was still at her grandparents' in Boston, and Bamie didn't think she could endure being at Sagamore Hill without her. The summer before, when she had been Bye's Baby Lee, Alice had filled the great Sagamore Hill house with the sound of her footfalls skipping up and down the halls, her squeals of delight galloping across the wide lawns. Beyond Bamie's missing her "little blue-eyed darling," she was also hesitant to tread on Edith's turf. It was not that Bamie was jealous of Edith but that she was aware of Edith's jealousy of her, of T. R.'s relying on her, needing her, wanting her input on pretty much everything. As children growing up together, Edith had been intimidated by Bamie's skills. She had once been filled with awe and admiration when Bamie made a bonnet for her doll, not just any bonnet but an expertly made bonnet. She had once even dreamed of Bamie's disapproving of her for doing something silly.

Both women were now ensnared in a transition of power. What Bamie first sensed at the wedding in London was now as readable as a message in ink, meant only for Bamie. Edith's feeling created the sense of an invisible presence between them. The tension, the suspicion, the feel of a threat was scorching. Edith could not share T. R.'s attention with someone so affectionately close to him as his beloved sister. No doubt, when T. R. and Bamie were together, their blazing-quick minds concocted sparkling repartee that could drown out any bystander. And Edith could never tolerate being a bystander when her adored Theodore was involved.

The tension even spilled over to T. R.'s younger sister, Corinne, who had grown up as Edith's best friend. Corrine could now see that Edith could misconstrue as a threat any interest she and Bamie took in what their brother did. And of course they knew that T. R. would have to side with his wife. Edith might even become so annoyed with them, she would forbid T. R. to ever see them again. After discussing the issue, Bamie and Corrine joined in a pact to tiptoe around the boundaries, never to give Edith a reason to think they were interfering—which would never be easy.

T. R. was squeezed between strong women who loved him more than anything, and he them. It also did not help that he started out that summer telling Bamie in so many words that she was . . . well, too fat to ride her favorite horse. (This is never a wise remark coming from any man, not even to someone as secure in her self-worth as Bamie.) It happened when T. R. began going over his household expenses, prodded by Edith, who didn't know how they could keep up so many servants and horses on a writer's salary. T. R.'s inheritance was not enough to sustain all they were taking on, especially with his losses in the Badlands and with a baby on the way. He wrote Bamie late in May that he might have to sell the entire stable at Oyster Bay, including his own beloved horse, Sagamore, and even Bamie's carriage horses. But he would not sell her favorite one, Caution, adding that he wished very much that "Caution were big enough for you to ride; but I am afraid she is much too light." However, he would not sell her "because Edith thinks she would like to ride her very much."

Bamie, now in her thirties, had grown stout without realizing it. As proof that T. R.'s letter had hurt her, it was later found split in half, secretly hidden in her desk drawer. But since T. R. sounded as if he missed her terribly, and Bamie didn't want the lack of feeling between herself and Edith to explode into full exposure, she agreed to visit Sagamore Hill, even though Alice was still not there. But she needed a buffer, so she invited Springy, assigned now to Washington, and together they went to Sagamore Hill. However, the subtle signs of Edith's resentment were evident every moment of the visit, so Bamie cut it short.

Then she tried again. This time, she took her adored Fergie, who came over on his first trip to America. This visit was cut even shorter. Simply, she and Edith found it too hard to be congenial. They were able to conceal it from most everyone else, but could not hide it from each other. Theodore, however, was catching on. He became miserable knowing what was happening between the two most important women in his life.

Bamie declined his invitations to visit Sagamore Hill the rest of that summer, saying she was too busy. He continued to write to her, his discomfort becoming increasingly evident. Bamie could read Edith's voice behind his words, and when he told her that Alice had returned from the visit with her grandparents, it was all she could do to keep from running out to Sagamore Hill. In a strained effort to reengage her, in one letter T. R. composed a scene between Alice and her stepmother, with Edith saying: "Well, what do you want to say [send?] to Auntie Bye? Little Alice smiled and said, 'A kiss.'" Theodore added, "We miss you dreadfully."

Bamie understood that Edith felt insecure following Alice Lee as T. R.'s wife. She also understood her brother's needs better than anyone. She realized that, in time, she would have to set Edith straight. When she would do it, and *how*, she did not know. But she knew for certain that one day, she would have to make Edith realize that loving T. R. must include what was best for his happiness. And T. R.'s happiness meant a career in politics.

She had engineered his new marriage. Now there was more engineering to do. Yet in the atmosphere of these new relationships and the complexity of feelings among the three of them, Bamie forgot, or was unaware, that Alice could have felt abandoned.

Nine

She Watched Him Shave

THAT SUMMER WITH HER GRANDPARENTS was the first time Alice sensed the life of her mother. In addition to their grand home in Chestnut Hill, her grandfather Lee owned a house on Beacon Street in Boston where the rear windows looked out over Back Bay. Each floor had a gloomy middle room except for one. And in *that* middle room her mother's dollhouse sat squarely on the floor, left just as her mother had played with it.

She touched the same tiny furnishings her mother's fingers had touched, saw the same pieces her mother's eyes had lingered on. These were the dollhouse rooms her mother's imagination had peopled, practicing for a future she could not know would vanish. And yet, no doubt, Alice Lee had envisioned her future children—as many little girls tend to do, practicing for a family—and now there was the one sitting there, whom Alice Lee had imagined and hoped for. Little Alice was feeling for the first time the presence of her mother.

It was her mother as a child like herself, not as the adult Baby Lee would soon miss, the mother who would have helped guide her through the fog of how she should be in the world; to make her feel special, singular; whose eyes would light up when she entered a room. Baby Lee was the child whose father could not say her name because it was tainted with death, creating a silence that felt like disapproval, like a designation that she was invisible. She was shared with the parents of a mother who had been taken away, grandparents who never spoke of her mother, either. And now she was expected to accept a stepmother who seemed to want her mostly to complete the picture of a perfect family.

Everywhere, Alice Hathaway Lee was a ghost haunting with her silence. Even in Alice's grandparents' home, Edith was referred to as Baby Lee's mother while Alice Hathaway Lee remained hushed, merely a connection to the child who visited every summer and every fall as a part of a family she struggled to feel a part of. It was Alice Lee's dollhouse that whispered of the girl who was very much alive, playing in joy. While Auntie Bye had told Baby Lee that her mother had been beautiful and kind, no one else had told her anything about her—no details, no sense of a real person who cried out "I love a little girl," just before she let go into the darkness of dying. But here, now, Alice could feel a real connection to the one who had brought her into the world.

The experience, while being comforting, was also, no doubt, unsettling. Soon Alice would be desperately searching for a lodestar, a mother to pull her through childhood into the complicated roles of grown daughter, wife, mother, world citizen—all the things a successful life is supposed to shoot for.

That summer when she was not yet four, little thought was given to the possibility that her mind was absorbing experiences that would write the script for much of her adult life. The Roosevelts accepted the Victorian confidence that infants and children were supremely adjustable. Most parents of that era followed John Locke's view—that children were to be "molded." The physician-philosopher described a child's mind as a blank slate, a *tabula rasa*. Some seventy years later, Joseph Campbell, who studied how myths help us understand childhood, pointed to the sharp truth in the age-old tale of the stepmother: that the child of a first marriage may feel thrown away or left behind when her father remarries. Without someone making that child feel special, loved unconditionally, there is no sense of a world center, of a script to follow, only one of living in the margins of a family. The child's journey then becomes one of making a world in which she alone is the center—which in Alice's life would mean the making of a life that would eventually see her become known as "America's Princess," the orchestrator of world-riveting mischief.

But on her first visit to her mother's parents' home, Alice had discovered the child her mother had been. For the first time she felt a sense of the life that had led to her own. In time, she would learn there was a piece of lace from her mother's wedding dress put in safekeeping for the day she herself would make it part of her own wedding dress. There was also that locket with her mother's hair in it that she'd worn at her baptism: a thumbprint of her mother's intended love.

After her grandparents left their Back Bay house to return to their Chestnut Hill home, Alice walked every morning with her grandfather Lee to the train station, where he caught the early train to town to his office at Lee, Higginson & Co., the investment firm in which he was a partner. He had silver-white hair, cut very short, and the clearest China-blue eyes. He loved to tease, especially Alice's grandmother, who seemed to look worried all the time. He wore a sunburned straw hat with the brim turned up, somewhat like a sailor's hat. He would return by train a half an hour before supper and read the *Evening Transcript.* Unlike the Roosevelts, he did not dress for dinner. And Alice noted that for the Lees, dinner was referred to as "supper." Learning the new people in her new family fed her nascent curiosity.

In the afternoons Alice accompanied her grandmother in a comfortable Victoria driven by a coachman and drawn by horses that looked far from dashing. Rolling along the shady roads in Brookline, they often stopped at the Woman's Exchange to buy a delicate cake with white frosting. And since it was barely twenty years since the end of the Civil War, the sense of the war could still be felt, especially during Alice's first visit. In that late May on Decoration Day, her grandmother took her to the bridge over the railroad tracks at Chestnut Hill to watch the parade march by. Men who looked like they might have come back from the wars the day before, and were fit to go into battle again, marched to decorate the Civil War dead.

Those six weeks of her first summer visit with the Lees gave her the attention she craved and the security she needed. Until her grandparents dropped her off at Sagamore Hill, her days had been spun to a secure rhythm. She was the center of her grandparents' lives, their every concern, the source of their every wish to keep her from further tragedy. Back at Sagamore Hill, everything took on a different tone. Edith was preparing for the birth of her first child, due in three months. She and T. R. had been arranging the house the way Edith wanted it. Alice had spent a summer there when she was two, but now a year older, Sagamore Hill became a principality. A huge house with extensive grounds and staff to maintain it—a maze she had to learn, the biggest world she had yet known.

Sagamore Hill had been built for Alice Hathaway Lee and finished by Bamie. Now it was the household for Edith to rule. Once, it had reflected the hopes of dead Alice Lee with its furniture and design. When Bamie supervised the final months of its construction, she put on the finishing touches, which she hoped would entice her brother out of his grief to join her there. And it did. But now it was to be Edith's house.

In the three months she put her stamp on it, moving in old family pieces as well as new ones she had bought in Italy on her honeymoon. She and Theodore had worked "like a couple of dusty, grimy beavers" placing furniture, hanging up game heads, and shelving hundreds of books. While Edith reluctantly realized she had to accept a heavy masculine décor, she took over one first-floor room as her personal parlor. Facing south, it looked out on the front piazza and lawns toward the blue water of Oyster Bay.

She moved in floral button-back sofas, two armchairs, two side chairs, delicate side tables and lamps and a small writing desk. Theodore put his study across the paneled hall in the library with a fireplace ready for warmth on winter nights. A collection of weapons and western memorabilia decorated the walls. A massive desk was set under the oil-painted gaze of Greatheart.

Edith spent the mornings organizing the household, sewing, and answering letters. She was a meticulous housekeeper, her personality always seeking perfection at everything she did. And she could absorb T. R.'s hyperactive personality with humor, such as the summer day the Sagamore Hill windmill got stuck and T. R. climbed the sixty feet to the top holding an oil can, hoping a squirt would get it going. When the wind shifted and the windmill blades accidentally sliced off a bit of his scalp, he headed into the front hall where Edith met him, scolding: "Theodore, I wish you'd do your bleeding in the bathroom. You are spoiling every rug in the house."

Those early days at Sagamore Hill, T. R. spent mornings in his study finishing his fourth book, the biography of the founding father Gouverneur Morris. He and Edith began teaching Alice her numbers and alphabet. In the afternoons they would walk in the woods, swim, or boat through the marshy lagoons, sometimes with Alice, sometimes boating alone, with T. R. pulling on the oars and Edith reading aloud from Browning, Thackeray, or Matthew Arnold. Sometimes they would go on Sundays across the bay to Christ Episcopal Church in the village.

On August 6, Edith celebrated her twenty-sixth birthday. Heavily pregnant, she wanted a female friend in the house to help her when the baby came. Bamie volunteered, more concerned about her brother than Edith's desire for a helper. She knew T. R. would be wracked with worry and tormented by his memories of Alice Lee. She wanted to be there to calm him. She thought it would be ridiculous to wait for an invitation from Edith and wrote T. R. that she would indeed like very much to come to Oyster Bay "if she could be of real assistance in this way to Edith." (Apparently, no one considered that she could also be of help to Alice, who certainly would feel the jar of adjustment to her only-child world.) Edith sent back word through Theodore that there was no need for Bamie, that she had arranged for her childhood nurse, Mame, to be there and stay on to be her own child's nurse.

"Just a line to say how very, very much we appreciate your proposal," T. R. wrote to Bamie, "you blessed blue-eyed Rogue; you always were true as steel in any tight place. Mame is devoted; you know how much she is to Edith: I do not think there is need of anyone else." This attempt to smooth the waters only ruffled feathers more.

Bamie was learning that she had to tread even more lightly in all dealings with Edith. She began doing anything to keep away from Sagamore Hill. Trying to live through others, she stayed on the go. She took on wanting to cure Elliott's self-destructive drinking. She traveled with friends. She embraced her loneliness and kept her distance from T. R. and Edith.

In early September, T. R. sent his book *Gouverneur Morris* to his publisher. With that no longer occupying his mind, he became wracked with the repressed terror of the approaching birth of his second child. It was then that Alice herself took him over. She positioned herself at his washstand. She watched him shave down to the last whisker. She demanded that he take her on long walks. She stood on the sidelines of the tennis court and supervised his playing. She waylaid him, jumping at his shoulders, enticing him to lift her up for a ride where, no doubt, she would hold on to his head as any three-year-old would, dislodging his glasses so he'd have to reset them. Sometimes her new mother went with them on walks, but Edith was heavy and sickly now. In most ways, Alice took charge of her father, keeping him busy while the sense of something momentous about to happen saturated the household.

The baby was not expected until the second half of the month, but T. R. was not surprised when at nine o'clock on September 12,

Edith went into labor. The nurse who was to help with the delivery had not yet arrived, but a cousin who lived nearby, Dr. James West Roosevelt, rushed over. At two fifteen, Edith gave birth to an eight-and-a-half-pound boy, to be named Theodore Junior. T. R. right away shared the news with Bamie, adding, "[Edith] was extremely plucky all through. Aunt Annie spent the night here and took charge of Baby . . . I am very glad our house has an heir at last."

In Victorian custom, Edith was wrapped from bosom to hips in muslin bandages to remain in bed for the usual two-week recovery from childbirth. She soon was set upon by postnatal depression, tearful for hours for no good reason. Even when T. R. took her for a drive, she wept and begged him to take her home. With her stepmother preoccupied and sad beyond explanation, Alice took hold of a rocking chair and pulled it up to her newborn brother's crib. She studied him carefully. She declared him "a howling polly parrot" and wanted to take him to Chestnut Hill for her fall visit.

In October Bamie was finally invited to come see the baby. Two days before she was expected to arrive, T. R. dashed off a quick note: "Edie is still pretty weak, and the small boy has colic, but I guess it will be all right. I probably hunt Saturday so I may not be able to meet you myself. Yours ever, Thee. P. S. Edie wants a pair of nursing corsets."

When Bamie arrived at Sagamore Hill, she found Alice sitting by the bassinet, guarding baby Ted, staying there for hours at a time. When asked why she was watching him so long, she answered that she was worried "lest someone should take baby brother away." Alice's haunted childhood was taking root as an indelible part of her.

Ten

Where *No* Did Not Exist

SHE HAD A SET RITUAL. As soon as she arrived at Chestnut Hill, she'd burst in and violently jump up and down on the sofa until the springs sagged. She never would have dreamed of doing that at Sagamore Hill, certainly not with Edith in charge. But at her grandparents' home, there was no "no."

As Alice was the only connection to their dead daughter, George and Caroline Lee were loath to deny her anything—certainly not anything if it would upset her or make her unhappy. Which covered pretty much everything. Alice Hathaway Lee's four sisters, who lived nearby, were the same—aunts so permissive that Alice would later declare, "I ought to have been spanked." When it came time to go back to Sagamore Hill, she dissolved in tears, partly because she loved her grandparents but also because she knew she would miss having the world swing about her. As soon as she got home, she would still be sniffly, eating her supper in the nursery with the crusts of her bread cut off while the memory of the delicious French rolls at Chestnut Hill danced in her head. She practiced being miserable until the misery became a habit. She gave herself a lifelong disease of self-pity. And in time it would crust over with a hard-heartedness that fooled everyone. Inside, the tiny girl was still longing to be special, especially to her father, who continued to avoid speaking her real name and began now simply calling her "Sister"—identified in relation to the male child in the household.

T. R. and Edith ignored her moods and privately began a running joke, reminding each other to be nice to Alice because she received her mother's portion of her inheritance in a lump sum, which her grandfather Lee doled out to her in an allowance. These yearly sums supplemented the household's tight budget. Every day, they read to Alice. They took on the responsibility of educating her themselves, teaching her numbers and the alphabet and the fundamentals of reading. They read from *Grimm's Fairy Tales* and *Tales from the Arabian Nights.* They eventually moved on to Dickens, Twain, Longfellow, and Kipling. And T. R., in his love for imitation and drama, acted out history through tales of George Washington, the War of 1812, Davy Crockett and the Alamo, the Civil War, and the fate of Custer—something like a living forerunner of *Sesame Street.* While Alice absorbed a good bit of the history he taught her, it was mostly the sound of her father's voice that she craved.

After turning four, Alice was most interested in living out her new name of Sister, or Sissy, and began asking for another brother or sister. Having another playmate to add to her Sagamore gang would be delicious, because she saw what a good playmate Ted could be. Adventuresome, he toddled after her in short pants all around Sagamore Hill, playing with two dogs and a litter of newborn kittens. She trooped with Ted into their father's room while he was dressing to go through the little box on his table, just as T. R. had done with *his* father—going through the trinkets in the "ditty-box." All the while, Alice would be teaching Ted how to get into their father's riding boots and clump up and down the room in giant strides.

The winter of 1887–88, Edith and T. R. took baby Ted and Alice to Bamie's New York house, as Bamie was traveling. At first T. R. found it great fun to play in the waist-high snowdrifts and hurricane-force winds, but being housebound, he soon felt the lack of doing anything serious and said, "I should like to write some book that would really take rank as in the very first class." By the end of March, he was well into the research on a four-volume history of America's expansion, from Daniel Boone through the Revolution, to be titled of *The Winning of the West.*

In April they moved back to Sagamore Hill, where Alice stayed until mid-May when she left for her visit at Chestnut Hill. While Alice was away, Edith became pregnant. In addition to liking sex, Edith enjoyed breast-feeding, and never balked at expanding her and T. R.'s family. T. R. was so delighted at his growing family, he was able to push aside his restlessness. As Edith noted in a letter to Cabot Lodge, her husband was writing "two lines a day and is fatter than ever." He wrote through the winter, snow falling outside his window, pushing his literary skills to their utmost, partly hampered by his drive for perfection. He had been brought up on Francis Parkman's seven-volume *History of France and England in North America*, in which men of force bent nations to their will. T. R. aspired to follow this style, to avoid historians' obsessive analysis of treaties and instead enthrall his readers with descriptions of the smell of campfire smoke or the sight of a sunset reddening the water of the Mississippi or the sound of a tomahawk thudding into bone. Yet he meticulously annotated his impressions for fear a scholar would accuse him of fictionalizing. He was always aiming to match Parkman's epic vision of whole empires contending for a continent.

When Alice was back at Sagamore Hill, she sometimes had Bamie's butler, Chamberlain, there with her, and she would hitch a ride on his tall shoulders to watch the sunset—igniting in her a lifelong love of the sky's changes at nightfall. That summer of her five-year-old year was calm and happy. Large hunks of ice had been cut from the pond to put in the icehouse and covered with sawdust, so throughout the summer ice cream was made with fresh fruit from the strawberry beds and cherry trees. There was a flourishing garden, giving luxurious suppers of mashed potatoes, string beans, corn, and spinach (disguised). There was also a dish the cook made out of eggplant, which T. R. called "fussy."

Since Alice learned to bellow in the Irish brogue of her nanny mixed with the British briskness of Chamberlain, T. R. often delighted to tell her, "Sister, go out and call for the carriage now." The stables were a quarter of a mile away, so Alice had to stand on the piazza, fill up her lungs, and let it rip. Her mixed accents always unleashed her father and Edith's belly whoops. Her ability to imitate accents was a talent she was proud of.

Her stepmother and father continued to school her every day. Edith was subdued and busy, blooming in her early pregnancy of the third child to be added to the family. "Sister" had little Ted as a playmate and the promise of another that she could guard, lead, boss, and love. On July 29, Edith went to watch T. R. ride in a polo match. His sister Corrine also came. Their troubled brother Elliott was on the opposing team, and in a burst of competitive fervor, T. R. chased him down the field, fighting for the ball. Elliott's life now was mostly made up of polo playing and drinking. Bamie, Corrine, and T. R. had begun to realize that Elliott was slowly but surely drinking himself to death. In fact, T. R.'s galloping after him with total abandon could well have been out of frustration at not being able to catch and save his brother. Suddenly, there was a horrendous thump of colliding horseflesh and T. R. was knocked unconscious. He lay, not moving or stirring, described by Corrine as being "like a dead man." After getting up, he staggered, rambling in his head for a couple of hours and not quite himself for days. Edith, though, as usual not outwardly perturbed, had a miscarriage two days later.

Rattled and sad, Edith stayed in bed for twelve days. As soon as she was up and about, T. R. left for a hunting trip in the Rockies and Edith's sister Emily came for a visit. Although others described Emily as vapid and obsessed with talking about her various romances that did not exist, Alice found her a good playmate. They forged an eccentric friendship, which planted the idea in

Alice that years later bloomed when she became the owner of a thin green snake she would name Emily Spinach.

Edith had started reading to Alice from the Bible, and Alice was also given free rein of the Sagamore Hill library, so that over the next years she became a voracious reader, like all the Roosevelts. She herself said she gobbled books. She became fluent in French and could speak a little German. Her governess, Mademoiselle Drouet, added another accent to her repertoire, so that her manner of speaking became a soup, seasoned by the cultures of various nannies. While she was "lightly nudged" toward Mark Twain, her father thought Twain was a vulgar old horror, so reading him felt like a stolen pleasure.

Eventually she would add a good understanding of music, geography, and some of the sciences, especially astronomy and geology. As her parents continued to educate her, T. R. recognized in her his own sort of creative intellect, but as she was a woman, it was not valued as promising of anything useful in the world except to enhance her attractiveness and charm. "Charm," however, was never high on Alice's list of aspirations, though the ability to tantalize would be.

On her trips to the Lees at Chestnut Hill, she bonded with her cousins. Since her mother's three married sisters lived close to their parents, she now had a set of resident playmates: Quincy and Louis Shaw, Alice and George West. Her cousin Molly was about Alice's age. They became ingenious in thinking up things that, as Alice said, would "make themselves felt in the neighborhood." They got into the pigsty and smacked the pigs until they squealed. They got into the coal bin in the cellar of the schoolhouse at the foot of the hill where they made such distressing sounds, the classes above had to be dismissed. When the noises were traced to Alice and her cousins, they were routed out and sent home.

When she returned to Sagamore Hill at the end of the summer of 1888, her father was packing up for his autumn hunting trip. He gave her a piggyback ride downstairs to breakfast every day and took great delight in Ted Jr., who, he said, "plays more vigorously than any one I ever saw." At the end of August, he left on his trip to Idaho's Kootenai country, where he slept above the snow line and feasted on bear meat. Two days after he returned to Sagamore Hill, he left again to campaign in Minnesota and Michigan for the Republican presidential candidate, Benjamin Harrison. This time Edith went with him, leaving Alice and Ted in Mame's care. T. R. wrote Bamie that the trip was "immense fun." By then he had finished the first volume of *The Winning of the West*, but it had been a struggle. The sedentary, lonely life of a writer was not suitable for someone as active and extroverted as T. R. And campaigning had again whetted his appetite for the bear pit. He longed for some official position of responsibility.

After President Harrison's inauguration in January, T. R. got his wish, thanks to his previous year's campaigning for the president-elect, paired with Cabot Lodge's help, who recommended to the new president that T. R. be appointed to some post. Offered the job of civil service commissioner, T. R. was thrilled; Edith was pleased with its salary of $3500 a year. She again was pregnant. Since she did not want to move to Washington until after the birth, she stayed at Sagamore Hill with Alice and Ted. T. R., who hated hotels, moved in with Cabot Lodge and his wife, Nanny, on Connecticut Avenue and threw himself into his new post in typical style. Within weeks he had investigated corruption in midwestern post offices and was gathering notice all around. Soon he was reconciling himself to a bureaucratic career, and even though he was not yet thirty-one he began describing himself as "middle aged, fat, and lazy."

When he left for his annual trip to the Rockies that August, he admitted to "acute physical terror" at the thought of climbing the first mountain. While he was gone, Edith fell into a deep depression, as she usually did when he was away. It seemed to her that when she was pregnant T. R. left for long periods, leaving her to manage his children, his household, his farm, and his finances.

This time she wrote him, "I sat a long time on the fence of Smith's field watching [the sunset] and wishing for you. I am trying to make Alice more of a companion. I am afraid I do not do rightly in not adapting myself more to her. I wish I were gayer for the children's sake. Alice needs someone to laugh and romp with her instead of a sober and staid person like me. My darling, you are all the world to me. I am not myself when you are away. Do not forget me or love me less."

He answered, "I never was in more superb health and condition. . . . I thus got my game much earlier than I expected . . . and I cannot say I am sorry, for I am dreadfully homesick without my darling, and now I hope to be home even before the 20th." Two months later he was back in Washington. Edith, feeling that the baby was near and T. R., though attentive and excited about the coming birth, was absorbed with his new job, sent for Bamie. By now Edith felt Bamie understood her boundaries, and she regarded her as a valued guest, especially since she was so helpful with the children.

The night of October 10, 1889, T. R. suddenly received a telegram from Sagamore Hill, no doubt sent by Bamie, telling him that Edith had given birth prematurely to a boy. Wracked with worry, yet ignited with excitement, he found he was too late to catch the last train and instead hired a special locomotive to reach Sagamore Hill at four in the morning. The baby was premature but healthy, and T. R. said to Bamie, "Edith can't say enough of what a comfort you were to her. Again, and again she says, 'Oh, that *dear* Bamie.'"

Little Ted announced that the new baby, Kermit, "miaows." Alice regarded him with pride, no doubt longing for the days of her babyhood when she was the center of undiminishing attention. In late December Edith left Alice, Ted, and Kermit with Bamie and joined T. R. in Washington to set up house. He rented a small place at Jefferson Place, which Edith soon made homelike and comfortable.

Now five years old, Alice had her first experience of a new city. Washington then was relatively small, only 200,000 souls who lived to the languid rhythm of the South. No one saw much reason to hurry. The streets were clean. Rotating twigs on horse-drawn machines swept debris to the roadsides to be bundled up and carried away. Streetcars hummed on rails where passengers entered at the back, dropped a nickel at the front, and settled into cushioned seats. Center Market was peopled with upper-class matrons with servants in tow as well as hotel chefs, boardinghouse owners, African American and white housewives—all mixed together when elsewhere in the city classes and races were separated.

Alice was finding her kingdom. Studies of childhood say that the years of six to twelve are latency—a period of supposed calm when the base instincts of early childhood are under control so the child is pronounced educable and sent to school. It is the time when fantasy and dreams are weapons to undo humiliations and hard knocks. Deprive a child of her fantasies and dreams and she is forever stunted. Symbols in our stories become the threads that hold our lives together, shepherding our sanity. So the business of six to twelve is to latch on to the idea of who we will become: Cowboy, Gangster, Thief, Fireman, Housewife, Movie Star, Chief.

Was it possible that Alice, who wore her dead mother's name, buried beneath the everyday names of "Sissy," "Sister," T. R.'s "Baby Lee," and Bamie's "Little Blue-eyed Darling," would soon be subconsciously deciding to be the hellion of Washington, DC?

Eleven

"I Tried to Be Conspicuous"

In letters, Edith described Alice as growing tall and pretty with golden hair; a straight little nose; and white, even teeth. Because her wealthy Lee grandparents paid for Alice's clothes, Edith could be extravagant. As she told her sister Emily, "I got Alice a beautiful dress—dark large plaid with navy blue velour." Yet growing up with brothers, Alice pestered Edith for trousers and wanted her hair cut short like that of Ted and Kermit, while also finding ways to distinguish herself from the brothers her parents adored. She liked to announce in polite company that she planned to give birth to a monkey—perhaps her first launch of a passive-aggressive spear. No doubt it made everyone in the room turn and take notice of her, perhaps even guffaw in shock: fair warning that she was more than capable of honing outrageous tweet-like comments to get under everyone's—and especially her parents'—skin.

T. R. described Ted as quicksilver, proudly telling how his son would plunge his toy sword into imaginary enemies and ride recklessly on a pony named Grant. He saw Alice as the instigator, though a timid one, and told friends how she would make a nest in a corn stack and Ted would take a header in after her in a thrilling dive. But Alice detested the physical activities her father thought up. He drove his gang of children, including various nieces and nephews, to master his challenges, and Alice never seemed to measure up. In swimming, which was hard for her, he egged her on, shouting, "Dive, Alice, now dive!" In his insistence that she master what scared her, she felt persecuted.

Her father's gun room at the top of the house was off-limits. The children were never allowed up there unless invited. Much to Edith's horror, as they grew older, he put rifles in his children's hands as they stood on the piazza, coaching them to shoot at a railing or a fence. In playing hide-and-seek, all her father had to do was growl and moan in what Alice called a "horrid, savage noise that petrified us," and the children would scamper away in horror.

From the age of six, Alice became a good horsewoman, even with the social requirement that women ride sidesaddle. She seemed to have a special feel for horses, which Edith wrote to Bamie about, telling how Alice woke before everyone and got her new toy horse and cart in bed to play with. In her letters to Bamie, Edith always included something about Alice, such as, "She looks splendidly, very clear, which means she feels well, and so bright and happy. She has improved much in her riding and seems to have more elasticity and spring of health than I have ever known."

Living part-time at Sagamore Hill, part-time in Washington, and six weeks with her grandparents in Chestnut Hill gave Alice the mistaken perception that there was something about herself that was shameful. She felt as if living at the edges of the family, not in constancy among them. Her ache to belong must have been searing. While her other family had Thanksgivings at Sagamore Hill, she was at Chestnut Hill, though she did, at least, on the holiday that was her favorite, meet scores of relatives on her mother's side, who paid her the attention she craved.

When she went for her visit with her grandparents in Boston, Edith's childhood nurse, Mame, would often go with her before returning to Sagamore Hill. Mame was intriguing to Alice, who later described her as having a face like a priest, austere and ascetic, but with great warmth of character underneath. Her real name was Mary Ledwith. Like Mary Poppins, she had the perfect combination of temperament for a nanny, strict but charming.

She was said to suffer from "milk leg," a condition women got from nursing babies. Most likely "milk leg" meant varicose veins. When Mame drove the pony cart at Sagamore Hill, riding the children around, Alice was intrigued by the sight of the lilac-colored elastic stocking she wore because of her condition. Since Mame had a delightful Irish brogue, which Alice added to the accent she learned from her earlier nurse, Ginny Jane, she found she could make her father laugh at her telling of her toy goat's death in a version of an Irish accent: "He lost *abl* its legs and *abl* its fur and *abl* its horns. That's the way the goat went." Seeing her father's delight in her bringing to life a comic moment, she no doubt filed away his laughter as a sign to mimic more and to exaggerate to make her father laugh.

When she was six, her grandfather Lee gave her a new dollhouse, green and pink. The original of her mother's doll house had faded in age and disrepair, as did her mother's dolls, dressed in the fashions of her mother's youth. Things that had belonged to her mother disappeared, too worn, too broken to mend, or too painful to display. Yet somewhere, hidden away, was lace from her mother's wedding dress. But for now, the new dollhouse became a cherished possession, a stabilizing anchor in her back-and-forth childhood, as she loved adding to its furnishings and never let it be put away.

At her grandparents' house she felt she belonged, though there was always an inner struggle. As she turned eight years old, she began to feel marked in a way that unraveled any strong sense of herself. Her brothers teased her, saying she didn't have the same mother, that she'd had a "sweat nurse." Since Edith breast-fed her newborns, Alice saw what her brothers described as their mother being "eaten by her newborn"—which, to Alice, stamped her as an outsider. Watching babies arrive at Sagamore Hill, she saw how a real mother cuddles her newborn and knew only that she had come into the world differently. Having Bamie, Corrine, Aunt Annie, the wet nurse—all those who, no doubt, fussed over her at birth—had not been a substitute for having those first few days of special bonding with a mother who sends love spilling through a house like scented air. There were no stories of *her* birth. The deaths of Alice Lee and T. R.'s mother on the same day swallowed any tales that spoke of the joy of her entrance into the world. In the prepubescent years that followed, those feelings struck with the force of a sledgehammer.

She was diagnosed as having weak ankles. The tendons were too short and turned her feet on the side. Alice herself would later explain it as an undetected case of polio, which seems unlikely since she didn't have the feverish infection that leaves the effect of a "foot drop." It is more likely her ankles were pulled out of alignment by a developmental growth issue; but no matter the cause, the cure was severe and the emotional damage was lasting, especially for a child entering those critical years when she is developing her body image.

Every night before going to bed, Edith would stretch each of Alice's feet in a contraption that rather resembled a medieval instrument of torture, turning a key to change the angle. During the day, Alice wore braces on each leg from ankle to knee. Even when walking on level pavement, the braces would sometimes catch and throw her, so after leaving them off, she was very cautious. Edith wrote Bamie to tell her of the treatment, knowing that Bamie, who'd suffered a childhood disease herself, would understand. "[The braces] reach half way up her leg, and consist of two iron bars screened to the bottom of her shoe and connected by a leather strap around her leg. They have a hinge so she can move her foot freely up and down but not sideways. . . . I fear there will be a long time before there is permanent relief—one day she will walk quite easily and the next can hardly bobble. The doctor thinks she does not have enough cartilage, but I feel there may be rheumatic pains beyond the muscular trouble which he recognizes."

The feeling that something was wrong with her seeped deep, so that she was never fully able to scrub it out. And whenever her father put her up to one of his physical games, that feeling emerged most. At Sagamore Hill there was a great oak near the path to the orchard. On Sundays the tree became a special treat—or a torment. It was then that T. R. liked to get his three children and an assortment of cousins worked up with the fantasy that they had to escape from some danger—a burning ship, bad men chasing them with guns, or a giant bear craving a child for dinner. T. R. would climb to the lowest branch, fifteen or twenty feet from the ground. The kids would then throw a rope up to him to make a noose, and he would haul them up, one by one.

Feeling awkward in her braces, Alice would hang back. The more-agile children stepped up eagerly, putting a foot in the noose and hanging on. But when it was Alice's turn, she tied the rope around her waist and let her father pull her up that way. By the time she reached the branch beside him, she felt cut in half and burning with the shame of being so inept. Even years after she shed the braces, the feeling of shame remained from that time she later described as being "an orthopedic case."

She was puzzled at how her father never seemed to pick up on her feelings. She was developing a hard-edged resentment at his never realizing she felt ostracized as his first child, with a mother who lived only in silent memory. She had an early remembrance from her toddler years in which she had watched him fall in a fox hunt and, at seeing him banged up and bloody, screamed uncontrollably. Shaking her, he yelled, "Stop, stop!" which set off her early awareness of displeasing him, a dangerous mix with her longing for him to pay attention to her every moment.

Having Bamie as an example of living with pain and never complaining, Alice began to shrug at those years of her physical troubles. Yet later she would say the experience left a scar, thinking that she was deformed, making her pathologically shy. She shuddered with terror when people tried to get her to speak publicly. Shy, yet she shared with her father a compulsion to be the center of attention. And when her brothers teased her about not having the same mother, her self-image sank to the bottom of who she wanted to be. She felt like a pathetic creature.

To defeat that feeling, she needed a counterweight—something that would distract, something that would rattle everyone. She set out to buck tradition, to be contrary, to be unruly. Hiding behind the curtain of her shyness she could yet pull the strings on the stage of her life as the star everyone was watching. She decided to be conspicuous.

Edith wrote Bamie, "I do feel quite as sorry for the poor child as for myself and other inhabitants of the nursery, for she realizes that something is wrong with her, and goes through a real mental conflict trying to get straightened out." While "Sister" was struggling with her self-image, there was yet another blow waiting. These were the years when Bamie was on the move. Starting with the Christmas of 1890, when Alice was only six, Bamie urgently took on the task of trying to save poor Elliott.

T. R. worried constantly that his brother would cause a public scandal. For some time, Bamie and Corrine even dreaded having him to dinner, for he would cause a scene. When Elliott moved his family to Europe, the project to save him became urgent. It started with Elliott's wife, Anna, writing to Bamie to say she was pregnant again and afraid of her husband's drunken rages. She begged Bamie to cross the Atlantic to keep her company and help with the birth. Edith encouraged Bamie to go, even though she herself was expecting a baby in August and counting on Bamie to be there to help.

The adult discussions of Elliott formed an undercurrent of sound in the house that abruptly stopped when Alice or others drew near. Alice was aware that her father worried about Elliott constantly and seemed always to be saving him from some predicament. As Elliott began to deteriorate, falling into mental illness, Alice began to listen through keyholes, which is how she learned of her father's abrupt departures to pull Elliott out of various dives and from the arms of women who contacted the family in hopes of saving him.

Now Elliott's wife, the beautiful Anna Hall, was pregnant with their third child, living in Vienna with their other two children: their son, Ellie, and daughter, Anna Eleanor. Edith described Eleanor in a letter to Bamie as "plain" with "mouth and teeth that seem to have no future." Indeed, Eleanor's plainness astonished everyone since Anna was considered one of the most beautiful women in New York. Eleanor and Alice were close in age, but Edith would not allow Alice to spend much time with her cousin, even though Elliott had a house near Sagamore Hill. Elliott's erratic behavior concerned Edith. Writing her mother, she pointed out, "As you know I never wished Alice to associate with Eleanor so shall not try to keep up any friendship between them."

Elliott was also the godfather to James and Sara Roosevelt's precocious son, Franklin Delano, who lived at Springwood in Hyde Park. There had always been much expected of Elliott, who was considered even more charming than his older brother, T. R., and always the favorite of the women in the family. Now, living abroad, he was headed for a crisis that required Bamie to take charge. She sailed early in February.

When she arrived, she consulted with a specialist, then escorted Elliott to a sanitarium outside of Graz, Austria. Since she didn't trust her brother out of her sight for a minute, she persuaded the clinic authorities to break their rules and give her a room in the same institution. By April, Elliott seemed well enough to move to Paris, where Bamie found a doctor to take care of Anna during her pregnancy, and on June 2, Elliott and Anna's son Hall was born.

But back in New York, Elliott's situation was seriously unraveling. One of his former servants claimed he was the father of her recently born baby and began legal action for financial aid. She wanted ten thousand dollars, an enormous amount by nineteenth-century standards. To see for themselves, T. R. and Edith went to meet the baby, and T. R. hired an investigator, who soon convinced T. R. the woman's claim was true. When the news made it to Elliott, he started on a bout of heavy drinking, becoming violent and suicidal.

Bamie cabled T. R., who advised her to leave Elliott in an asylum outside Paris and come home with Anna and their children. By then, T. R. was staying at their house in Washington by himself, living like a bachelor, working as a civil service commissioner and waiting out the family crisis. Cecil Spring-Rice witnessed T. R.'s eccentric habits under pressure, which he described as "walking up and down in creaky boots and eating chicken like a wild animal," but added that he was doing fine and really was "one of the people who are absolutely dependable and sure." As Edith's due date drew near, T. R. and Springy went to Sagamore Hill. On August 11, 1891, Edith's labor began, and after a long, difficult night, a healthy girl, Ethel, was born. Leaning over her for a good look, T. R. announced that she reminded him of his stocky Dutch ancestors and nicknamed her "Elephant Johnny."

Edith began worrying even more about their finances. They had two houses to keep up, along with the travel expenses back and forth to Washington, and four children to provide for: Alice, Ted, Kermit, and Ethel. To make their strained budget worse, 1893 unleashed a financial panic. The US Treasury's reserves of gold had been depleted by excessive imports, and between May and July three hundred banks failed, prices and wages fell, and the markets for many goods vanished overnight. Unemployment and strikes multiplied, and there were breadlines in major cities. T. R. again agonized over Sagamore Hill. Should he give it up? Should he rent a simple room for himself in the capital and live there alone while Edith and the children stayed at Sagamore Hill? Edith put her foot down about that. She saw too little of Theodore as it was.

In a last-ditch effort to bridge his financial crisis, he sold a field behind the Sagamore Hill barn to a relative. Edith took the financial pinch personally, saying she thought her management had been an evident failure. To punish herself, she began making her own tooth powder from ground-up cuttlefish bones, dragon's blood, burnt alum, orrisroot, and aromatic ingredients. Then a boon arrived: a payment from her father's estate. Of course, the rest of the country was suffering more than a Roosevelt would ever experience. Mills and mines closed by the hundreds. Paper money was so scarce, Edith paid the servants in gold. She wrote her mother: "I am more thankful than I can say that Theodore is not in business. I believe that he would go mad with anxiety."

Theodore was depressed for other reasons. It seemed his early years in politics had not prepared him to support a family. To him, his future looked bleak. Edith's mother commented to Edith that perhaps Theodore could run for Congress, to which Edith shot back, "That is a dream never to be realized." With Elliott's seeming improvement in the sanitarium in France, T. R., Bamie, and Corrine decided to bring him home and let him try to stay sober. Through connections, they found him a managerial post in Virginia. By then Anna, with sons Ellie and Hall and daughter Eleanor, were living in a townhouse in New York.

Elliott wrote charming lies to his mother-in-law, knowing his news would circulate: "Neither from heat or fatigue, thirst or weakness, from despondency, discouragement or hopelessness or any other cause have I experienced the slightest inclination to drink." That fantasy of serenity was heartbreakingly short. In that same month of November 1892, when she was only twenty-nine, Anna Hall died of diphtheria. Soon after, his son, Ellie, died of scarlet fever. After that Elliott deteriorated rapidly, had attacks of delirium tremens, and, finally, suffered a convulsive attack that killed him.

Corrine wrote Bamie, again in London, saying, "Theodore was more overcome than I have ever seen him—cried like a child for a long time." Bamie thought of adopting Elliott and Anna's orphaned children, especially Eleanor, who was nine. But Eleanor's grandmother Hall wanted her, and so Eleanor went there until her drunken uncles threatened her safety, which is when her grandmother sent her to a school in Allenswood, outside of London, run by the same woman, Marie Souvestre, who had run the school in Paris that Bamie had attended. This would be the time in Eleanor's life when she would receive the extraordinary tutelage of Souvestre, helping her to become the independent woman who was revered for generations as the partner-wife of President Franklin Roosevelt.

Alice, fascinated and curious about Elliott's demise, would remember the grief that ripped through the family. She heard of a picture somewhere of her Aunt Corrine standing at the foot of a bed with dead Elliott lying there, while two of his mistresses stood on either side and a picture of his dead wife hung on the wall behind him. Living in the vortex of these family troubles, Alice no doubt became acquainted with the idea of shame veiled in silence.

If, in her childhood understanding, Alice became aware of the effect of Elliott's wild behavior on her father—even to the point of T. R.'s becoming unraveled—there is no way to know. But certainly the lesson was there for her to absorb, to become aware that when a family member's wild antics intruded on her father's life, he turned to it with complete attention. Perhaps she filed *that* away in her mind—the wild antics, the unorthodox shenanigans, the embarrassment as ingredients to capture her father's undivided attention.

And what about the cousin? Were there any lessons in compassion or concern in thinking about Eleanor? Did Alice ever think of her cousin, Elliott's daughter, only eight months younger than herself, now an orphan? Apparently not. Not until Bamie supported a friendship between the girls when they were much older did Alice become aware of her cousin's life. It would eventually become an awareness that would lead to Alice's delicious sense of competition, a jousting for men's affection and her father's attention. And it sprang from that time when there was enough free-ranging emotion from the family tragedy of Elliott's death to seep down to Alice through keyholes and whispers to add to her self-absorption, to a stalled heart longing for any crumbs left from her father's unconditional love for her dead mother.

At the beginning of 1893, Edith was yet again pregnant. The new addition was expected in April, and, as usual, whenever her step-mother was pregnant, Alice reveled in the house awash with an air of contentment and cheer, which would evaporate with the depression Edith always suffered after the birth.

That year, Alice's grandparents gave her a pony and cart, setting off a lifelong love of new things and a shiny life, especially when the family's focus was elsewhere. When Edith and the children were in Washington staying with T. R., the older children's nanny would take them to the Capitol to play on the steps and to the grounds of the White House that were open to everyone. The park at Lafayette Square was a favorite, as well as Dupont Circle, McPherson Square, Farragut Square, Franklin Square, and Washington Circle. Since there were no playgrounds, Alice, Ted, Kermit, and Ethel used their imaginations to act out fantastic plots, and sometimes on their way home they waited on the corner of Farragut Square to meet their father coming from his office. He'd often get off the streetcar with a small toy animal in his pocket, which at home he would brand with a heated hairpin (he gave these toy animals brands from his ranches—the elk horn for Ted's toy, the Maltese cross for Kermit's, and the triangle for Alice's). It made her feel she had taken part in one of his roundups that he loved to tell them about.

On April 9, the family took a strenuous family walk through Rock Creek Park, and ten days later, when they were back at Sagamore Hill, Edith went into labor. In the middle of the night, Archie was added to the family. Theodore wrote Bamie, who was in London helping out yet another family member in need: "Ted waked up . . . and rushed in to tell Sister. They sat up in Mame's bed chattering like parakeets and hugging two large . . . rag dollies which they always take to bed. Kermit said he liked his new brother because 'he had such berry tiny feet.'"

Soon T. R. was off on his usual hunting trip to the Badlands. It was then that trouble between T. R. and Edith erupted, not only threatening the family's stability and happiness, but also offering the moment Bamie had been waiting for. Bamie would now have her chance to confront Edith and straighten her out about T. R.'s destiny in politics.

Twelve

"It Could Scorch the Paper It Was Written On"

It started with Bamie receiving a letter from Cabot Lodge telling her that Theodore had been asked to run for mayor of New York City on the Republican ticket but had turned it down. Edith was against such a run. His income as a writer and his inheritance from the Roosevelt estate were not enough, she pointed out. What if he resigned from the Civil Service Commission in order to run and then lost the election? They couldn't afford to lose his secure salary.

Cabot Lodge confided to Bamie that when Theodore had written him, he sounded morbid. "It was much worse than I imagined possible." Ordinarily, Bamie would have sped to Sagamore Hill and straightened everyone out. But she was in London, where she had gone when her friend Rosy Roosevelt sent for her after the sudden death of his wife, Helen. Their two grieving children were foundering. Rosy, one of the Hyde Park Roosevelts and half-brother to Franklin, had begged Bamie to come help him. He was an assistant secretary to the American ambassador in London and he desperately needed someone to run his household, to keep up the expected social events. With Helen gone, he was helpless. Bamie couldn't bear to say no. She had been a bridesmaid at Helen and Rosy's wedding, and she was their daughter's godmother.

So when T. R. hit bottom after Edith refused to support his return to politics, Bamie was far away, charming the British Empire. As soon as the official mourning period for Helen was over, Bamie unleashed her charm and spread her influence. She began with hosting tea parties and soon became so noted an organizer that the ambassador's wife asked her to arrange and supervise all social functions at the American Embassy.

Bamie was bridging British reserve by hypnotizing her listeners, sprinkling her magic in making everyone feel at their best. Her art of listening was completely genuine—she truly found all sorts of people fascinating—and gave her great force. When she began losing her hearing, she cleverly covered it up, reading lips, making her an even more astute listener. Her renown led to her presentation at court, where she curtsied before Queen Victoria at an event that she would write about to T. R., comically describing how some who presented to the queen were so overcome with nervousness they threw up in their shoe!

But not Bamie. She carried off the presentation with aplomb and grace. But now, with her brother and his rambunctious family in trouble, she aimed her take-charge know-how at Edith. Not only was her brother's marriage about to crumble—or at least cease to make him happy—he was even describing himself as a "fat political has-been," hiding out, living the life of a reclusive writer. Edith had managed to throw his life out of balance.

Bamie may have shrugged at life in all other arenas, but not when it came to her adored Theodore. She was infuriated when she learned what T. R. had written Cabot Lodge about turning down a chance to run for the New York mayoralty: "It was the one golden chance, which never returns; and I had no illusions about ever having another opportunity; I knew it meant the definite abandonment of any hope of going on in the work and life for which I care more than any other." That her brother had taken the view that his whole future had ended because of one decision was simply unacceptable. And she was resolved to do something about it.

She urged Cabot Lodge to write to Theodore and assure him he would have many more chances. Then she sat down and wrote

Edith a scorching letter. We don't know exactly what she said in the letter, as Edith destroyed it, but Edith's response gives us a good idea:

> Dearest Bamie,
>
> I cannot begin to describe how terribly I feel at having failed him at such an important time. It is just as I said to you he never should have married me, and then would have been free to take his own course quite unbiased—I never realized for a minute how he felt over this, or that the mayoralty stood for so much to him, and I did not know either just in what way the nomination was offered; in fact, I do not know now for I did not like to ask too much. I am too thankful that he is away now for I am utterly unnerved and a prey to the deepest despair. . . . If I knew what I do now I should have thrown all my influence in the scale with Corrine's and helped instead of hindering him. You say that I dislike to give my opinion. This is a lesson that will last my life, never to give it for it is utterly worthless when given. . . . It has helped to spoil some years of a life which I would have given my own for. I shall be myself again by Saturday when the darling gets back.
>
> Much love—E.

Bamie had made her point, but it was too late for T. R. and the mayoral race. When William Strong won on the reform ticket, T. R. sent feelers out, and in response the new mayor offered him the position of commissioner of street cleaning. T. R. let his reply hang for three days—much like Alice contemplating diving off the swimming dock—then turned it down, saying the work was "out of my line." Yet he hinted that he wouldn't mind being a New York City police commissioner. That was a role he could "afford to be identified with." The new mayor came through for him.

Soon, the whole large family was on their way to take up residence in Bamie's old Madison Avenue house while she was in

London. Bamie continued to be a guiding light for the whole family, especially for Alice, her "blue-eyed darling," and her niece Eleanor, now orphaned. From London, Bamie sent the two girls identical sets of Shakespeare's works for Christmas, cunningly keeping the girls connected in ways that would not rock the family boat.

Bamie's house was a family home for the children and their needs while their father served as police commissioner: Alice in leg braces; Kermit "a cranky little mortal," also in irons because of "water on the knee"; Ted, about to be sent to serious school; Ethel, whose legs were as "sturdy as bedposts"; and little Archie, still a baby in need of everything. T. R.'s salary was $6000 a year, which was a comfort to Edith. Furthermore, she would never again squash Theodore's passion for politics.

This expanded family meant that Alice had to compete for T. R.'s attention in the waning years of her childhood. While she didn't doubt her Auntie Bye's affection for her, there came a stinging moment when it seemed the anchor in her life had slipped away. It came in the form of a cable from Bamie to her father, who announced that his sister was getting married! She had met an American naval officer, Will Cowles, in London, and she would soon be home to see everyone before returning to London to be married.

Married! Bamie, married! To go away forever into a family she would call her own! To be lost to all of them! The news was shocking. Bamie, however, knew what she was doing. She knew how she was regarded as a physically challenged old maid, but she had never been one to let the agenda of others dictate her life. At thirty-nine, she longed to be a mother. Looking after Alice had awakened this desire in her, and it was now the driving the force of her life. She relished the idea that a "dashing old maid" might marry a naval attaché at the American Embassy. "I am so glad it wasn't an Englishman!" Theodore wrote her. "I should have hated that. And I am glad it was a naval officer. I have a very strong feeling for the navy."

Bamie's news struck every Roosevelt dumbfounded. Commander Cowles, whom Bamie affectionately called her "Mr. Bearo," was nine years older than she was. But though portly he was also dashing, especially on the dance floor, where he cut quite a figure with his great walrus mustache and his naval uniform, complete with gold epaulets and a sword sash. Most importantly, Mr. Bearo adored Bamie. He was besotted.

Bamie came home only long enough to pack up things she wanted for her new house in London. On the day in 1895 when Alice went with Bamie to the ship that would carry her to England for her wedding, Alice cried uncontrollably. It seemed that Bamie was leaving her to start a family in which Alice would have no part. She would now be forever on her own. It was Ted Jr. who best expressed how all the children felt. "Aunty Bye won't love us as much now." Of course, no one thought that Bamie would have a baby, or was even physically able to. After all, aside from her physical differences, she was nearly forty. But Auntie Bye having a husband was enough to convince the children that she had a new family.

Bamie would not forsake Alice, however. She would never turn away from her blue-eyed darling. But Alice, about to move into her teen years, felt at the bottom of the list of five children (with one more to be added) and a father who didn't speak her name. It was no wonder that a few years later she would write in her diary a note that could also scorch the paper it was written on: "Father doesn't care for me. That is to say, one eighth as much as he does for the other children. . . . We are not in the least congenial. . . . Why should he pay any attention to me or things that I live for, except to look upon them with disapproval."

Thirteen

In Love with the Rogues' Gallery

When T. R. started work as police commissioner in New York, the family moved to Bamie's house on Madison Avenue. Alice had Central Park to play in, where she perfected "rolling the hoop," a popular toy at the time, and drove her Auntie Bye's "little yeller wagon." But mainly Alice was soaking herself in the drama of what her father was doing, loving the gore and danger in the stories he told of dealing with criminals. Indeed, for the next two years, she would revel in feeling that, with her father in charge, the New York police force somewhat belonged to her. Each week, when one of the policemen escorted her and Ted to music lessons in Brooklyn, she begged her policeman escort to stop by headquarters so she could indulge her obsession with the "Rogues' Gallery." There, she stared at the photographs of murderers, thieves, and the worst of humanity, who, full-face, stared back at her. Like any child fascinated with the seamy side of life, she also stood over the display cases of the weapons of evil: guns, knives, ropes that had hanged someone. The police station was a never-ending fascination.

In her reading, she relished stories of Mary Queen of Scots, Lady Jane Grey, and the French Revolution, when heads rolled off the guillotine like melons at a street market. She fed her appetite for thrills, feeling certain she would end in some similar way, and spent hours wondering what someone would be thinking as they walked to their execution.

At home in Bamie's house, her father told funny stories of what went on with policemen and criminals, peppering his tales with deeds of bravery as well as his ideas for reform. Every night Alice studied his clothes for clues, noting that when he dressed in day clothes rather than dinner clothes, he was about to start out on one of his nighttime walks through the tenement house districts and crime-infested streets.

What she didn't know was that her father was coming up against an impenetrable wall of political corruption. New York City was thick with it and impervious to his passion to fix it all. Saloons defied the Sunday blue laws, serving alcohol at all hours. At night, prostitutes walked around the saloon tables in long dresses, offering dates for a dollar. Crooked cops took bribes and kicked back a portion to the political machine that ran the city, known as Tammany Hall. As a member of the assembly nearly a decade earlier, T. R. had declared his passion for smashing corruption. But never before had he faced anything like this.

He battled back by putting in a system of merit to reward officers for enforcing the laws. He instituted a bicycle squad and target practice. He tried to upgrade the cop on the beat to a respectable profession. But he was up against men who were ingenious at finding ways around rules. The blue laws that his fellow Republicans had put in place to crack down on Sunday drinking at hotels were a good example of what he was up against. Raines laws allowed drinking only on Sundays in a hotel with a meal. Crafty saloon keepers thumbed their noses at the law by serving ten beers with one hard-boiled egg.

T. R. wrote Bamie that the Sunday law was "altogether too strict, but I have no honorable alternative save to enforce it and I am enforcing it, to the furious rage of the saloon keepers, and of many good people too; for which I am sorry." He had started a quarrel with his colleague on the board of police commissioners, and explained to Bamie how he regretted that he could not "shoot him or engage in a rough-and-tumble with him." After nearly a year and a half of trying to reform the police, T. R. was reduced to handing out awards to police officers for stopping runaway carriages. His failure ate at him. Not being able to be effective aroused his old dreaded feeling of helplessness. Cabot Lodge wrote Bamie, "He seems overstrained and overwrought. That wonderful spring and interest in all sorts of things is much lowered. He is not depressed but he is fearfully overworked and insists on writing history and doing all sorts of things he has no need to do. He has that morbid *idee fixe* that he cannot leave his work for a moment else the world should stop."

What Cabot Lodge did not say, for fear it would alarm Bamie unnecessarily, was that a distinguished Boston doctor had seen Theodore several times and told Cabot Lodge bluntly that unless Theodore were "shifted somehow to an easier place, it was only a question of time when he has a breakdown and when he does, it will be a bad one." Even T. R. himself admitted to a friend, "Though I have the constitution of a bull moose, it is beginning to wear on me a little." Yet while he was supposedly inches from a meltdown, his complex personality was being infused with a new awareness. He was spending time with Josef Riis, a photographer and social critic who had written *How the Other Half Lives*, a pioneering book documenting the squalid living conditions in New York City slums. Riis showed T. R. the hellish conditions suffered by the city's struggling immigrants, awakening him to the desperation of the poor. He would never forget those times he spent with Riis, traveling through the slums, igniting his compassion for the left-out Americans who seemed to never get a fair deal in improving their lives.

Cabot Lodge may have wanted to spare Bamie's knowing of T. R.'s near implosion, but the seriousness of her brother's mental state did not escape her awareness. Better than anyone, she knew Theodore's ups and downs. His agony in his weekly letters got through to her. She also knew he was distressed over cattle losses at his ranches and bogged down with family cares and duties. He had no time for exercise or fun—sorely needed to keep him on an even keel. She wanted to flee to America and tend to him right away, but she was now Mrs. Will Cowles and still cautious about Edith's suspicions of her tendencies to barge in.

Instead, Bamie paid attention to something else Cabot Lodge had mentioned. As a member of the Senate Foreign Relations Committee, Cabot Lodge knew firsthand what no other world citizen knew: that the United States and England were close to war over a crisis in Venezuela. Nothing of that was in the London newspapers, but Bamie knew from being in political circles that Britain was in an uproar over President Cleveland's message to Congress in December 1895, when he said that Britain must respect the Monroe Doctrine and keep its hands off Venezuela. Cabot Lodge told her, "A spark would kindle a blaze. The situation is very grave." He urged her to "try to make some of the people you see who are sensible understand it, for we don't want war."

The crisis grew from a surveyor-set boundary between Venezuela and British Guiana established half a century earlier, a boundary the British government did not want to accept. Cleveland's speech had been blunt. The Monroe Doctrine forbade European powers from colonizing or interfering in the affairs of the independent nations of the Americas. In return, the United States would stay neutral in wars between European powers and their colonies.

Bamie took Cabot's request as a command. She suspected that the American ambassador had grown too deaf to hear what British officials were saying to him. In addition, he had become so thoroughly British himself, he may not have been viewing the crisis with the seriousness it called for. So she began a private campaign to enlighten not only the ambassador but British political leaders as well. She began going over her guest lists. Her frequent teas, intimate luncheons, and dinners were highlights in the London social circles. She created a plan of attack, reminding herself that the longer she lived abroad, the more she realized how much she loved her native land and wanted it to take its proper rank among the other great powers. She also recognized how much disdain she had for American expatriates who tried to endear themselves to Europeans by denigrating America. She understood thoroughly the underlying pattern of European politics and recognized that the British fleet held in place the balance of power in the world. Wishing that same power for America sparked her question: wouldn't Theodore be brilliant in charge of the American navy? Of course.

After Cabot Lodge's request, Bamie went into high gear. She revised her guest lists to include not just royals but also the bright young men from the Foreign Office. She made her tables irresistible. She hired a superb French chef. She served excellent wines and magnificent food on English china with exquisite silverware and crystal. No one turned down her invitations. Her home became the go-to spot for the real news from America, where the powerful and influential rubbed shoulders while Bamie, being Bamie, spread conviviality as no one else could.

When she found that many of the leading English politicians had no idea what the long-forgotten Monroe Doctrine was all about, she tactfully reminded them. Her subtle suggestions eventually convinced the English to forgive President Cleveland's rude speech to Congress. She chalked the blunder up to Americans' ignorance and inexperience, and they believed her. They accepted her explanation. Their stance softened. They trusted her. There was nothing phony about Bamie; her reputation was stellar. As the crisis dissipated, Bamie knew she'd played a large part in not allowing the two countries to drift into war. She didn't mind when the London newspapers summed it up by saying that "Americans had given themselves up to a delirium of jingoism." She never needed her ego stroked or to give in to a feeling of revenge. She quietly pulled the strings. Three years later, in response to her subtle interventions, a tribunal met in Paris, and a year later the disputed territory was awarded to British Guiana.

Cabot Lodge soon wrote Bamie again, saying that Theodore was in fine form, all himself again—alert, energetic, and full of interest in everything. "The Venezuelan crisis has taken his mind off the police work and he seems to have recovered his tone entirely." But Bamie had moved on—now she began to rally Cabot Lodge to start promoting Theodore as a perfect secretary of the navy-in-waiting. She knew her brother's political potential.

So Alice was growing up in a family that was not only rich but growing closer and closer to the power centers of American politics. Cabot Lodge began working behind the scenes on Bamie's secret plan, and soon T. R. himself had sent word to an influential backer of William McKinley, who had won the presidential election of 1896, to suggest himself for the position of assistant to the secretary of the navy. He also began giving speeches supporting the McKinley presidency. Enthralled, his audiences embraced him. His anticorruption reputation gave him credibility with ordinary people. They didn't hold his Harvard accent against him. They didn't mind his wealth and privilege. His unleashing passion on the side of right against wrong resonated with everyone. Rather than being a devout political party member, he was a moralist, appealing to all voters.

At the same time, he despaired that he would be forever stuck on the board of police commissioners and lamented to friends, "This is the last office I shall ever hold. I have offended so many powerful interests and so many powerful politicians." And McKinley, though he had begun to pay attention, was on the fence. He sent back word to those petitioning for T. R., saying "I am told Theodore is always getting into rows with everybody. I am afraid he is too pugnacious." But just as T. R. was nearing the end of two years on the board, the president gave in.

So Alice moved with the rest of the family back to Washington. The *Washington Post* wrote of T. R., "He is a fighter, a man of indomitable pluck and energy. A field of immeasurable usefulness awaits him. Will he find it?" Even the secretary of the navy said that while he looked forward to having Theodore on board, the job of assistant secretary was really too small for such an able and brilliant man. Others nursed their opinions of him, fearing "he would want to fight somebody at once."

Delighted with his new position, T. R. exploded into action. He set out to increase the number of American battleships to eight and to acquire more cruisers and torpedo boats. He had the president's ear and promised McKinley that the Department of the Navy would be "in the best possible shape" if war with Spain should come. The president laughed. T. R. was all for Cuban insurgents throwing off Spanish rule and considered it a disgrace to America for permitting the bloody conflict to go on so long. By 1898, the so-called war in Cuba "had dragged along for years with unspeakable horror, degradation, and misery—not war at all but murderous oppression." Furthermore, there were America's interests in tobacco and sugar and Cuba's proximity to the projected isthmian canal.

Edith, happy to be back in her favorite city, eagerly took on organizing their rented house opposite the British Embassy. She was becoming good friends with historian Henry Adams (grandson of President John Quincy Adams and great grandson of President John Adams), who said that "the American woman of the nineteenth century was much better company than the American man." Soon, when Edith became pregnant again, she returned to Sagamore Hill, leaving T. R. to get more settled in his new job. In October she was back in Washington to celebrate T. R.'s thirty-ninth birthday, and on November 9, 1897, she went into labor. T. R. sped on his bicycle to get the doctor. Their sixth child entered the world, and within two hours of Quentin's birth, T. R. had him on the list for Groton. And though he wrote to Bamie, saying "Edith is doing well," in fact she was critically ill with an abscess in her abdomen.

Fourteen

In the Hormone Jungle

ALICE WAS NOW THIRTEEN. The attention she craved was simply not there—not with a father preoccupied with a new job and the prospect of a war with Cuba; not with a stepmother who was ill. And her need for attention was being altered by her time of life. Her changing biology was igniting a fascination with boys and with her body. She was also becoming enthralled with the dark side of life—such as Elliott lying dead on a bed with his mistresses crying over him. She was well aware of the danger of her uncle's behavior, but she could not help wondering what it would feel like—especially if flirting with the dark side would catch her father's attention. And not just *catch it* but *keep it*; and maybe, if necessary, even become a form of torment for him.

She was physically developed enough to wear a corset, which made her feel like an "animal in a cage" and added to her feeling of being an outsider in a family that shared the same mother but who was not *her* mother. This feeling must have felt like a splinter in her skin only she could see. She was attending school for the first time and getting to know others outside the family. She would ride her bike up and down the hills of Washington with her feet on the handlebars. She led a gang (in which she was the only female member) that roamed the neighborhood and cooked up mischief.

Her changing body only stirred the emotional confusion she had felt all her life—that she was different, left out, with too much money, too much privilege, too many on her mother's side of the family holding out a bottomless bag of treasure to waste and drown in. She had everything but the emotional validation she wanted and needed. She was like a cherished pet testing how far the family leash would stretch. For this time in her life, Alice left historians little to draw on—at least not a deep draw into her inner turmoil. And yet, the inner turmoil of adolescence is universal, one every young girl comes to know, suffers from, and is enlightened by, so that more often than not she looks back on it smiling at her ignorance and confusion.

Alice suffered from her fears of being deformed from the two years she wore braces. She suffered feelings of being the child of a first marriage that set her apart in a freakish, confusing way. All the while, she was living the complicated mores of the 1890s, in which women were misled about their bodies, and a slip-up of passion could result in religious and social ostracism. Elliott and men like him could have children out of wedlock, but a young woman who broke the sexual mores of the time and risked pregnancy faced the prospect of a dangerous abortion or the scarlet letter of unwed motherhood. Such a scandal would destroy her father—not only in heartbreak, but also by dynamiting his political chances. And while she always liked to torment him with her antics, she never would have done anything to *really* hurt him. Deep down, she longed for his approval and affection more than any other longing in her young life. Actually, his unconditional affection was the holy grail that drove her.

Alice's desire for attention from the opposite sex only heated up. Her ability to flirt was incendiary. In 1897 she wrote her cousin Franklin, "I want to know the name of the girl who James told me you were stuck on instead of me. Have you proposed and has she accepted? . . . I suppose James told you all the pleasant little things I said about you, they are all true. I hope you have given me up, if not you had better. Ta ra ra boom de ay, Alice Lee Roosevelt."

She enjoyed flirting with Franklin and using the power of her sexuality. At a dance at the Essex Country Club, after dancing a polka with him, she stood on tiptoe to whisper in his ear that he should go over and speak with their cousin Eleanor, who was looking forlorn on the sidelines, staring at the ceiling. Was this the first truly kind gesture Alice made toward her orphaned cousin? Or was she bored with the "feather-duster" Franklin. In either case, when Franklin asked, "Eleanor, may I have the next dance with you?" she answered, "Oh, Franklin, I'd love to."

Alice liked to sit with a girlfriend on the doorstep of her parents' house in DC after dark and whistle or make remarks to passersby. The two of them took a cab just to ride around and wink at men they passed. By now, Alice was looking so much like her mother, she was no doubt a constant torment to her father, as well as to Edith, who never completely vanquished her insecurity of following Alice Hathaway Lee in T. R.'s desires. Edith had told Ted Jr. that Alice Hathaway Lee had been empty-headed and frivolous, that had she lived, his father would have grown bored with her—a comment Ted passed on to Alice as a form of young-brother torment. Edith wanted Alice to adopt the docile behavior of a Victorian girl, to be the perfect daughter in the perfect family she was obsessed with presenting to the world. Alice would have none of it.

She set out to do just the opposite. She became dedicated to not doing whatever her stepmother demanded. She resented more than ever that neither of her parents mentioned her mother. In rebellion, she preferred fun over duty. She thought of Bamie as her role model, living independently, in charge of a renowned salon, married but powerful in her own right. Her behavior infuriated her father; not being able to control her aroused his greatest fear: that he was helpless. The final straw was the day a boy from her gang, dressed as a girl, knocked on the Roosevelts' door and asked for Alice. T. R. exploded. He called Alice a "guttersnipe" and forbade her to meet with any of that gang of boys ever again. From that day, Edith's voice toward Alice grew cold. She said their house now resembled a home for delinquent children. She spoke to Alice in a high slight whine, "Oh *yes*, my dear, Mother says you must."

With her reserved personality, Edith was never able to be warmly demonstrative, and on any day had little patience with a tempestuous adolescent. Not long after Christmas, as if in sympathy with the household tension, Ted Jr. came down with ghastly headaches. Edith's firmness with both Alice and Ted added to a crippling repression of their natural rambunctiousness.

Edith and T. R. threatened to send Alice to Miss Spence's New York boarding school. That talk made Alice go on a strike. She said she would not go, and if they sent her, she would do something disgraceful. Every afternoon she cried about it. From her room, the sound of her sobs floated down the hall. Her sheets and towels were packed for her departure, her name marked on all of them, when her parents suddenly relented. Knowing that something had to be done with her, however, T. R. made plans to send her to Bamie in New York. Bamie always wanted Alice, whenever, however, no matter her outrageous behavior—though everyone agreed that with Alice, Auntie Bye would have to perform a miracle.

On February 13, a day after her fourteenth birthday, Alice was put on the train to New York. She was forewarned by Bamie's letter: "Now darling, I am too happy you are coming, but there will be a few rules and regulations. . . . You know, dearie, Auntie does not believe in a great party just tearing around all day, and so you will have a couple of hours of music and reading. . . . To put everything nicely in order whenever you have put it wrong, hats, etc. all must be put in their places and help Auntie about everything."

Bamie was being clear about what she expected, but she also knew how to relate to a teenager. She would join in Alice's adolescent obsessions, not as much to enjoy them as to contain her. In the meantime, she was going through a life-changing moment herself. At the age of forty-three, Bamie was pregnant. Despite having to adapt to this huge change, she was pleased that her household would be rounded out into a family with Alice, and soon Ted, who was dealing with high anxiety, driven by his father's ambitions for him, and suffering horrendous headaches.

Two days after Alice arrived at Bamie's, the battleship USS *Maine* blew up, setting off the Cuban war that T. R. longed for. Tensions in the family were multiplying, and as T. R. talked of going off to war, Ted, only eleven, began to suffer even more. His father had told him he expected him to take care of the family while he was away. A family that included a mother who was recovering from surgery. Ted was overwhelmed. His headaches became so debilitating that T. R. and Edith consulted a specialist at John Hopkins. No cause was found, and Edith and T. R. took the doctor's advice and sent Ted to stay with Bamie a while to ease his high-strung personality. They arranged there for the renowned Dr. Alexander Lambert to examine Ted and give his opinion.

Alice at first resented living under Bamie's firm hand and having to attend a regimen of lectures and concerts. She wrote to Edith, complaining that it was "worse than boarding school," to which Edith replied that that was why she'd been sent there. Soon, though, Alice admitted she enjoyed the intellectual stimulation of Bamie's friends and said she had no desire to return to Washington. Alice always acted better when she had someone's undivided attention, and Bamie certainly gave her that. Bamie would chat and play, talking on with Alice about her little love affairs, discussing this boy and that, laughing together. Alice felt that Bamie really understood her. Best of all, Bamie's eyes would light up whenever Alice was near. Here was the unconditional acceptance she craved. And now that Alice was old enough to see the world more completely, she considered how odd it was when one of her friends told her how Bamie was seen: "Very nearly ugly—almost a cripple, and yet no one for a moment thinks of these things. One is only aware of her charm." When her friend spoke of Bamie in that way, Alice realized that she had never thought of Bamie as anything but beautiful. She saw her aunt's extraordinary gift with people. No one ever had so many devoted friends. Everyone who was important in America found their way to Bamie. Alice thought of Bamie as her own special aunt and recognized the same peppery high spirit within herself.

Alice had a chance to observe Bamie's "spicy" side firsthand when Bamie referred to people she disdained as "utterly incompetent" or "so very pale yellow." When Edith sent Bamie a small present, Bamie would drop it in the wastebasket and say, "another one down the oubliette." No doubt the up-and-down moods of Bamie's pregnancy exacerbated this spiciness. One day she said that Alice, "with her amber-colored hair . . . shed an amber-colored tear." Bamie criticized "Mr. Bearo," her husband, for failing to share her interest in world affairs and falling asleep during conversation with her friends. He preferred magazines to the volumes of history piled by her bedside. She teased him for being helpless; once, after she helped him into his navy uniform, he turned to her and said, "Someone forgot to put a scarf on me."

Alice must have absorbed Bamie's exquisite combination of brilliance, warmth, and acid observation. She must have longed to have the same influence over people and events. T. R. saw the influence as positive. Alice's letters prompted him to write to Bamie and say, "Her letters are really interesting and amusing. Evidently you are doing her a world of good and giving her exactly what she needed. I quite agree with what you say about her; I am sure she really does love Edith and the children and me; it was only that running riot with the boys and girls here had for the moment driven everything else out of her head."

He also wrote to Alice of family matters: the pets, his and the children's romps. At the end of March, Dr. Lambert delivered his diagnosis for Ted: he'd had a kind of nervous breakdown. And Dr. Lambert made T. R. know that he himself was the cause of it. He admonished T. R. to let Ted grow up at his own pace and not push him, which was apparently what Edith had been telling Theodore all along. "Dear Alec," Theodore wrote Dr. Lambert remorsefully.

"I shall give plain proof of great weakness of character by reading your letter to Mrs. Roosevelt, who is now well enough to feel the emotions of triumph. Hereafter I shall never press Ted either in body or mind. The fact is that the little fellow, who is peculiarly dear to me, has bidden fair to be all the things I would like to have been and wasn't, and it has been a great temptation to push him." To Bamie, he wrote: "Evidently you have done as much for Ted as for Alice by taking him into your house."

Then world events gave T. R. other things to think about. When on February 15, 1898, three days after Alice turned fourteen, the *Maine* was blown up in Havana Harbor, killing 264 Americans, the crisis consumed him. Here was his chance, seeded from his childhood days when he'd dreamed of battle heroics, not only to take part but to also wipe the shame of his father having "bought" a replacement for his service in the Civil War. *That* to T. R. had always seemed a stain on the Roosevelt name. The *Maine* had been sent to Cuba to protect the interests of Americans there after a rebellion broke out against Spanish rule. Since Mr. Bearo was commanding a ship in Key West, he was ordered to Havana to provide a floating headquarters for an investigative team. Right away, a naval court of inquiry ruled that the ship was blown up by a mine, and though there was no evidence to implicate Spain, Congress and public opinion believed otherwise. The country demanded war.

On March 27, the day before the naval report became public, T. R. wrote Ted: "Today I took a hard walk with Doctor Wood and we both discussed how we could get into the army that would go to Cuba." Two weeks later, President McKinley sent the message to Congress to declare war. The secretary of war offered T. R. command of one of the regiments. While all of T. R.'s friends were against his decision to enlist, they knew they had no power to influence him. One said, "I really think he is going mad. The President asked him twice to stay in the Navy Department instead but T. R. is wild to fight. It is really sad. . . . this ends his political career for good." Other friends wondered how he could desert his wife and children at such a dangerous time. He answered, "You know what my wife and children mean to me, and yet I made up my mind that I would not allow even a death to stand in the way of my one chance to do something for my country and for my family and my one chance to cut my little notch on the stick that stands as a measuring rod in every family."

Bamie understood the root of her brother's feeling—his shame in his father's not joining the "absolute fighting forces" in 1861. She knew that to make up for that, he felt he had to go to Cuba. "My heart aches for him," she wrote Cabot Lodge. With it all decided, T. R. came to Bamie's in New York to say good-bye to Alice and Ted. He told them that his regiment was called the "Rough Riders" because that is what they were: a group of fighting men cobbled together from the various classes of Americans that T. R. had befriended over the years, a group as hodgepodge as a granny quilt.

Bamie gave him her blessing. It was the only decision in his career that he made on his own without her, and she was the only one who believed that going to war would not hurt his future, saying, "he cannot help being a power." She pointed out to his friends and colleagues that he had made his decision out of "unselfish thought of the country and not self-interest." He resigned from his post as assistant secretary of the navy and got ready to head to Texas to purchase horses for his regiment. When he came to say good-bye, Alice found herself weepy. She had grown up knowing that if ever there were a war, her father would be in it. But now that his chance had come, she was shaken.

Gathering in San Antonio, T. R. helped train and drill the eight hundred Rough Riders before they headed with their horses to Tampa, Florida, in May before embarking for Cuba. Edith let her anxious feeling slip when she wrote: "Come back safe darling 'pigeon' and we shall be happy, but it is quite right you should be where you are." And she added: "Always I have the longing and missing in my heart, but I shall not write about it for it makes me cry." To relieve her distress, she and T. R. agreed to meet June 1 under the rotunda of the Tampa Bay Hotel for a last night together before he headed for war and Cuba.

On that date, he was waiting for her in the lobby, looking thin but rugged, amid the bustling town taken over by the army as a headquarters for the Cuban invasion. The next morning, she went with him to his camp, ten miles away on a sandy spot rimmed by palmettos and pine, where khaki-shirted Rough Riders emerged from their white tents, lining up to drill. T. R. wrote to his children from Tampa:

> Blessed Bunnies,
>
> It had been a real holiday to have darling mother here. . . . Yesterday I brought her out to the camp, and she saw it all—the men drilling, the tents in long company streets, the horses being taken to water, my little horse Texas, the colonel and the majors, and finally [our mascots] the mountain lion and jolly little dog Cuba, who had several fights where she looked on. The mountain lion is not much more than a kitten as yet, but it is very cross and treacherous . . .
>
> Mother stays at a big hotel about a mile from camp. There are nearly thirty thousand troops here now, besides the sailors from the war-ships in the bay. At night the corridors and piazzas are thronged with officers of the army and navy; the older ones fought in the great Civil War, a third of a century ago, and now they are all going to Cuba to war against the Spaniards. Most of them are in blue but our rough-riders are in brown.

Edith returned to home in early June, and Ted and Alice moved back to Sagamore Hill to wait out the war. While Edith trembled with anxiety, Alice and Ted embraced what they always knew about their father: that he would one day go to war. They tramped

Alice Hathaway Lee, Theodore Roosevelt's beloved wife and Alice's mother, about four years before her death

Alice as a baby

Alice at about the age of two with T. R.'s older sister, Anna Eleanor, known as Bamie, who cared for her until the age of three

Alice at six, when living at Sagamore Hill with her father and stepmother

Alice with newborn Ted Jr., standing guard
"lest someone take baby away"

Alice and her siblings in fancy dress in 1898
(left to right: Ted Jr., Ethel, Kermit, and Alice)

The Roosevelt children with their pets (left to right, Ted Jr., Ethel, Alice, Quentin, Kermit, and Archie)

Edith, T. R.'s childhood friend and second wife, taken about five years after her marriage

The Roosevelt family at Sagamore Hill

Alice as a young woman, fully in White House Wild Child mode, 1902

Alice's wedding in the White House, with her husband Nicholas Longworth and her father. Some biographers have speculated that T. R. is leaning away from Alice because she is wearing part of the lace from her mother's wedding dress.

Alice, now Mrs. Longworth, wearing pearls the government of Cuba gave her as a wedding present

Family portrait at the White House in 1908

Alice with Paulina, close to Paulina's second birthday. By then Paulina was the most famous baby in the world.

Alice at eighty-five, wearing her "crowded hour" pearls

up and down the broad veranda of Sagamore Hill yelling verses from the opera *The Saga of King Olaf*, which Bamie had taken them to see in New York. "*Unleash the dogs of War! The enemy will find us unrelenting, When our cannons roar, The little king of Spain will be repenting*!"

Bamie, five months pregnant, also came to Sagamore Hill but could not avoid the need to feel useful. Ignoring Edith's worries for her pregnancy, she returned to the sweltering New York City heat to become a member of the executive committee of a Red Cross auxiliary to oversee the training of nurses for the field. Alice amused herself by learning to ride astride her father's saddle instead of in the customary sidesaddle for girls.

The story of the Rough Riders' charge up San Juan Hill—their bravery and key role in the outcome of the war, T. R.'s leadership—has been told many times. T. R. would call his moments of being in combat the best moments of his life, labeling them with a poetic, lasting description: his "crowded hour." He called it "the time of my life." And the public saw it, too. The victory secured Cuba's independence from Spain and made it a protectorate of the United States. A letter to the editor of the *New York Sun* from three Democrats argued that the people of the state of New York State nominate Theodore Roosevelt for governor. A rolling ball of political force was set in motion that would forever change his life—and Alice's. Best of all, her father was headed home.

On August 15 Edith got a message by the new technology of telephone to come to Camp Wyckoff on Long Island, where the Rough Riders were in quarantine. She took a five-hour train ride to see her Theodore and stayed in a Red Cross hut. For four days she worked as a volunteer in a hospital, then went back to Sagamore Hill to get the children. Two weeks later, on a spectacular September day, Edith took the children to see their father for a twenty-four-hour visit.

Alice loved the glamor of it all. The regiment was mustered out on September 15, ending T. R.'s four months as a soldier and beginning a most glorious time in Alice's young life. Even though she was in pigtails and short dresses, her budding sexuality could not be hidden. She went with her father as he reviewed the troops, where she was reviewed too, bathed in the admiring looks of men who had faced death and won. In her private journal, she wrote, "If I was in love with one Rough Rider, I was in love with twenty." And when the family was back at Sagamore Hill, a steady stream of Rough Riders visited. Alice basked in their attention during picnics and long walks, listening to their tales of war.

As soon as T. R. was home, he met with the Republican senator for New York, Tom Platt, who encouraged Roosevelt to put himself forward as a New York gubernatorial candidate. His "crowded hour" triumph was translating into unstoppable political power. Soon after, T. R. wrote Cabot Lodge to tell him, "Apparently, I am going to be nominated." It was only Bamie who was not surprised. Yet Bamie was on the verge of her own profound life change. That autumn, at the age of forty-three, she gave birth to her son, Sheffield.

Fifteen

The Script Is Set

Alice had no sense of politics, nor any interest in it. But her father's run for the governorship awakened in her a dazzling novelty. To be adored by a throng of many was not unlike the buzz of an elixir. His political success sparkled in her life with the allure of a new jewel. It began to give her a rock-solid feel of belonging, to be in a circle of power not unlike European royalty, born into it rather than earned. She was emerging from Bamie's influence and feeling the effect of that loving hand over her life—as well as viewing up close the way Bamie orchestrated events through her connections.

Alice was now consumed with her looks and the burgeoning influence of photography. It would not be long before the hungry eye of the camera would begin stalking her. She adopted what was called the "Gibson Girl" look: shirtwaists and voluminous skirts with a neat belt held in place by a pin at the middle of the back. She loved hearing her father speak at political meetings; she loved the press of the crowd and the admiration of her father that trickled down to her. She and her siblings tramped around Sagamore Hill robustly singing the Roosevelt campaign song, set to the tune of "Hot Time in the Old Town Tonight": "*Ro-see-velt, and his riders bold and rough, showed that they were made of good old stuff.*"

Good old stuff. She was good old stuff too. At least by association. And that was okay. Okay, because it fit perfectly into a culture when women's names were never to appear in the newspaper unless they were "coming out" as a debutant, getting married, or were already dead. Being in search of the campaign's trophy of a successful win, she felt as if heading into battle.

John Pierpont Morgan gave ten thousand dollars to "the boy candidate," and T. R. defeated the Democratic opposition on November 8. A month later, Edith was on her way to the executive mansion in Albany to look it over (and pleased with the steady salary of the governorship). Alice loved the inauguration, the glittering uniforms, the big but ugly mansion. She moved in with her governess, Gertrude Young, who had been hired as part of a bargain with her parents for not being sent away to school.

Six months into T. R.'s term, Alice began assisting Edith and her father's secretary with the correspondence. Edith wrote a friend, "We have never been happier in our lives than we are now"—contentment arising partly from the simple fact that Alice was mostly well-behaved. T. R. wrote to a friend, "My big girl is very big indeed now, almost grown up. . . . Alice, I am sorry to say, does not show any abnormal activity, but is a good rider, walker and swimmer, and has an excellent mind and I think I could say that she is by no means bad looking." Edith agreed and told her friends that Alice was "pretty and she is certainly intelligent."

Here was the rub: Victorian culture signaled she was supposed to marry and have children. Her debut, the official signal that she was in line for that role, was only a few years away. Her father always thought women should each have four children to keep the nation populated. He even talked of the lack of children as a form of "race suicide." The social boundaries of Alice's culture were like a gilded rope that hobbled her. When her father wrote that she showed no "abnormal ability" he meant depth and ambition. Did this attitude seep down to her? That she was a disappointment? And how was that disappointment connected to his inability to say her name?

The most she could aspire to was to follow in Bamie's footsteps: to have influence in the world by influencing men. If her father had been able to talk privately about her mother—to escape the strange love triangle between him, Edith, and dead Alice Hathaway Lee—if he had been able to share that love with Alice, would it have changed her? What would *that* have meant to her sense of herself, to her personality so much like his, with its need to be front and center? Being born two days before her mother's death on Valentine's Day created a black hole of silence. She would forever be connected with great loss, if not a reason for it. Her birthday was never a day of celebration.

To stuff that hole with something, if not meaning, she filled her life with frivolous things: lunching, shopping, hoping to be pretty. Even though her father wrote his friend that "she is by no means bad looking," she didn't believe it. She didn't feel "pretty"; one can't anoint oneself with that adjective; it has to be spoken by someone who matters, preferably in face-to-face honesty—even as it promotes shallowness. She followed her father's love of a strenuous life by playing tennis and basketball, ice-skating, and horseback riding. After she read *Antigone*, she fell in love with the story and thought about taking up Latin again. But there was no offer of being educated in Europe as Bamie was. Or like her cousin Eleanor. Eleanor, her dead uncle's child, hung in abeyance without a family to call her own—a much more stringent situation than Alice's complaint of being a stepdaughter.

Maybe Alice was not offered those opportunities. Maybe Edith didn't want to spend the money. Maybe Alice wouldn't have gone in any case and would have thrown one of her glorious fits to change her parents' minds. If her grandparents, the Lees, offered a Bamie-like education, there is no evidence of it; besides, their pattern was already established: being soft with her, gentle to the point of kid-glove handling without a hint of tough love, fearing rattling the silence around Alice Lee's death. Nor was she instructed to feel compassion for her cousin Eleanor, to be awakened to the depth of her grandfather's feelings for others, especially for those in need. Not even to what her own father had witnessed as police commissioner, learning for the first time the harsh conditions in which immigrants scratched for a living.

For a while, Alice played the role of the New York governor's daughter, helping Edith at official teas. She babysat, giving her parents a laugh when Quentin, while sucking his thumb, took it out of his mouth and offered it to her, saying: "Do you want some?" To which Alice, in typical Alice style, sucked her own thumb and offered hers to him. She reveled in the atmosphere of the circus she could always create.

Alice's life, on the cusp of womanhood, was set. She was selfish. Her heart was crimped by resentment and grievance. She had no real interest in being *good*. When she was—fulfilling others' expectations of her—it was only a flicker in a full-length play that would take decades to reach its final act. Her great transformation would not happen for many years—years filled with her father's career and his enormous personality sweeping everyone into it.

That career was now rocketing. During the second winter of his governorship, talk cropped up of T. R. being nominated for the vice presidency. He hated it. He loved being governor and wanted to be reelected. He believed the vice presidency was an empty position that would make him "a symbol of obscurity." But his resistance was no use. The big boss of the Republican Party, Senator Platt, and the monied interests thought of him as a menace to their power and wanted to get rid of him. Burying him in an office that would have no real power would be an acceptable move, especially since the people loved T. R. too much to squelch him. It was a clever move. Yet Bamie and T. R. came up with their own move to thwart it.

By then Bamie had moved to New York, as her husband had been reassigned stateside. She settled herself, Mr. Bearo, and her baby, Sheffield, in the old house where she had lived with baby Alice. She had never sold it, and now it was convenient for her governor brother to spend weekends, saying he wanted to play with his nephew. Actually, he and Bamie were a force to cleverly counteract the political pressure from the party boss, Senator Platt. Following Cabot's advice never to force an open break with the party, T. R. agreed not to make any decision as governor without consulting Platt. However, when Bamie opened her New York house to host weekend breakfast meetings between her brother and Senator Platt, these consultations were cleverly managed. Whenever Platt walked in, T. R. gave a disarming grin and explained that his sister would sit in on their discussions because "she takes such an interest in what I am doing." Platt felt uncomfortable having a lady present when crass matters of patronage were discussed; furthermore, he suspected T. R. of planting Mrs. Cowles on him as a witness to his underhanded ways.

Round one of Platt and T. R.'s confrontation began with Platt wanting T. R. to give the job of the Erie Canal administration to *his* choice. T. R. didn't want to place Platt's man in that position, knowing Platt's chosen fellow was vulnerable to local pressures. Over one of Bamie's British breakfasts, which could go on for half a day, T. R. took over, talking and talking. Even when Platt came close to losing his temper, T. R. kept talking. Platt just sat with his head in his hands while T. R. lectured him about ethical principles. Bamie sat quietly, her presence restraining Platt's temper by the Victorian culture that insisted a woman never hear foul language.

Having won this round, Bamie and T. R. moved on to round two when T. R. sent a bill to the assembly urging immediate passage of a franchise tax on corporations, explaining, "I believe that in the long run here in this state, we should be beaten if we took the attitude of saying that corporations should not, when they receive great benefits and make a great deal of money, pay their share of public burdens." Platt could no longer restrain his anger. He called T. R. a dangerous "altruistic" man (for Platt, "altruistic" meant "socialistic"). T. R. and Bamie bent over with laughter.

Since shelving T. R. in the vice presidency was an acceptable way to get rid of him in New York, the maneuvering to get him on the presidential ticket for McKinley's second term started. Despite T. R.'s reluctance to get mired in second place, where do-nothing seemed the schedule of the day, he changed his mind when Cabot Lodge advised, "Take it." Lodge pointed out that the vice presidency would lead him straight to the presidency in 1904. At age forty-one, T. R. could afford to mark time in the vice presidency. Soon he heard that McKinley had wired the powerful senator Mark Hanna, saying he would not stand in T. R.'s way at the convention if he were nominated to run with him. In response, Hanna warned McKinley, "All right then, but it is your duty to live."

That, of course, would be a promise McKinley would not be able to keep. Platt himself stepped up the pressuring, telling T. R. that if he turned down the vice-presidential nomination, Platt would block his renomination for governor. When Platt said that, T. R. left the room. But after all the finagling, T. R. was nominated at the convention in Philadelphia in June. Platt said, "Roosevelt might as well stand under Niagara Falls and try to spit water back as to stop his nomination by this convention." T. R. wrote Bamie, "The thing could not be helped."

Edith felt he had done a foolish thing getting mixed up in the "vice-presidential business," but she soon realized that "Theodore himself is quite convinced that he's in for a good and useful time of it. There are big questions in the world that interest this country and the campaign is to be fought out on many of them." Bamie agreed with an "Amen." They then made plans to give a bang-up party when Theodore won the election.

Alice, however, was disgusted when her father was nominated. She thought of it as second place, an offense to her family. She wanted her father to become the governor general of the Philippines, where she could live among palm trees in a palace, where young officers in dazzling white uniforms would adore her. Instead, she was pushed back beyond public recognition, since it wasn't considered "nice" for members of a politician's family to talk to the press. With photography becoming more advanced, it would soon become a matter of course that politicians' families would be known by their photographs in newspapers, and *only* by their photographs—a perfect fit for her incurable shyness and fear of speaking in public. She could be a paper-thin presence, a personality born of short articles and scintillating pictures, even as her father admonished all his family not to talk to reporters.

However, not even he would be able to stop her when it came to the public's appetite for the spectacular. She was an image waiting to explode in the public consciousness on the front pages of every newspaper. It was only a matter of time.

In the fall of 1899, Bamie moved from New York to Washington, where Mr. Bearo had been appointed assistant chief of the bureau of navigation. She locked up her New York house, much to T. R.'s regret. He would miss those breakfasts at the house that had gotten him and Bamie through many trials. It had been where he had reunited with Edith. It was the house where Bamie had moved when she assumed she would be childless. But the new Washington house would be just as important to T. R., for Bamie soon began the elegant breakfasts and dinners where she and Theodore would "keep the conversation rippling."

March 4, 1901, was inauguration day. Florists arrived at Bamie's house with a wagonload of flowers. The price tag, already paid for, was $3500, but the florists would not reveal the sender, only that they came from a New York admirer. Immediately Bamie realized it was a sarcastic joke from Senator Platt, who had often said he would not miss being in Washington on inauguration day to "see Theodore take the veil." Bamie's house was already overflowing with houseguests and flowers. The new delivery swelled the rooms with an unmistakable sweetness—and laughter—as T. R. and Bamie realized they were arranged as funeral wreaths.

With T. R., Edith, and all their six children; as well as Corrine, her husband, Douglas Robinson, and their three children; along with Mr. Bearo and Sheffield; the household was stuffed. At breakfast that inaugural morning, others joined: Cabot Lodge and his wife, Nanny; the secretary of state, John Hay, and the secretary of war, Elihu Root; and an English journalist T. R. invited at the last minute. They celebrated a champagne toast at breakfast, gave hot chocolate to the kids, then climbed in closed carriages to ride to the Capitol in a heavy drizzle. Each of their coats was decorated with huge McKinley and Roosevelt buttons.

To watch the parade, Bamie had reserved rooms above a manicure shop at Fifteenth Street and Pennsylvania Avenue. There, they had a bird's-eye view of the presidential reviewing stand in front of the Executive Mansion, as the White House was known at the time. Just as McKinley's carriage rounded the corner onto Pennsylvania Avenue, President McKinley ordered a halt to put the carriage top down. There beside him sat T. R. The Roosevelt children leaned out of the shop window, shouting "hurrah" and waving American flags. Alice noticed how overweight and pale President McKinley looked next to her father, with his military bearing and ruddy complexion. Her father was now a heartbeat away from taking the place of the older, clearly unhealthy man. The image whispered that her father may not be in second place for long.

T. R. stayed another week at Bamie's, while the Senate was in session. Then he returned to Sagamore Hill since he didn't have much to do until Congress reconvened in December. Earlier, he and Edith had rented the Washington house of Ohio friends, only a few blocks from Bamie's N Street home, where he could stay when in Washington. But the rented house would never be needed. In six months, circumstances would upend T. R.'s life and that of every member of his family. With no warning, no signal except the contagion of anarchy sweeping through the nation and around the world, McKinley's presidency would be over. But on the day of

McKinley's inauguration, Alice watched her father accompany the president down Pennsylvania Avenue, oblivious to what would come. Bamie was thinking of giving Theodore a celebration in Mr. Bearo's ancestral home in Connecticut, where they could begin collecting supporters for T. R.'s own run for the presidency in three years. She was preparing to make history at her Washington home, just as Marie Souvestre had prepared her to do.

Alice too was plotting. If she was not exactly deciding to break the rule of staying in the political shadows, she was certainly savoring her future in figuring out how to dynamite the boundaries of "being good." No one could look at her and look away.

Sixteen

"Bored, Shy, and a Little Resentful"

Despite Alice's lack of interest in politics, being the daughter of the vice president gave her a sense of living close to history, and *that*, soon, would become important to her. Especially when history, in a matter of months, elevated her father to the presidency.

In September of 1901, just six months into T. R.'s vice-presidential term, the Roosevelt family was vacationing in a cabin on Mount Marcy in the Adirondack Mountains—all the family except Alice, now seventeen, who was staying some distance away with friends. On September 13, runners rushed three telegrams up to T. R., one after the other, at the cabin. He knew that McKinley had been shot eight days before by Leon Czolgosz at a reception open to the public during the Pan-American Exposition in Buffalo, New York. And from the moment T. R. learned it, he was seething. He knew the bullets had been aimed not just at McKinley but at what McKinley represented: government, government of any kind, and especially representative government and civilized order. Anarchy had become a virulent strain in America, born of social unrest circling the world, and it was spreading. Only recently, an old man had taken T. R. by the hand and said, "Look out they don't get you, Mr. Vice President."

The first telegram brought the grim news that gangrene was spreading throughout President McKinley's body. The second was worse: THE PRESIDENT IS CRITICALLY ILL. HIS

CONDITION IS GRAVE. OXYGEN IS BEING GIVEN. ABSOLUTELY NO HOPE. Rain began falling. If T. R. rushed down the mountain in the dark to start the journey to Buffalo, it would be treacherous. Waiting for clearer weather would be wise. But then the next telegram was bleak: THE PRESIDENT APPEARS TO BE DYING AND MEMBERS OF THE CABINET IN BUFFALO THINK YOU SHOULD LOSE NO TIME COMING.

At midnight, T. R. pulled on a hat to keep rain from his spectacles, left Edith and the children in the vacation cabin, and climbed into a buckboard beside the driver to head down the mountain. In good weather it was a seven-hour journey to North Creek for a train to Buffalo. In the rain, in the dark, with no light but from a lantern that T. R. held, bouncing on the seat of the rough buckboard pulled by two horses that would need to be swapped out for fresh ones, the trip could be a disaster. As the descent grew slippery, one of the horses stumbled. The driver slowed, but T. R. yelled, "Oh, that doesn't matter! Push ahead."

The road was invisible. The horses' eyesight and memory of the mountain road were all they could gamble on. At five o'clock that morning, after rushing since midnight and exhausting the second set of horses, the driver announced they were two miles from North Creek. T. R. ordered a stop to let the horses rest. Knowing that notables might be waiting at the station, he straightened his tie and smoothed his suit. Then once again, rushing, the buckboard rattled over the bridge into town, as voices began shouting, "There he comes!"

At the station, T. R.'s private secretary, William Loeb Jr., waited with a special train car. Loeb handed him eight words sent from Washington, written by John Hay, Lincoln's former secretary, his father's old friend, and now McKinley's secretary of state: THE PRESIDENT DIED AT TWO-FIFTEEN THIS MORNING. T. R.'s mind flooded with all he had to consider. First, he sent a telegram, "Darling Edie . . ." She would know what to do. He stepped up into the train that soon began speeding at sixty miles an hour to Buffalo.

Up to that point no vice president who ascended to the presidency through assassination had successfully run for reelection to the presidency. And T. R. wanted his own term. He wanted it badly. In fact, this historical truth would soon become an obsession. He *had* to be elected by the people to his own term. There was so much he wanted to do for the nation, and when all his strengths were boiled down, the one that really stood out—the one he was really good at—was leadership.

But from the beginning, the contradictions of American culture would create difficulty for the Roosevelt presidency. For this was still a time when women could not vote, when their limited role in American life was carefully defined. It was a time when segregation and discrimination against African Americans, especially in the South, was the de facto law of the land. These two realities would come together in the opening months of T. R.'s tenure and make it clear that leadership in a divided country was no easy thing. And Alice, without even being aware of it, would be sucked into the controversy.

Right away T. R. knew it was important to solidify the Republican voting bloc. The Southern delegates to the Republican National Committee included many Black delegates, loyal members of the party of Lincoln, and their support had been crucial in McKinley securing his party's nomination. T. R. knew that cultivating Black delegates would continue to be essential, and before he even reached Buffalo that September morning, he already had his eye on the 1904 election. He decided that after he reached Buffalo, he would send a telegram to Booker T. Washington, the most famous Black man in America, asking him to come meet him at the White House. He would make Washington his unofficial adviser, not only to acknowledge and help the Black community but also to serve his own political interests.

Meanwhile Alice (who had recently been described as "a young wild animal who had been put in good clothes") barely registered the fact of McKinley's death. She was having a delightful time with a "band of cheerful young people," greedy for sensation but not of the kind brought by a political assassination. She was properly horrified but also fulfilled because she'd been wishing for her father, in some way, to leapfrog the vice presidency into the higher spot. When one of the girls at the party mentioned to her how wonderful it would be for her to "come out at the Executive Mansion," she felt bored, shy, and a little resentful.

She didn't even think of sending a telegram to her parents. Nor did she realize that her nonchalance at the change in their lives would hurt their feelings. Instead, she made plans to go stay at Commander Cowles's family home in Farmington, Connecticut, known as Oldgate (though Bamie and the commander were already in Washington). She didn't think of anything but pleasing herself. When Edith sent word to stay away until they were settled, she began to think she wasn't rejecting them as much as they were rejecting *her*. She decided that if her father wanted her to come to Washington, he would just have to come get her himself. The ongoing, tangled misreadings in their relationship continued, and she stayed at Oldgate, stewing.

Of course, the assassination was a momentous change for everyone in the family. Edith rushed to Washington for McKinley's funeral services. Trying to control her emotions at the sudden jolt upending their lives, she had managed to get down from the vacation cabin and back to Sagamore Hill, where she got funeral clothes for herself and Ted Jr., who was old enough to attend. When Bamie went to meet her at the ferry slip arriving from Sagamore Hill, she saw Edith in a closed carriage with the curtains drawn, then climbing out wearing a long crepe veil with Ted Jr. beside her, a mourning band on his arm.

At Jersey City, where she was to transfer for a train to Washington, Edith got her first taste of what it meant to be famous. Somehow people heard that the new president's wife would be at the train station and rushed there. As the crowd descended on her, she flinched, then held herself erect as she, with Ted Jr., made it through the throng of people onto the Pullman car named "Olympia" for their ride to Washington. The press quickly noted she had "made her hurried trip unaccompanied by a maid," praising her as an example of one "having simple habits and democratic tastes."

But Edith would never get used to the staring, the eyes that perused her, the unwelcome attention she would always get as first lady. She held herself aloof, clearly uncomfortable. At the funeral at the Capitol, some lawmakers whispered, "He's too good a man to win on a foul—but there he is and thank God for it." The powerful senator Mark Hanna railed, "Now look—that damned cowboy is President." Edith stood next to former president Grover Cleveland, saying in a voice choked with tears, "Oh, Mr. Cleveland, my husband is so young!" The former president smiled, comforting her, "Don't worry, he's all right." Already noticing how Theodore was trying to escape Secret Service surveillance, Edith fretted. Over and over during those first days of T. R.'s presidency, she would hear, "Poor Mrs. Theodore; I'm afraid she is heartsick with fear for him."

Soon after McKinley's funeral, Edith returned to Sagamore Hill, promising to return as soon as she could. T. R. stayed at Bamie's house. A week or so later Edith was back, with Ethel and Kermit. Ted had gone back to school at Groton; Archie and Quentin would come later with their nurse. Alice was still at Oldgate. Over the next few days, more of the Roosevelt menagerie would appear: more children, more animals, more excitement, similar to watching a circus tent go up. On the same day, Booker T. Washington, who had accepted the president's invitation, arrived at the White House. The president's first crisis was about to occur.

Washington was wary of the telegram T. R. had sent from Buffalo. He surmised that the president wanted Black delegates who could help him win the future nomination. And he knew what he would request in return: judges and officials who would protect the right to vote of African Americans, who had been consistently disenfranchised by Democrat-controlled Southern legislatures.

He knew the numbers. He was also aware that by the next presidential election not one Black man in a thousand would be eligible to vote, and a hundred lynchings a year would continue terrorizing the African American community. So he concluded that accepting the new president's invitation was worth exploring, and the night when Edith's arrival was attracting the lion's share of press coverage, Black servants escorted Booker T. to T. R.'s library in the Executive Mansion.

Right off, T. R. said he wanted to strengthen Black rights—mainly by protecting the Black vote—and by appointing judges accordingly. Booker T. was relieved. Though T. R. said that his offer would promote "a policy of quality rather than quantity," Booker T. considered it the first step in making a good deal, especially when T. R. added that, with Booker T. as his adviser, he would appoint several African Americans to federal jobs. In a courageous move, T. R. also suggested changing the practice of denying white Southern Democrats federal civil service positions, a policy that had been part of Northern reform imposed on the South. Booker T. agreed. He wanted to help create a new political force in the South that included moderate white Democrats.

While T. R.'s highest priority was to make African Americans part of national life, it is important to remember that he was a man of time, with all its prejudices. His mother was from the antebellum South and raised him to believe that the Fifteenth Amendment had been a mistake, that not allowing African Americans to vote was justified. T. R.'s viewpoint may have progressed, but he still believed that patience was needed as the country strove for racial fairness. He was horrified by lynching, but he felt that change would come as those who had been enslaved strengthened themselves by cultural influences, which would be a stronger change than any wrought through legislation.

As T. R. and Booker T. Washington concluded that meeting in the Executive Mansion's library, T. R. invited him to come dine with him on October 16. No Black person had ever been invited to dine with the president at the mansion, but since Booker T. had just returned from Europe, where he'd had tea with Queen Victoria, he saw no reason to decline T. R.'s invitation. Worrying about what to wear, he sent a friend speeding to the White House to ask someone he knew working there. Learning that T. R. always dressed in formal attire for dinner, Booker T. dressed carefully in the best suit he had.

That evening he arrived at what T. R. was now calling the White House and was escorted to the dining room. Edith and the other children were now living there, except for Alice, who was still in Connecticut. Usually Edith sat between the children at dinner, across from T. R., but that night the children were left upstairs. Edith sat down at the dining table with T. R., Booker T. Washington, and Philip Steward, T. R.'s hunting pal from Colorado. Who was not there turned out to be as significant as those who were.

An Associated Press reporter, as the White House was shutting down, stopped by the official desk to ask about the day's guest list. When he learned that Booker T. Washington had dined with the president, he got the news out on the wires before the night was over. It was big news worldwide. And the front-page reaction from the Southern newspapers was predictably racist. A comment from the *Memphis Commercial Appeal* was typical: "This is a white man's country. President Roosevelt has committed a blunder that is worse than a crime." The *Nashville Tennessee American* wrote: "T. R.'s beloved mother was raised on a plantation in Georgia—had she been present when he seated Booker T. Washington at his table, she would have doubtless declined to sit."

Another feature of Southern racist outrage was the belief that Alice had been at the dinner. The thought that she had been sitting next to a Black man was scandalous in Southern culture. Despite the fact that she was not even in the White House that night, but some three hundred miles away, didn't matter. No one looked into the fact of where she really was. The harm was done. T. R.'s presidency would never recover as far as racists were concerned. Hate mail and death threats rained down on the White House and on the Tuskegee Institute, where Booker T. worked as its founder. Fear of miscegenation had spawned the rumors—fear of the sexual, fear of mixing the races. At seventeen, sexually mature, Alice became a symbol of this fear. T. R. was, according to the *New York Times*, "vastly amused, while also regretting that anyone would find fault with his conduct . . . that he feels he has nothing to apologize for and nothing to be ashamed of."

But the Southern press would not let it go, running articles not just about the dinner but other scurrilous rumors, including one that Alice had suspiciously received a hundred-thousand-dollar gift from an old bachelor, insinuating that she herself was scandalous. Alice, still at Oldgate, was unaware of the backbiting. She was shielded by her self-absorption, and she didn't look at headlines—not yet.

Booker T. and T. R. decided that the best way to stifle the scandal was to be silent. But when the White House schedule revealed that the two men were expected to be at the Yale University Bicentennial a week later, and that the president's daughter would be accompanying him, the story picked up a second wind. T. R. was being given an honorary degree, and as a revered educator, Booker T. Washington had been invited, too. With banquets scheduled over several days, the likelihood that the president, Alice, and Booker T. would be seen sitting beside each other, and even dining together, was an enticing, believable prospect. To try to squelch the rumors, Yale released a statement saying that Dr. Washington would only be marching behind the president in the academic procession.

Bamie was already masterminding her brother's run for his own term as president. She had planned a fund-raiser for her brother at Oldgate ahead of the Yale event, so while he was there he could pick up Alice on his way to Yale. It would be the first time Alice would see her father as president. When he arrived, he walked up the entrance to Oldgate with his usual buoyance and zest. But Alice couldn't believe the stir at his arrival. A crowd of politicians, newspapermen, and others hugged the streets. The Secret Service protection was thick and obvious. If Alice could glean the split motivation of her father, glad-handing potential donors while pretending to be there to pick her up, there is no record. But a child can always sense when a double goal is present, a sense of something other than the joy of their existence. It would take her a while to realize that her father's love of the bear pit was in his blood. And little did she know that she was about to step into the bear pit herself.

Seventeen

Clearly Her Father's Daughter

THE WHOLE ENTOURAGE headed to New Haven. That night at the festivities, as soon as T. R.'s name was called, the crowd exploded with a roar of affection. His speech, none of which Alice remembered, was soaked with his enthusiasm. Feeling the excitement of the crowd, savoring the cheering for her father, she sat in a box beside white-suited Mark Twain. She was loving everything about being there. During the public reception, whenever T. R. and Booker T. Washington were near, T. R. stayed aloof, twirling his hat. Later he reached out to Twain, asking in his sweet naiveté whether it had been right to invite an African American man to the White House. Twain answered that a president was not as free as an ordinary citizen to entertain whomever he liked. Later, Twain would give his real opinion on T. R.—saying he should "refrain from offending the nation merely to advertise himself and make a noise." Likely, Twain's sarcastic remark had more to do with his misanthropic disposition than a racial view.

If the appearance of Booker T. and T. R. together at the Yale event was meant to water down the scandal of their meeting in the White House, it partly worked. But the whole controversy went right over Alice's head. She was focused on the perks of her father's new job. On their way back to Washington, she was absorbed in the luxury of the private train car, where she stood on the back platform, basking in the lovely October weather. Then there was the drama of arriving in Washington. A crowd was waiting. When she and her father stepped off the train, the cameras flashed to capture the moment. Few eyes followed the president. They were riveted on her.

It was a significant moment. Everything was changing between father and daughter, heating up to a degree impossible for him to ignore. As she felt this sudden burst of power with everyone looking at her—*her*, not him—the resentment toward him now caught a new energy. The feeling had the potential to become addictive, and it happened so suddenly! In the flash of a moment, she had abruptly been placed on a playing field where she could compete. And eventually win. Her malignity was hardening. We might ask why couldn't he let her know, in some way, how much his love for her mother was now his unconditional love for her? Of course, he loved her as his daughter—in his way—but it was a love out of duty, not a love born of his singular sense of her value, swelling with the sweetness that only a father can give, of the sort T. R. and Bamie received from their father: an indelible sense of self-regard. She had never felt that, nor could she loosen the hard shell of his silent grief, entangled in his shame of remarrying, which felt like a husband's betrayal. Had she caused this? Was it her birth that had shut him away like this? Was she to blame? Alice's confusion at not knowing why she felt the way she did, having no clue how to unlock his love, was a puzzling veil she could not see through.

Much later in life, T. R. would write a letter to his sister Corrine, who had asked his advice about a friend whose life had taken "a tragic turn." He answered: "The only thing for her to do now is to treat the past as past, the event as finished and out of her life; to dwell on it, and above all to keep talking of it with anyone, would be both weak and morbid. She should try not to think of it; this she cannot wholly avoid, but she *can* avoid speaking of it. She should show a brave and cheerful front to the world, whatever she feels, and henceforth she should never speak one word of the matter to anyone."

Never speak one word of the matter to anyone. T. R.'s advice may have been characteristic of the age, but this way of handling tragedy was no help for Alice. For her, his words could have combated the haunting of her mother's death. He might have healed them both. There was one thing above all else Alice intuitively knew her father cared about: his image. How he was perceived mattered almost above everything else in his life. Soon after he walked into the White House the first time, he gathered the press and announced he would bar any correspondent who betrayed him or misquoted him. He even tracked down letters he had written in his youth and asked the owners to keep them private. A joke went around the White House about his obsessive keeping of records: "If the remains of his grandmother were discovered in his cellar, T. R. would immediately produce written evidence that he was elsewhere at the time of the crime."

Yes, he carefully managed himself, just as Bamie and Cabot Lodge had carefully managed his image while he'd been writing overblown heroics in the Badlands. Like Bamie pulling strings behind the scenes, now Alice, suddenly on the global stage as she stood on the Washington train station, saw clearly how she could exert her own control of her father and their relationship by managing *her* image as part of *his*. She bore the physical evidence of their relationship, of course, but now she saw how she could undermine that closeness by mocking the Victorian mores he adhered to with an ossified, almost religious acceptance. Slender and beguiling in a wine-colored traveling dress, she sent signals of ripe sexuality. Violets tucked into her belt bowed as she moved. She paused gracefully with all eyes on her that October day in 1901, unaware, or at least not caring, that many of those eyes looking at her saw her disparagingly as a young white woman willing to share a dinner table with an African American man.

Later, she would become famous for saying that her father wanted to be the bride at every wedding and the corpse at every funeral. But she was cut from the same cloth. She heard the flashbulbs pop. She basked in their glow. Following her father out of the station, she saw he had spiffed up his personal carriage with his initials painted on the side. The driver and footmen were in new blue uniforms with doeskin trousers. He was clearly getting into this thing of being president. And loving it.

As Alice walked into the White House for the first time since her father became president, she was struck with how dowdy it was. Everything seemed left over from President Grant. The only other time she'd been there was at President McKinley's inauguration, when she'd committed the faux pas of sitting on the arm of Mrs. McKinley's chair. Edith had pointed out her rude behavior to her. But this time, with her father the president, her awareness was changing. Everything he did was becoming of interest to her. In what she called "a monkey-like quickness" to catch on, she began listening to what officials said who dropped in to speak to her father.

However, she was not too old to join in the shenanigans of her brothers and sister. Since the private rooms were on the same floor as the president's offices, stilts and bicycles were propped against the long upstairs hall. Quentin, who was only four, played hide-and-seek on the floor above. A blue macaw lived in the conservatory. Archie, Kermit, Quentin, and Ethel filched tin trays from the pantry and slid down the stairs on them.

Alice's bedroom, assigned by Edith, was across from that of her parents, furnished with two brass beds. A window looked out onto Lafayette Square. Her father had been president for just two months—just enough time to settle into a routine, the family eating breakfast together at 8:15, followed by her parents walking together in the garden, where Edith picked a rose to put in Theodore's buttonhole. She also stuffed a few dollars in his suit pockets that he never knew what he did with. All morning he would work furiously, then call early in the afternoon for the barber to give him a shave. He tackled the nation's business with a torrent of letters, all the while working on his message to Congress, to be delivered December 3. A tag team of stenographers sweated to keep up.

Showing off his extraordinary mind, he called four naval officers to give him an oral briefing, then wrote detailed summaries of what they told him and had the papers waiting for their signatures by the time they got back to their offices. For seven weeks he worked on the message to Congress, reading drafts to his cabinet, churning out pages. In his daily public reception of people seeking appointments, he was curtly efficient, calling office-seekers forward with the command, "Tell me what you have to say, quickly, quickly!" or "Glad to see you. Dee-lighted!" Or, on more than one occasion, "Haven't you a jail record?"

On December 3, T. R. sent his secretary to deliver his message to Congress—an eighty-page document edited by Senators Mark Hanna and Henry Cabot Lodge and signed by T. R. on the last page. Congress had rarely seen such polished competence. Usually, presidents collated reports from executive departments; but T. R. was a writer. Each of the twenty-five thousand words was his, and he wanted to put his name to them. In the Capitol, one clerk began reading aloud until he had to be benched for hoarseness, then another came on. All through the afternoon, T. R.'s words set out what he hoped for the nation. He called for a new department to regulate commerce and industry. As he loved to say when challenged on the relationship of business and government, the Constitution was to serve the people, not the people to serve the Constitution. In his message, he stated: "The railway is a public servant. Its rates should be just and open to all shippers alike"—a startling statement laying the groundwork for what would eventually be one of his most substantial legislative successes, the Hepburn Bill.

His call for federal protection of America's natural resources struck everyone as a visionary new request. He wanted forest resources to be under the control of several agencies, with more power given to the Department of Agriculture. No doubt the action came from his boyhood obsession with nature, as well as his voracious reading, such as the writings of travelers in the 1700s who described America's forests as having "treetops so close to one another for many miles . . . [that] it seemed almost as if the sun had never shone on the ground since the creation." Sailors at sea could smell the pine forests before they could see them. White pines were two hundred feet tall and sycamore trunks fifteen feet in diameter. Grapevines as thick as a man's thighs looped through treetops. Coastal waters nourished oysters the size of dinner plates; crabs were big enough to feed four men. Streams of clear, cold water produced "fishes as big as two-year-old children." In conclusion, he wrote: "Conservation is a great moral issue, for it involves the patriotic duty of ensuring the safety and continuation of the nation."

The night of the final reading of his message, he held a reception in the White House. Congratulatory telegrams poured in. The next day, the stock market surged. The *Chicago Record-Herald* gushed: "This remarkable piece of writing . . . has raised up a new intellectual force, a new sort of leader, against whom the older politicians are afraid to break a lance lest he appeal to the country . . . and take the country with him." Hanna warned T. R. to "go slow" about business, reminding him to follow in McKinley's footsteps. T. R., however, told Bamie he would "rather be a full President for half a year than half a President for seven." Bamie sat on the secret, known by few, that in the new year T. R. intended to file a lawsuit against the Northern Securities Trust, the railroad company formed by Harriman, Hill, and J. P. Morgan. As usual, Bamie always knew what T. R. was doing before he did it. She weighed in with her advice, then breathed not a word of it.

Alice followed all this activity closely. She noted that her father had moved an enormous globe into his office, either as inspiration or guide for his vision for the nation. He tilted it at an angle so that the Americas faced up. Without being aware of it, Alice was learning about politics firsthand, a new interest stirring within her, pushing at her mind, which was so much like her father's. Though she would not be allowed to vote for nineteen more years—not until she was thirty-six years old—she was being schooled in the exercise of power.

The family was now settled, wearing their new roles as the nation's first family with a certain amount of grace. On Sundays, Edith with the children would go to the presidential pew at St. John's Episcopal Church, across from Lafayette Park. T. R. would follow the Dutch tradition of the Roosevelt family by going to Grace Reformed Church at Fifteenth and O Streets, then walk briskly back to the White House. On his way, he often stopped at the home of the Lodges on Massachusetts Avenue, where his favorite rocking chair would be waiting at the tea table in the library. There, and at the houses of others he knew—John Hay and Henry Adams, among others—he would talk politics. He liked to take vigorous horseback rides with his cabinet through Rock Creek Park, so Cabot Lodge began taking riding lessons in order to keep up. Henry Adams would stand on his porch and cackle at Roosevelt's shenanigans. Adams, who had became a good friend of Edith, noted that she helped the new president much as Henry's great-grandmother, Abigail Adams, had helped President John Adams, curbing her husband's natural impetuousness and helping him round out his judgment of people.

By the family's first Christmas in the White House, Bamie's house had become an annex, accommodating the overflow of White House guests who arrived in droves. Bamie would also always be ready to receive T. R. to talk over his complex problems, especially when Bamie and Edith's opinion about someone did not agree. That first Christmas, the family's tradition of madcap dancing traveled with them from Sagamore Hill, and the White House resonated with their loud clapping and hooting. When T. R. took to the floor with the buck-and-wing steps of a Virginia reel, Edith fell back in laughter and the children yelled, "Go to it, Pop!"

On New Year's Day the Executive Mansion, now called the White House, was thrown open, as usual, to receive the public. Edith held a bouquet of violets so she would not be expected to shake hands. Alice stood beside her in a white taffeta gown with a train and high collar fastened with a diamond crescent. Her hair was arranged in a pompadour, looking sophisticated. And while she and Edith were overwhelmed by the numbers of people waiting in the cold to get in, T. R. would not leave until he'd shaken the hands of nearly 9,000. The Executive Mansion withstood it all, but it was clear that it was in great need of renovation, which the family would have to live through.

It was not only shabby, it was unsound. T. R. didn't care; he liked it just as it was. But there were only two antiquated bathrooms for the family of eight, and a low-ceilinged attic housed the serving staff brought from Sagamore Hill. T. R.'s valet, Henry Pinckney, was tasked with keeping up with the children, riding a bicycle after them, and partnering with Mame to take care of the younger boys. Miss Young was still there as the governess. The family cook, Annie O'Rourke, brought two Irish sisters from Sagamore Hill to help her. One of their first tasks was, along with the kitchen workers left from the McKinley White House, to prepare the food for Alice's debut, scheduled to take place at the White House during the first week of that new year.

The mansion's floors were propped up with timbers to prevent them from falling during the weight of a reception. Worst of all were the rats, which were kept secret from the public. They had moved in and stayed through several administrations and were often heard gnawing through the night. (President Harrison had hired "ratologists" whose special poison was no help.) By the time the Roosevelts moved in, the rats were living with confidence—much to Kermit and Ethel's delight, who made a deal with the head gardener to let their colony of white rabbits have free rein over the grounds too.

Bamie encouraged Edith to hire Belle Hager as her social secretary, the first social secretary to a first lady, setting a precedent for every first lady thereafter. Smart and popular in Washington, Belle often threw back the curtains to open the windows after an administration meeting, saying she needed to let the politicians out. Belle would manage Alice's debut. She had lovely handwriting for the invitations but also, no doubt, had to intervene in the quarrels between Alice and Edith that frequently sent Alice to Bamie's house to fret.

Bamie was careful not to intercede with Edith. And Alice and Edith butted heads over everything. The cotillion. The drinks. The dance floor. To lead the debut, Alice wanted a cotillion—a formalized dance ending with the host handing out favors of jewelry, watches, combs, purses, and stickpins of silver. Edith said that was too expensive. Alice wanted champagne; Edith wanted punch. Alice lost both battles. The dance floor was covered in a mustard-yellow carpet, which Edith wanted to overlay with coarsely woven linen, waxed for dancing. Alice said that was not enough and wouldn't let it go. She wanted a hardwood floor. Finally, Edith told Alice to go see the Speaker of the House and charm a new floor out of him. Alice used her every ploy on him, enjoying her first taste of lobbying, but the Speaker held firm, refusing the funds.

On January 2, six hundred people lined up at 10:00 p.m. to go down the reception line in the Blue Room. More than two thousand roses, carnations, hyacinths, and narcissus decorated the mansion. Green leaves wrapped around the chandeliers and the portraits of George and Martha Washington, Abraham Lincoln, and Thomas Jefferson. Alice wore a white dress appliquéd with white rosebuds. Her honey-brown hair was in a pompadour. Edith stood by her as all of New York and Washington society filed by.

Alice began honing her developing sense of the absurd, feeding her sense of humor by thinking that at least she wasn't having her debut in false teeth. The previous summer, when she'd been in the Adirondacks, she'd had an acute pain in her jaw and was rushed to a hospital in New York. When an abscess was found in her jaw, the doctor recommended that her lower teeth be removed. Edith refused. Alice underwent surgery and her teeth were saved. So that night of her debut, she moved on the dance floor in her lovely white dress, her own teeth shining. She made sure her cousin Eleanor had been invited, especially since lately they had spent time at Bye's having tea, going to the theater, renewing their friendship.

It was her new friend, Marguerite Cassini, a niece of the Russian ambassador, who mattered most, though. Maggie, as she was called, was exactly the opposite of the kind of girl Edith wanted Alice to have as a friend—so of course Alice was determined to have Maggie as her partner in mischief. Already fast, wild, beautiful, and irresistible to men, Maggie would play a large role in Alice's next few years. Watching Alice that night, Maggie called her "the [most] tomboyish-looking girl I have seen around Washington . . . transformed into an assured, sparkling young woman in a stiff white satin gown and long white gloves. . . . Her eyes are . . . a phosphorescent grayish blue, changing color according to her mood. Her smile curls up in mischief."

Another guest was Franklin Delano Roosevelt, who danced with Alice several times (as well as dancing with Eleanor, at Alice's suggestion). Franklin called Alice's debut ball "glorious from beginning to end," though Alice would say afterward, "I myself enjoyed it moderately." But she must have been thrilled at how her life had become the center of society's attention. She'd been surrounded by potential suitors, including young men from the "400s," a tribal group made up of what were considered the richest, most blue-blooded families in America. T. R. denounced them as the idle rich, considering them vulgar. Alice retorted that they were the only people with big houses and big dances.

The next day's headlines shouted out the nation's new obsession. The *New York Tribune* anointed the first daughter "Princess Alice." Hundreds of requests for her autograph and photograph poured in. Even Quentin asked for one. She was an instant celebrity, the likes of which would not be seen until a half century later when Jacqueline Kennedy stepped onto the world stage, to be followed decades later by Princess Diana. Her father was on his way to becoming the most popular person in America, and Alice was on *her* way to becoming the most popular girl in the world. Yet while it may have seemed that she was a self-obsessed, silly-headed girl, she was actually absorbing political skills, amassing the tools to one day be a power broker herself. After all, Bamie had led the way.

Eighteen

All-Out War

THEODORE ROOSEVELT BECAME PRESIDENT at the beginning of a new century. It would eventually turn into the American Century, and the constraints that marked an older, European way of doing things were starting to fall away. Victorian culture was up for revision. Bamie was one of the first to see how silly it was for women to stay out of the newspapers except at the mention of their marriage and death. With her crafty intelligence and remarkable social skills, she understood the time's shifting dynamics, an understanding she passed on to Alice.

Edith accepted the Victorian constraints, at least on the surface. Writing to Springy in 1902, she told him, "I count on long misty moonlight evenings on the White House porch, Theodore in his rocking chair, you and Cabot settling world affairs over your cigars, while Mrs. Lodge and I meekly listen as becomes our sex and position. Being the center of things is very interesting, yet the same proportions remain." She was T. R.'s gatekeeper, an acceptable role for a wife, warning him about certain people, labeling them not of their world. Yet he was always open to his Rough Rider friends and found associating with the average American a priceless education. Edith put up with them because Theodore loved them so much. Now that he was president, many wrote him letters beginning, "Dear Colonel: I write you because I am in trouble . . . ," which always made his heart sink. One letter-writer went on to explain: "I did not take the horse, but they say I did." Another lamented that his mother-in-law had put him in jail for bigamy. Yet another began: "I write you because I have shot a lady in the eye. But Colonel, I wasn't shooting at the lady. I was shooting at my wife."

T. R. especially chuckled over what he learned at a regimental reunion, when one Rough Rider greeted him by saying he was happy the judge had let him out of jail in time for the reunion. When T. R. asked what was the matter, the man answered with surprise, "Why Colonel, don't you know I had a difficulty with a gentleman, and . . . er . . . well, I killed the gentleman. But you can see that the judge thought it was all right or he wouldn't have let me go." Still curious, T. R. asked, "How did it happen?" Not fully understanding the question, his friend answered, "With a .38 on a .45 frame." This so tickled the president that he adopted it as an excellent answer to explain any shooting.

Though she kept her own counsel, Bamie watched the workings of her brother's administration closely. She also spent time with Alice and Eleanor, who frequently fled to the freedom of Bamie's house whenever they needed it. They went to baseball games, to the theater, to New York to shop. The girls learned from their aunt's sharp mind and tongue. The only time Bamie reduced her shine was when she feared she was taking too much away from the first lady. When she learned that Edith was keeping a scrapbook entitled "Social World" and that the numbers of clippings about herself and Alice were eclipsing those of the first lady, she worried. Yet she could no more stop advising her brother than Alice could stop soaking up newsprint.

After her debut, Alice continued to attract attention. The German kaiser asked that she christen a yacht he had ordered from an American company and sent his brother, Prince Heinrich, to pick up. Immediately, the French ambassador accused the kaiser of requesting Alice to christen the yacht in order to win over America's opinion of Germany. But T. R. didn't mind. Creating a little jealousy between Germany and France would give him some diplomatic artillery when dealing with the two powers in the future. Even the Russians were worrying about who would gain most favor with the new president. Knowing that relations with Germany would be a major challenge during his presidency, T. R. decided that using Alice to smooth the future relationship with the German royalty would be beneficial. He already knew that the kaiser was "vain, coarse, romantic, often foolish, xenophobic, anti-Semitic, given to fits of rage so violent as to make onlookers sick." So T. R. approved of Alice's christening the yacht, and she practiced by smashing bottles of champagne in Bamie's backyard.

The newspapers covered the boat's christening, including drawings of the yacht, the *Meteor*, and a description of the women's dresses. Reporters counted exactly how many times the German prince took Alice's arm. The *Times* reported, "Miss Roosevelt was the most self-possessed person on the stand." The *New York Tribune* wrote, "It is only a few weeks since Miss Roosevelt left the schoolroom and in a day she has become one of the most regarded women in the world."

The prince gave her a diamond bracelet as a gift from the kaiser. Collecting expensive baubles for her jewelry box would become a mission. Under her father's orders, as soon as she had christened the *Meteor*, she sent a telegram to the kaiser telling him that the world-shaking event had been accomplished. At lunch, the prince made a speech directed to T. R., and T. R. made one in return. The prince toasted Alice. Everyone wrote their names on the menus.

Almost as soon as the *Meteor* was baptized, Alice was invited to attend the coronation of Britain's Edward VII. Word came that England wanted to seat the Roosevelt daughter in Westminster Abbey with the rest of the world's royalty. The *Literary Digest* stated that Europeans believed that Alice should be thought of as "a princess of blood" deserving "the honors due to the oldest daughter of an emperor." This was too much for T. R. He had worked fervently to appear to be a man of the people—insisting on sending his children to the public elementary school at Oyster Bay, and in all other ways stifling perceptions of his privileged upbringing and life. Alice begged to attend the coronation, but he turned a cold shoulder. Bamie went instead.

That winter, Ted fought a severe case of pneumonia at Groton. When Edith wrote Alice that Ted had called loudly in his sleep for "Sissie," she traveled to be with him. Even T. R. went to him for a week, leading the nation from his son's sick room. He had secured the rights to build a canal through the Central American isthmus from the French, who had abandoned the project after twenty years of mismanagement, lethargic workers, rusty machines, unforgiving jungle, and disease. T. R. asked the Colombian government to lease land in Panama to the United States for the purpose, and when the Colombian government raised their annual fee for the lease by half a million dollars, T. R., incensed, appealed to a representative of Panama—whose citizens had been itching for independence from Colombia—indicating that if Panama rebelled, the United States would quickly and willingly recognize Panama as a sovereign nation. It was a bold move dangling on the edge of reprehensible, but T. R. was always willing, like Lincoln, to bend convention toward whatever was best for the United States, now in his care.

As he involved himself more and more in global politics, T. R. recognized the value of Alice as a decoy, an aide in foreign relations whenever needed. Her celebrity was climbing. As a young woman under the impending pressure to embark on marriage and motherhood, Alice saw the opportunities of celebrity differently. She was ready for all-out war against her culture. And against her father. She was set to take him on in a duel in which she now held the advantage. And her celebrity had certainly surprised him. He hadn't seen it coming. Whenever Alice appeared, crowds gathered to cheer her. Dresses and gowns appeared in "Alice blue."

Her face gazed out from cards packaging candy bars. Songs were written about her, and her picture was featured on their sheet music. Her face was centered on magazine covers.

Edith hired a staffer to vet the photographs, which confused Alice. She couldn't understand her parents' attitude. As she later wrote, "The family was always telling me, Beware of the publicity! And there was publicity hitting me in the face every day . . . and once stories got out, or were invented, I was accused of courting publicity. I destroyed a savage letter on the subject from my father, because I was so furious with him. There was he, one of the greatest experts in publicity there ever was, accusing me of trying to steal his limelight."

Soon after the christening of the *Meteor*, T. R. sent Alice on a trip to Cuba, where his old friend Dr. Leonard Wood was now the military governor in Havana. The American occupation of Cuba was to end in May 1902, a month after Alice's scheduled visit. She was magnificent in representing him; her appearance was impeccable. In her diary, she wrote, "Several awfully nice Cuban men and girls out there. Had bully fun as I always enjoy meeting them." Intoxicated with how the world saw her but not fully understanding it, Alice was looking for suitors without really understanding what those suitors might want, or what she was stirring up. Obsessed with sex, yet terrified in her ignorance of it, she was well suited to both attract and repel. Her culture told her to attract men while denying she wanted anything to do with sex. It was a recipe for a sweet, comic, dangerous craziness. No one could deny that she had quickly become an expert in tantalizing. She wasn't, however, as interested in dynamiting Victorian culture as wanting to bend it. Nor was she trying to break her father's heart—only to bend it too, completely, steadfastly toward her. What she could do to please them both was to be perfect as his ambassador. As she wrote in her diary, "I feel that I want something, I don't know what. . . . When I come down to bedrock facts, I am more interested in my father's political career than anything in the world. Of course I want him re-elected . . . but there again, I am afraid it is because it would keep me in my present position."

By April of 1902, newspapers speculated that one or another man was in love with her. Rumors spread that she had been engaged five times in the last eight months. Erroneous news stories had her in love with the crown prince of Sweden, the prince of Greece, and even two of the sons of the German emperor. She wrote in her diary that she "had a foolish temper fight with mother this morning. A newspaper saying [two men] were in love with me." When Edith expressed the damage to Alice's reputation, Alice exploded in another temper fit. After a few days, she found out that Edith was pregnant, retreating to her room with headaches, which perhaps provided an explanation for her stepmother's short temper. But their mother-daughter explosions left scars on their relationship.

T. R. was so excited about Edith's pregnancy that for weeks he had been joyously hinting to everyone that a very special event would take place the following October. That special event, however, disappeared in May when Edith had a miscarriage. The lost baby sank T. R.'s spirits. Edith stayed in bed, recovering physically and emotionally, clearly unable to keep up her schedule. That week, she was supposed to be with T. R. when the French ambassador arrived to pay a visit. With Edith unable to make public appearances, T. R. wondered how he would handle the important visit without Edith. As he contemplated the problem, he lay on a sofa in the executive office when suddenly, he kicked his heels in the air, he shouted, "Alice and I will go. Alice and I are toughs."

"Toughs." Yes, they were toughs together. Happy and behaving perfectly, Alice filled in for Edith, charmingly standing beside her father at the official reception. She continued on while Edith was down and out, going with her father and the ambassador to Annapolis to admire the French ship *Gaulois*. She attended a dinner at the French embassy. She did all things right, looking beautiful. Never a misstep. Her toughness impressed him. They were two of a kind. She could have taken another path to win his admiration, as some children do—being accident prone or hypochondriacal, subconsciously sprouting health problems to require a parent's full attention. But none of that would have ever worked with T. R. She knew that. No wild death wish or fabricated illness would gain his attention, at least not for long. Her toughness, though, impressed him.

No doubt, seeing her grit stimulated the same sort of admiration he had for wounds earned in battle. He himself even said he wished he had come home from Kettle Hill with some sort of disfiguring scar. He was so ashamed of his invalid childhood, he buried it under silence, transferring it to his disdain for sickness. And his humiliation was sealed by his stated hatred for "sissies," "cripples and consumptives," for anyone who could not measure up physically. He told his sons he'd rather see them dead than grow up to be weaklings.

With his friend and fellow Rough Rider Leonard Wood, T. R. would play what they called "singlesticks." The two men put on padded helmets and chest protectors and hit each other with ash rods as if they were beating carpets. In the White House T. R. joked that they looked like Tweedledum and Tweedledee. General Wood noted that T. R. was too excitable to remember the rules, saying it was "almost impossible to get him to come to a guard after having been hit or delivering a blow." T. R. also boxed with an invited opponent in the White House, until he blinded his left eye during a match.

Telling the story of a Rough Rider who had been a sheriff, T. R. would light up, dramatizing the conversation by asking, "Ben, how did you lose that half of your ear." Ben responded, "Well, Colonel, it was bit off." "How did it happen, Ben?" "Well, you see, I went to arrest a gentleman, and him and me mixed it up, and he bit off my ear." "What did you do to the gentleman, Ben?" And Ben, looking more coy than ever, responded, "Well, Colonel, we broke about even!"

Over the next few years, Alice and her father would break about even. And the fight was intense, measured not only by the degree of T. R.'s consternation but in how much newsprint each could generate. To get the best of him Alice took up smoking—becoming the first woman to smoke openly in Washington. She would drop her compact to shock people when cigarettes spilled out. A relative tried to cure her by giving her two black cigars to smoke, but she smoked them both all the way down, without showing any sign of illness, only enjoyment.

When T. R. said she could not smoke under his roof, she climbed to the roof of the White House and smoked there. Often her friend Maggie Cassini was with her. When her father spoke of the need for large American families and said that childless marriages were "race suicide," Alice invented what she called the Race Suicide Club, whose members vowed never to have children. She ate asparagus with her gloves on. She carried a green snake, allowing it to slither over her young body while observers stood frozen, horrified and dumbfounded into silence. She named the snake after Edith's frail, skinny sister, Emily. And since it was green, it made all the sense in the world to make "spinach" part of its name. Often wearing Emily Spinach as a bracelet when walking among the politicians at her father's gatherings, she never flinched, never batted an eye while Emily explored the folds in her dress, the skin of her neck, slithering anywhere to shock and capture attention. Alice's purse always included four things: a copy of the Constitution, Emily Spinach, cigarettes, and a fertility image.

She learned how far she could go without tipping over, avoiding real damage to either herself or her father's presidency. When she learned how gossip ruined a girlfriend's reputation when the girl came back from a drive with friends with her buttons undone, Alice obeyed when told she wasn't to see that friend again. She always revised her antics if they put her in danger of being expelled from society.

On the other hand, rattling female conventions was her definition of fun. Since young women were not allowed to go on a date or attend a dance without a chaperone or offer a man a lift, she did them all. Maggie, the countess Marguerite Cassini, introduced Alice to car culture. Maggie drove a four-cylinder red convertible and loaned it to Alice when she herself was not joyriding with young men. Maggie said that her friendship with Alice had the "violence of a bomb." She led Alice down the path that Alice thought she wanted to go—but only so far. Alice wanted to harden herself to achieve the toughness her father wanted, but Maggie's behavior was not just adventuresome, it was dangerously outrageous.

Maggie had no moral compass, only a desire to exhibit herself as much as possible. She had accompanied the Russian ambassador to the United States, but their relationship was a mystery. He introduced her as his niece. It seems she may have been his illegitimate daughter. Her lasting mark on history would be not as Alice's wild friend but through her son, Oleg Cassini, who would become the designer of Jackie Kennedy's stunning wardrobe. But in her teens, beautiful, sexy, tantalizing Maggie was bent on ripping apart Victorian culture—and taking Alice along for the ride. She taught Alice how to gamble and they bet on horse races. When the inventor George Westinghouse became sweet on Maggie and offered to throw a ball for the two girls, Alice and Maggie turned in a guest list so long George had to build an extension onto his ballroom. He ordered hundreds of orchids to attach to the walls. As soon as the flowers began wilting, Maggie and Alice skipped out, rudely leaving their guests.

It was not unusual for a crowd to form wherever Alice went, calling out, "There she is! Hoorah for Miss Roosevelt." Girls copied the way she dressed and the way she behaved. She broke the Victorian restriction on a woman smoking in public. The substantial allowance from her Lee grandparents (which she never considered enough) allowed her to order a customized car with trim and upholstery she had chosen herself. The *Los Angeles Times* got wind of the order, and T. R. demanded she cancel it. He was not a fan of automobiles, influenced by his love of horses. He also disliked telephones, and when one was installed at Sagamore Hill, he refused to answer it. But Alice was a woman who embraced the modern. Her father hated her socializing with the Four Hundred, whom he regarded as the idle, vulgar rich, but she was becoming one of them, rushing to be with them whenever she could, for she loved how much it troubled her father. She would rather have his criticism than his silence.

Eleanor, who was now engaged to Franklin, often sought solitude from his mother by going to Bamie's. The relationship between the cousins remained strained. Eleanor wrote chatty letters to Franklin about Alice, once telling him that she ran into Alice in New York, "looking well but crazier than ever." Alice mocked Eleanor's good works, calling them "do goody." The only thing they had in common was the loss of their mothers. But since Alice, like her father, hated the thought of arousing pity, she had long ago shrugged off sympathy associated with her mother's death.

Concerned about Alice's direction in life, T. R. and Edith warned her that she was choosing to be with people who had money to burn. Her Hathaway Lee grandfather, also concerned, threatened to cut off Alice's monthly inheritance from her mother. To test her, he gave her a thousand dollars and asked T. R. and Edith to tell him if she spent it in less than four weeks. She did. He put her on a restricted allowance—a quarterly stipend—for the rest of her life.

Alice did not worry about interrupting her father's personal or presidential business. During his first term as president, he was in his private office visiting with his old friend Owen Wister, author of *The Virginian.* Alice rushed in with Emily Spinach, said hello, then bounced out. As soon as the men's conversation resumed, Alice barged in again, asking a question that didn't matter to anyone. Then quickly left. While T. R. and Wister were searching for their train of thought, lost by Alice's interruption, she bounded in a third time. "Alice!" T. R. warned, "the next time you come I'll throw you out the window!" He then apologized to Wister for his daughter's manners, adding, "I can run the country or I can control Alice. I can't possibly do both." The most famous comment he would ever say about Alice, it was notable for its blend of admiration, pride, and exasperation.

By the time he made that comment, he could at least say her name in public, although he usually referred to her as "my blessed girl" and within the family still called her "Sister." Wister described the event differently in his own memoir, writing that the "I can control Alice" remark was in response to a question someone asked the president. Whatever the case, the telling and retelling of the president's remark delighted the American public, who saw Alice as a typical teenager driving her parents crazy.

Behind the jousting between T. R. and Alice was the shadow of Alice's mother. The silence that enshrouded Alice Hathaway Lee haunted both father and daughter, raising the question of how *she* would have mothered Alice. And how would Alice Lee have been remembered in the White House as the wife of a president? Who would *she* have been if she had lived, maturing, wearing the scars and triumphs accrued through the normal span of a lifetime? Never spoken of, her mark on the relationship between her husband and daughter would nevertheless never fade. Even though she was denied the privilege of mothering her fierce daughter, Alice Hathaway Lee left her mark on history.

How would Alice be tamed? The expectation of the age was that a husband would do it. No doubt many feared for him at the same time they hoped for his appearance. But for those years, the central relationship in Alice's life was the one with her father. She took him on in a battle of wills that began to shift their relationship. In spite of his concerns, his regard for her was growing, while her regard for her own power—even if it was only through the influence on men—was becoming her new definition of fun.

Nineteen

His Blessed Girl

As the anniversary of McKinley's assassination approached, marking T. R.'s first year as president, his auburn hair was streaked with gray. The young, ruddy-faced politician who had been the governor of New York had matured, and an indefinable something washed over him: a dignity, a seriousness, a sense of carrying great weight. Edith and Bamie agreed that T. R. appeared like "a prophet who is charged with a message to deliver."

Taking care of his own security, he carried his personal pistol wherever he went. Edith was still haunted by McKinley's assassination and worried about Theodore all the time, especially since he liked to walk and ride by himself. So did Bamie, who privately asked friends to enhance Secret Service protection at large public events, which gave her and Edith some comfort. In addition, a decoy railroad train always went ahead of the president's train in case of anarchist bombs or other threats.

The two women joined up in helping him where they could. During T. R.'s White House meetings, Edith sat knitting quietly in the room, then afterward in private gave her counsel on what she had heard. She knew Theodore's most top-secret subjects, especially the delicate diplomatic negotiations he was in the midst of or wanted to take on. She enlisted Cabot Lodge to help her keep T. R.'s bluster and impulse in check. She also helped him keep up with newspaper coverage. Some news articles he had planted himself, so Edith reviewed the others, reading them in her library next to his office. She had firm opinions and often said about someone, "I don't dislike him. I just don't want to live in the same world with him." T. R. would often protest, "E-die!" and retreat into a dark silence until he began talking about how much he liked the fellow whom Edith had just dismissed. If Edith then went to lie down with one of her headaches, T. R. would feel doubly guilty.

Bamie also had good judgment about people, though driven by her interest in the power play of politics rather than in social standing. She lived by the principle "You must show your affection, or it will dry up." As the world's most sympathetic listener, she didn't give specific advice, only offered it in general terms. She believed one should "never propose a solution to another's problem, for your solution might fit neither the will of the person seeking advice nor the real circumstances, since those who sought advice usually distorted reality in their own favor." When Eleanor sought refuge at Bye's house during her engagement to Franklin while Franklin's mother was being difficult, Alice saw how closely Bamie listened to Eleanor—as she always did for Theodore. As Eleanor would later say, "Uncle Theodore made no major decision in foreign or domestic policy without first discussing it with Auntie Bye." As a nod to Bamie's influence, T. R. once wrote to Alice, "Bye is as dear as ever and oversees the entire nation." When Bamie noticed that T. R. took too long deciding who should get government jobs, she took on vetting those seeking posts, leveraging her deep connections in the diplomatic service and navy.

While the White House underwent its renovation, which would take six months to complete, T. R. moved to a temporary residence and Edith and the children escaped to Sagamore Hill. In August 1902, he headed off on a speaking tour to rally the people's support behind his trust-busting policy and also campaign for those Republicans whose congressional seats were up in the fall. His private train made whistle stops, where up to 20,000 people gathered to hear him. Traveling with him were five reporters, four typists, two assistants to work the telephones, an aide from the Navy Medical Corps, and his usual bodyguards. Among these guards was William Craig, known as "Big Bill," an immigrant from Britain who had protected Queen Victoria. Bill was six foot three and as muscular as a bull. At forty-six years old, he was close friends with four-year-old Quentin, who shared his love of reading comics.

Alice joined him for part of the journey, and though she was more focused that summer on meeting friends in the Berkshires, she saw enough of her father's public speaking to get a sense of the raw personal power he brought to the presidency. At each whistle stop, brass bands played and large crowds gathered. T. R. began his speeches by balancing negatives and positives, working up logically to his main ideas. Following his instinct to seek out the center, he would explain that "human law encouraged moneymaking, but natural law prevented equal gain." Punching his left palm in emphasis, he'd spin on his heel to point a finger at those directly behind him. "If wealthy men abused their good fortune, or the needy sought to penalize them, both groups would be buried in the crash of the common disaster. General progress depends on stability . . . the fixity of economic policy." Bringing the crowd's attention to the moment of history in which they were living, he bellowed, "We are passing through a period of great commercial prosperity. . . . Such a period is as sure as adversity itself to bring mutterings of discontent. . . . Good fortune does not come solely to the just nor bad fortune solely to the unjust. When the earth is good for crops it is also good for weeds."

He worked up to his policy of creating a "square deal" for all Americans, where each could thrive under laws applying equally to every American. Born from his father's fears for the loss of the government to corruption, T. R.'s political philosophy never stayed for long in the margins. When the crowd responded with shouts or applause, he held up a hand to stifle them—so eager to be understood. However, his trait of talking on and on could wear his listeners out. As he would slide into the bog of his plans for regulating trusts, much of his audience could wander off.

Taking his tour up the East Coast, he switched from train to carriage, a barouche pulled by four elegant gray horses. On the last day of the tour, September 3, the air was bright and crisp and the carriage driver put the top down to allow T. R. to enjoy the ride to Pittsfield, Massachusetts. The governor of Massachusetts and other officials sat beside him. Big Bill Craig sat beside the driver, and a mounted escort rode alongside. Nearing Pittsfield, bugles and cheers sounded as soon as the carriage came into view.

T. R. gave his speech, got back in the carriage, and headed to the Pittsfield Country Club for another stop. As the carriage crossed a trolley track, Big Bill heard rumbling behind them and turned to see a trolley bearing down on them at great speed. "Oh, my God!" he yelled as the trolley hit them, hurling everyone onto the street. T. R. lay facedown on the side of the road. Dust and screams hung in the air. A navy medic rushed to him, saying, "Are you hurt, Mr. President?" T. R. got up, talking through bleeding lips. "No, I guess not." The governor was unhurt but the coachman lay unconscious, bleeding from his ears, and the horses lay on their sides, kicking in harness. The trolley wheels were covered with blood and tissue. All eight of its wheels had passed over Bill Craig, killing him.

When T. R. saw the trolley engineer staring in shock at what he had done, T. R. shook his fist and said, voice trembling, "Did you lose control of the car? If you did that's one thing. If you didn't it was a God-damned outrage!"

"Well, I had the right-of-way," the engineer shouted as deputies led him away.

T. R. knelt beside Bill Craig's body, mumbling, "Poor Craig. How my children will feel."

A charge of manslaughter was filed against the trolley engineer. Stories flew that passengers on the trolley had bribed him to pursue the president. Another claimed he had been coming down the slope on schedule and could not brake fast enough when the president's carriage got in his way. The driver pleaded guilty. He was heavily fined for failure to control his car and jailed for six months. Laments for "poor Craig" permeated Sagamore Hill.

On the day after the first anniversary of McKinley's death, T. R. and Edith held a reception at Sagamore Hill. Several thousand of their Nassau County neighbors showed up, wanting to shake the president's hand. Popcorn and a raspberry punch in glasses engraved with the date were served for three hours. With his face still marked with bruises, T. R. greeted everyone with his trademark, "Dee-lighted!" and shook two hands a minute, bragging: "It takes more than a trolley accident to knock me out. And more than a crowd to tire me."

But the accident had left him with an injury to his left leg that was not healing. Soon, he was having trouble bearing weight on it. On a trip through the Midwest he appeared unsteady, and at Indianapolis he had to go to St. Vincent's Hospital for surgery. In the operating room, T. R. joked. "Gentlemen, you are formal! I see you have your gloves on." He refused anesthesia. As the surgeons drained the wound he muttered to himself, then, with the surgery completed, he lay stiff and sedated on a stretcher to be taken to his train and whisked to Washington.

Bulletins through the night assured the country that the president was not in danger of blood poisoning. The surgeons who had treated him were not so sure. When he arrived in Washington, Edith met him and moved him into his temporary quarters, taken while the White House was under renovation, overlooking Lafayette Square. Soon he was rolling around in a wheelchair, carrying on with business. The wound was not healing, however, and on September 28 the surgeon general decided another surgery was needed. This time, cocaine was rubbed around the wound, and T. R. allowed himself to be semi-anesthetized with whiskey. But the most stunning fact was that he wanted Alice to sit with him. Taking her place by his side while the surgeons operated, she knew that talking politics would be the perfect distraction from the pain of his surgery. From the day of the trolley accident, she had followed his progress in her diary: "Father having a hard time." She gave up her partying schedule—at least for the time being—to stay home with him, telling her diary, "Have begun to get up for breakfast."

Now as the surgeons scraped his bone, cleaning it more completely of infection, she—Alice, his "blessed girl"—was the chosen one. She was the one whose toughness he admired, the one who would not flinch, the one whose beloved stature in the world would soon become so very valuable to him. The accident and Craig's death had shaken her, awakening her to the realization of how close her father had come to being killed. She was also realizing the weight of his decisions, noting in her diary, "Father very busy writing speeches for his western trip. Father and senators going over revisions of the tariff. He is having a pretty hard time."

While the surgery was being performed, she talked to him about the coal miners' strike, knowing it was very much on her father's mind as the first crisis of his presidency. She also realized how it threatened the whole nation as winter approached—at least as much as a privileged young girl might imagine Americans being without coal to burn in their homes. Hospitals, schools, homes without heat—all would suffer. She had followed the crisis enough to keep up, becoming somewhat educated in the art of politics, realizing for the first time the complex problems her father faced. While she understood that her father had no legal right to intervene, she also noted in her diary, "I think it is time that the government should have something to say about a thing which so much concerns all the people as the great coal industry does."

Now in its fifth month, the strike had begun in the spring, when 147,000 anthracite miners quit work in the coal fields of eastern Pennsylvania. Vowing not to return to their jobs in the fall unless management gave them an increase in wages and recognized their union, they were hamstringing the nation. The mine owners refused to consider either demand. Others in the bituminous industry struck in sympathy until a quarter of a million men were refusing to work, the greatest labor stoppage in history. One economist predicted that if the standoff lasted until cold weather, it would be of "such a consequence as the world has never seen." Despite the danger to the public, T. R. felt that he should not intervene in what was basically a private dispute between labor and management. But the level of violence became too horrifying to ignore: Fourteen murders; sixty-seven aggravated assaults; eye gougings and attempted lynchings; riots; ambushes; bridges blown up; and trains wrecked. The governor of Pennsylvania authorized state troopers to shoot to kill. John Mitchell, president of the United Mine Workers and a former miner himself, vowed his men would make the ultimate sacrifice, if necessary. He accused mine owners of not allowing workers to "live the life of a human being."

With violence as his bargaining tool, Mitchell sent a secret, desperate message to T. R.'s commissioner of labor, proposing that he would not push union recognition if management agreed to reduce the workday from ten to eight hours, establish an equitable system of assessing each miner's output, and give an overall wage increase of 10 percent. In response, T. R. sent a telegram to both Mitchell and six owners of the biggest mines: "I would greatly like to see you on Friday next October 3, at eleven o'clock, here in Washington."

Alice followed it all, keeping up with the newspapers howling that his "interference" was unconstitutional. She was seriously intrigued by her father's job for the first time. When both the mine owners and John Mitchell sent back word that they would come, T. R. felt that their agreeing to meet under the same roof meant he had already won round one.

All of this was a good subject for Alice to have at her fingertips. As she sat beside him during his surgery, she discussed the situation with him to keep his mind off the pain. And she did it well.

When he was up and about in a wheelchair, recuperating successfully, she headed back to her social life, partying with friends and shopping until her funds ran dry. She went on with the shallow life that made her seem popular, distracting herself from feelings of emptiness as she had distracted her father from physical pain. She told her diary, "Father getting on splendidly." But she also descended into feeling sorry for herself: "What wouldn't I give to be a most marvelous belle and be more run after than any other girl."

The meetings with Mitchell and the mine owners were prolonged and fraught. Now that the weather was flirting with winter, Americans in the upper reaches of the nation began heating their homes with anything they could find to burn: coconut shells, slats from fences, pieces of furniture. T. R. ordered the head of the army to plan to take over the mines. Ten thousand soldiers were at the ready. When T. R. mentioned his plan one morning to a leading Republican, the congressman accused him of "seizing private property for public purposes without due process!" Roosevelt took him by the shoulder and almost shouted, "The Constitution was made for the people, not the people for the Constitution!"

The financier J. P. Morgan helped solve the crisis. It didn't hurt that Bamie knew him well enough to ask him to get involved. The mine owners trusted him, so when he met them and spoke bluntly, saying they had to face bitter facts, that while they had a right to conduct business as they pleased, they could not do it if it led to ruin or a government takeover. It was time to end the strike while they still could. After learning an impartial tribunal would work out a settlement's terms, the mine workers agreed to go back to work to supply American homes with heating fuel while the tribunal met. And though the formation of the tribunal would provide further drama, the strike was settled and the crisis averted. The United Mine Workers won a 10 percent wage increase, fairer and safer working conditions, and the right to arbitrate disputes even though the union had not been recognized.

Mediating between capital and labor made T. R. famous; he was the first head of state to confront that most pressing problem in the twentieth century. He revealed his true feelings about the crisis in a letter to Bamie. "May heaven preserve me from ever again dealing with so wooden-headed a set. . . . Our great trouble was that the little world in which the operators moved was absolutely out of touch with the big world . . . the excellent gentlemen who said they would far rather die of cold than yield on such a high principle as recognizing arbitration with these striking miners, was that *they* were not in danger of dying of cold." Edith, commenting on his alliance with J. P. Morgan to solve the crisis, remarked that "Theodore has tied so many knots with his tongue that he can't undo with his teeth."

T. R. had set an example for fierce, skillful negotiations, which Alice had been privileged to witness. Even if she did not yet understand the bargaining, she was on her way to being an irreplaceable cog in the wheel of his diplomatic maneuvering. Without her knowing it, she would soon be employed in her father's secret negotiations leading to his being awarded a Nobel Peace Prize. Yet, as she approached her twentieth birthday, Alice had more personal issues on her mind. Marriage.

Twenty

Seeking Attention

THE DAILY LONGING for a father's unconditional love had hardened Alice. She was always watching where his eyes landed, always wanting to draw them to her. She sensed that he admired her lust for life, so much like his own. Yet she was destined never to be satisfied, and as she was now at the age where marriage was what the culture expected of her—and as she decided to enter the hunt for the perfect husband—she quickly decided that perfection was mostly down to the size of his bank account.

For years she had been eager for money. "I want more," she scribbled in her diary. "I want everything. I care for nothing but to amuse myself in a charmingly expensive way." And so she thrust herself into the chase for one young man after another. There were Carpenter, McCoy, Van Ness Philip, de Chambrun, and Iselin. At least those were some mentioned in her diary. There could certainly have been others. She enjoyed tantalizing them until two of them proposed, to which she answered "positively no." Since she seemed to be totally enraptured by Arthur Iselin, who preferred "beautiful Southern girls," she began lamenting in her diary about "poor Alice. No hope for Alice." She even wrote about how unattractive she thought she was. "I pray God make him love me. Oh Arthur Arthur Arthur my love and my life."

The hunt heated up with her spiraling mood changes, sending her to bed to sleep too long too often. Edith told her she was going through a phase. Always aware when she had her father's attention and when she did not, she filled in her sadness with the lusting eyes of cameras and reporters. And soon another item was added to the list of qualities of the prefect husband: the ability to command the same sort of public adoration that she and her father could command at the flick of a fingertip.

With the White House's renovation complete, Edith moved the family back in with her own ideas on decorating. Next door to the cabinet room, T. R.'s writing "den" was set up, with leather chairs, a deep fireplace, books upon books, and of course the huge globe. To honor his love of the navy, Edith found an old desk carved from the timber of the British ship *Resolute* and put it in the center of the room, establishing it forevermore as "the Resolute Desk." When T. R. put some of his favorite things on it, sun would slant through gauze curtains to glint on a miner's pan, a silver dagger, and an inkwell decorated with a bust of Abraham Lincoln. Bearskins lay on the floor. A clock ticked with subtle music.

Alice came and went, keeping up her travels and her manic social life, biding her time until the perfect husband-candidate should appear. She bought a pocket gun and fired it off whenever she thought it would shock someone. She considered herself among the first bootleggers when she bought small round flat bottles of whiskey and hid them up her gloves, fishing them out to delight a man sitting beside her. She stayed on the go, taking trains from Boston to New York, traveling to the Harvard-Yale Races with a party of people, becoming furious when her father stopped her traveling on the trains without buying tickets since railroads gave free travel to the president. She became an expert at feeling sorry for herself. "No one paid very much attention to poor Alice," was a common lament to her diary. The glow from those moments when her father needed her during his surgery had long since worn off.

To make matters worse, as if it were a marker in the passing of her youth, Emily Spinach was found dead. Likely murdered. Alice had taken the little green snake on her visits from one friend to another, until it seems Emily wore out her welcome. She got lost in curtains at one house and at another shed her skin under the bed. When Alice arrived at the door of a friend at Bar Harbor, wearing Emily on her comely body, the friend made a face of disgust, which Alice was used to. But then, when she came in one afternoon and found Emily on the roof outside the window, dead, Alice expected her party mates to give her sympathy. When none did, she suspected foul play.

In a bid for attention, she and a girlfriend drove without a chaperone from Newport to Boston. When the newspapers chronicled the outlandish trip, her father sent her a scorching letter. He listed the "iniquities she had committed," adding even the sin of omission in that she had stopped writing to the family. He said that she did not appear to have "a particle of affection for any of them, that she thought only of her own pleasure." He commented sternly on her general character or lack of it. She answered him promptly, promising to mend her ways. Then, in a temper, burned his letter.

Yet Alice was always conscious of her father's position and his future prospects. His nomination in 1904 was a foregone conclusion, though her rich friends weren't planning to vote for him (trust-busting was not in their interest). She would never break from him in politics or in any other way. In her longing to be ever closer to him, it was as if she were trying to inhabit the spirit of her mother. And she did look so much like her mother. And she was constantly invading her father's world. It seems safe to assume that as she entered her own womanhood, he chilled in her presence, terrified that she might open that pit of grief he'd climbed out of—complicated even more by Edith's jealousy, which was likely driven by her own fear of how much Alice looked like her mother.

The 1904 election was critical. Above all, T. R. wanted to be elected in his own right—to wipe out the fact that he was an "accidental president." He was even willing to break tradition to make that happen. Usually, to avoid the unseemly spectacle of a candidate campaigning for his own office, a presidential candidate placed his campaign in the hands of party professionals. McKinley had sat out two successful campaigns on his porch in Ohio. But now came T. R.—irrepressible, certainly not a shrinking violet. As Henry Adams said of him, "If you remark to him that God is Great, he will naively ask how that will affect his election."

Party conservatives asked him not to do anything that would crank up the tabloids, which were dying to feature him riding his stallion Bleistein in Rock Creek Park as if he were racing in the Kentucky Derby. Or go skinny-dipping there, which he never did, but it was fun to think he would; or play tennis, that effete pastime of the rich. Obliging his advisers, he replaced his outdoor exercise with Japanese wrestling. When his coach taught him three new throws that were "perfect corkers," he set a goal of strangling his instructor. However, he only succeeded in acquiring bruises all over, wounded toes, a lame ankle, his left wrist, and a bum thumb.

On election day, Alice and Ted fought so violently from sheer nervousness that they spoke only to insult each other. When the first returns from upstate New York came in, they rushed to their father and tackled him in joy. Alice called it a "smashing victory." "Victory. Triumph. My father is elected," she wrote in her diary on November 8, 1904. "Carried New York State by over 200,000. It's all colossal." Indeed, T. R. had trounced his Democratic opponent, Alton Parker, winning every state except the Democratic-solid South.

The landslide erased T. R.'s fears of being an accidental president, and he planned to start his new term introducing policies he no longer felt he had to hold back. He intended to lead his country into the twentieth century just as he had vigorously led his Rough Riders up Kettle Hill. He wanted to use the federal government to solve problems brought by the industrial age. He'd learned how public opinion could make Congress cooperate. As he thought through these hopes for his second term, he often went to the

Washington Monument late at night to run around its base while Secret Service men stood guard.

The inauguration on March 4 bubbled over with T. R.'s ebullient personality. It was unlike any inauguration America had ever seen. Alice's cousins Franklin and Eleanor stayed at Bamie's and rode to the Capitol in a procession of Roosevelt carriages that included his entire cabinet, escorted by Rough Riders. The first carriage took Edith, Alice, and Ted. The rest of the family and staff followed, including Mame, looking not a day over sixty though she was at least eighty. At the Capitol they all sat a few rows behind the president as he recited his most memorable inaugural line: "Much has been given us, and much will rightfully be expected from us."

At the inauguration, Alice wore a white toile dress with a white hat edged in black satin spouting ostrich feathers, swaying in the wind. T. R. wore a ring enclosing a lock of Lincoln's hair, which John Hay had given him. During the inaugural parade, Alice stood behind her father on the viewing stand, waving to her friends. When he chided her for making a spectacle of herself, she threw back at him, "Well you do it. Why shouldn't I?" He retorted, "But this is *my* inauguration!" They continued the sport of upstaging one another.

The excitement and strain of the campaign had aged Bamie, diminishing her hearing, stiffening her body with arthritis, but never lessening T. R.'s need for her. He used her to clarify his mind. She was so pleased that Theodore would be serving in his own term and not that of another man that she changed the opening in her weekly letters to him from "Best of Brothers" to "My dearest Mr. President." She reminded him that he had beaten the political machine their gentle father had been too ill and politically inexperienced to cope with.

Two weeks after the inauguration, the family gathered in New York for Franklin and Eleanor's wedding. Bamie asked T. R. to "give Eleanor away," and Alice, who was a bridesmaid, watched her father hold court, drawing all the attention away from the newlyweds. It was then that she made the comment that her father wanted to be the bride at every wedding, the corpse at every funeral, the baby at every christening. The wedding must surely have made her think about her own marital prospects . . . or her refusal to settle on any man as the "perfect husband." Did they not have enough money? Or was it simply that she remained self-absorbed? Her diary heard the same old whining: "I am bored to extinction." She returned to her social life with manic vigor: parties, dinners, balls. She continued to feel sorry for herself. "No one paid very much attention to poor Alice." Then on another diary page, she admitted the most awful truth: "I feel that I want something, I don't know what." How little she knew about herself—her sexual needs, her addiction to resentment, an unquenchable thirst for love.

The glow from those moments when her father asked for her during his surgery had long since worn off. The rigors of a presidency—issues of labor and race, international and domestic politics—took virtually all his attention, just at the point in her life when she was to make her most important decision.

Part III
Paulina and Joanna

Twenty-one

Nick

A DEBUTANTE WAS EXPECTED TO MARRY within three years of "coming out." That put Alice on a fast track, which was not easy for her, since most young men were intimidated at the thought of marrying Theodore Roosevelt's daughter. Living up to the expectation of a man of T. R.'s accomplishments was . . . well, off-putting to say the least. For his part, T. R. felt that as long as his daughter married in the general realm of the society to which the family belonged, he would not fear the dissolution of Alice's inheritance through marriage. He knew how much Alice prized the value of money.

At the time, she confided to her diary, "I swear to literally angle for an enormously rich man. . . . I cannot live without money." And again later: "Vow. That I will accept the next man who proposes to me. I have run over a thousand over my allowance."

Then her father introduced her to an impressive young congressman from Ohio. Nicholas Longworth. Nick. And their paths continued to cross. At her nineteenth birthday party, celebrating with friends, he was there. She later told her dairy: "After supper we all sang and Nick played. [He and another] were the stars. Perfect marvels." He was an accomplished violinist. How serious was she about Nick? One night Alice and her partner in crime, Maggie Cassini, skipped out on a soiree given by one of the most eligible bachelors in the country. It was a Versailles-themed party in New

York that cost the guy $100,000. At the last minute, Alice and Maggie sent a telegram with their regrets . . . then rushed to have dinner with Nick Longworth.

Soon she was writing in her diary: "Please love me. Please, please love me. . . . Would you not love me enough and ask me to marry you?" And finally, "Nick love me be kind to me."

It was an impossible mission she was taking on, for while she was in the midst of choosing a man who seemed to be cast in the image of her father, she was actually letting a man of dubious character into her life. Like a figure in a Jane Austen novel, T. R.'s "blessed girl" was about to make a catastrophic decision. Everything she sought from her father she now expected her chosen husband to provide. And that was not going to happen with Nick.

He was fifteen years older than she was. He was handsome and dashing and an artful politician. Born in Cincinnati, he was the eldest child and only son of a founding family of Cincinnati's art, music, and charitable societies. He had a suffocating, possessive mother who never wanted to share him, keeping him emotionally stunted and self-absorbed. She even moved part-time to Washington to be part of his daily life. His father had been for a while on the Ohio Supreme Court. Nick seemed to have it all. In a sense he was a mirror image of Alice herself—especially in his reputation as "a bad boy."

He loved all outdoor sports. He practiced amateur photography. His family summered at Newport and toured Europe in the autumn. When he was five, he began studying the violin and by the time he entered Harvard was an expert player. He attended Harvard Law for a year, then finished at the University of Cincinnati like a good Ohio son. A contemporary periodical summed him up this way: "His path has been lined with roses because of his money and family influence. . . . He turned to politics for diversion." He was also known as Cincinnati's Don Juan, so well versed in the art of pursuing women that the city matrons were on guard. One of his objects of desire told him, "My mother has been informed by many well-wishers of your past and she pleads with me to see you in your true light." A society column stated, "The gay young representative . . . is as familiar with the role of Romeo in everyday life as he is with politics on the floor of the House."

Edith told Alice, "Your friend from Ohio drinks too much." Of course that was part of his appeal to Alice: he knew how to party. Furthermore, he had credentials her father approved of. She endorsed her family's view of drinking as dangerous, that it was the cause of Elliott's ruin, though she was too young and distracted to know what her stepmother's comment really meant. Alice herself "never had the faintest inclination toward stimulants other than tea and coffee." She drank champagne at parties, and some told her that her "spirits were high and she had better not take any more." But no one was able to say her gaiety came out of a bottle. A glass of sherry, or Madeira, or white wine, or claret was a matter of course at dinner. Whiskey and cocktails she never would have thought of taking, but Edith had experience with the damage that addictive drinking could impart on a family. Being the child of an alcoholic and seeing the damage Elliott had done to the Roosevelt family, she had reason to warn Alice about Nick.

An excellent chef, Nick was knowledgeable about wines and threw the best parties, which soon began to include Maggie Cassini as well as Alice. Just as Alice was becoming interested in him, he became intrigued by Maggie and began pursuing her. Maggie was first introduced to him by the hostess at a lavish Washington dinner, who said, "Here is someone who wanted to meet you. Be careful; he's dangerous." Then the hostess said to Nick, "And you be careful because she is *very* dangerous."

They became a toxic threesome. As Washington royalty, Alice, Maggie, and Nick held court at embassy parties, went on yacht outings, gossiped at lunches, and spent time at Nick's bachelors' club. For Maggie it was all good, dirty fun because she prided herself on being able to take away any man from any woman with her skills as a temptress. Then after she made her conquest, she would dump the poor manipulated fellow. Gossip fed on the three of them like pond fish rushing toward crumbs. Everyone was certain that Nick would marry either Alice or Maggie. Maggie said, "The reporters were in a spin trying to keep up with the latest development."

All of which sharpened Alice's feelings that she was falling in love with Nick. "Nick, oh dear Nick. I am sure she has him. Revenge on her." When Maggie skipped out on a horseback riding date to meet Nick at the Congressional Country Club, leaving Alice stranded, Alice wrote, "Old nasty Maggie. I'll get even yet. See if I don't."

The sad complication was that Nick really did fall in love with Maggie. He proposed to her more than once, the last time during a sleigh-ride party in snowy Washington near Lafayette Square. He had stopped the carriage to fix the horse's harness and asked her to marry him, looking up from where he held the horse's bridle, earnestly wanting her to say *yes* as she looked down at him from the carriage. She shouted, "All right, here's my answer!" She took up the reins, flicked the whip at the horse, and bounded away, leaving Nick in the snow. "How he got home, I do not know," Maggie told Alice the next day, while they smoked on the White House roof.

Maggie admitted later, "It became more and more fun to tease my friends by trying to take their beaux away from them." She herself didn't love Nick; nor did she love Alice. She simply loved toying with them.

What Alice didn't know was that another woman, Miriam Bloomer, nicknamed "Hooty," had a thing going on with Nick well before he took up with Alice. Hooty sent Nick notes constantly: "I'll come on the 4:30 train and you can meet me and we'll dine quietly, any old place, for I'll have on a street dress and then if you like you can come out here with me and stay all night?" She was once described as "a former fiancée of Nicholas Longworth," but the word *former* would never really apply. Nick was schooled in the art of deception in relationships. Some reports even had him regularly visiting prostitutes on K Street.

In January 1904, Alice recorded in her diary: "Had lunch with Nick at the House of Representatives, then went back to N. L.'s for an hour." Christmas Eve 1904 was a turning point. "Had a long talk with Nick. . . . He made violent love [to me] all day long. Well, well, Nick." "Violent love" was an exaggeration; later in life, Alice often said she never kissed a man until she was married. Given her fears, born in childhood when she worried that she was "deformed," it is likely that Alice was a tremendous flirt yet reluctant to open up physically and give affection, much less receive it with abandon. The year passed with continued flirtation. When she confided to her dairy on January 9, 1905, "Nick and I in a very dark corner afterward. It was quite wonderful but I know that I will wish I hadn't. I know he doesn't really care for poor little me," she was most likely indulging his sexual appetite in order to keep his interest.

When she turned twenty-one a month later, Nick wrote her, "May I be permitted to call you 'Little Alice' this last time, for tonight at twelve o'clock you will become of age and be an heiress and then I suppose you won't be little anymore." He included a photograph of himself. In tune with her need for excitement, she soon quarreled with him so she could enjoy the drama of making up, confiding in her diary: "Oh, Nick I love you passionately Nick—I want to see you—have you with me always for every moment of this day and night for ever and ever."

This was to be the year when the romance would reach its destined conclusion. In June she went to stay with Nick and his family in Ohio. After she returned to the White House, leaving Nick in Cincinnati for a longer visit with his mother, he wrote her: "You were more charming than ever here. You were sweet to everybody and everybody was crazy about you. There wasn't a minute that we were together that I didn't wish was an hour . . . and not an hour that I was away from you that I didn't wish was a minute. It was a beautiful world when you were here. I love you and I always shall."

Convinced that Nick would give her the love she had always craved, Alice had fallen completely, trustingly in love with him. And if her stepmother didn't approve of him, Bamie did. She began hinting to friends that she was engaged. While her father was obsessed with international affairs, Alice took a giant personal leap into momentary happiness and, ultimately, a choice between allegiance to her father or to her husband.

The following month, Alice and Nick would have a chance to get to know one another even better. At the end of January 1905, T. R. had engineered an Asian tour in which the secretary of war, William Howard Taft, would make an inspection trip of the Philippines and then visit several other countries, including Japan. The region was in considerable turmoil, and the Russo-Japanese War was in its second year. T. R. had strong hopes of brokering a peace deal between the two countries (and would eventually win the Nobel Peace Prize for doing so). But before negotiations could begin, he needed a decoy to distract the media while Taft could slip off to meet secretly with the Russians and Japanese to find out what each would accept in a deal. When the Japanese and Russian governments sent word that they would accept Roosevelt as a mediator, T. R. realized he needed Alice. He needed her to do what she did best: to be a distraction, to capture all attention, to draw all eyes to her. Especially the eyes of newspaper reporters so Taft could slip off unnoticed. T. R. couldn't risk anyone knowing what he was up to. Not only was he an artful politician, he also relished the intrigue and use of power to advance the role of America on the world stage.

If Alice knew that she was to be a decoy, no record reveals her knowledge. She clearly knew that her father was up to something between Russia and Japan, but that was minor to the fact that she would be front and center. She understood that her greatest talent was in being conspicuous. She was a perfect ally for her father's artful diplomacy. As she saw it, she was only to enjoy herself and was "primed and ready for all that came her way." And coming her way mostly would be Nick.

Since Nick was a member of the House Foreign Affairs Committee, with a special interest in Hawaii and the Philippines, he would be on the trip, billed as a "friendship Tour." The newspapers loved it. The *Cincinnati Herald* put out a front-page headline: *ALICE IN WONDERLAND, How First Maiden of Land Will Travel to Orient.* "Her father will pay her expenses," the subhead continued, "across the Pacific, stop at Honolulu, reception in Japan, through the Inland Sea, tour the Philippine waters, Representative Longworth to go along—tropical romance anticipated."

The junket began when Alice and the congressional party of some eighty people headed by train to Chicago, then on to San Francisco, where they would board a steamer that would take them across the Pacific. She had three large trunks; two big hatboxes; a steamer trunk holding white linen skirts, three-quarter coats, blouses, and riding habits; and a separate box for her sidesaddle. Her maid, Anna, would see that her clothes were laundered, mended, and pressed. Alice had a little atlas that she marked her journey on, and as they traveled cross-country she recited words she had memorized from Kipling: "We lead the iron stallion down to drink/ through the canyons to the waters of the West." She had trouble sleeping, so excited thinking of the trip ahead.

During the earliest days on the tour she displayed her ability to size up people with pithy descriptions, which would eventually make her renowned for one-liners. One man was a "massive old fellow who looked a little like a Bismarck gone to seed." Another was a "little old Santa Claus–bearded man." On July 4 she set off firecrackers on the train's back platform and shot her revolver at telegraph poles. She had a gold vanity case with a compartment for hairpins that she filled with cigarettes. Since no woman on the trip smoked—at least not in public—she delighted in dropping her case so it spilled out the cigarettes, to the outrage of all those who saw her. And of course, there was Nick. She had an eye on him every minute.

As often as she could, she paired off with him for day tours or lunches. After they boarded the steamer *Manchuria* in San Francisco, Alice caused a ruckus when she jumped into the canvas pool rigged up on deck. The newspapers made much of the story by saying she went in fully dressed. Alice thought the whole thing was overblown, though she still loved being conspicuous. Actually, she had simply handed her shoes to bystanders and splashed in, while daring Nick, who was watching at the rail, to jump in fully clad with her. To her the ruckus seemed ridiculous, because a bathing suit in 1905 was a linen skirt, a shirtwaist, and long black stockings, covering about the same of her shapely body as the clothes she had on. Nick was watching but didn't follow her in, though a childhood friend joined her. The report of her swan dive, fully clothed, was so outrageous that fifty years later Bobby Kennedy would mention it to her. Alice told him that at least she didn't go in naked.

In the middle of July, her father's first letter reached her. He'd illustrated it with his comic stick drawing of a horse, a girl smoking, and a knight's long ax. On the top he wrote, "Not a posterity," because Alice liked to tease him that he was always writing "posterity letters," meaning he meant them for history, not for the person they were addressed to, evidenced by his signing "Theodore Roosevelt." His letter was written on White House stationery, posted from Sagamore Hill, and struck an ironic tone: "Alice, at present travelling in particular for her health." Later, he sent another of his "picture letters" with a quaint sketch of Alice with the Chinese empress dowager exchanging ceremonial puffs of opium. He titled it: *Hits the Pipe with a Possibly Congenial Friend.* At the top of the page, he drew Alice being pursued by bicycle cops and drew himself as a toothy, grinning bird, described as *The White House Dove of Peace.*

T. R. followed her tour in a daily newspaper column entitled "Alice's Adventures in Wonderland." Edith too sent letters with political views, perhaps hoping to elevate Alice's interest in the history she was living. Behind the scenes, her father was coaxing along the peace process between Russia and Japan, mixing soft and hard speech with white lies and what he called "a big stick," (T. R. famously said that in foreign diplomacy it was best to "speak softly and carry a big stick"). He shared his frustrations with only Bamie and Edith, including the comment that one of the men he was dealing with had the "intelligence of about eight guinea-pig power."

Taft had a clear brief from T. R. with respect to his dealings with the Japanese. When Alice and Taft—an odd couple, indeed—dined with the Japanese prime minister, Katsura Tarō, Alice had no idea the men were conducting business. Soon after, Taft cabled to the White House a memorandum that stated, in essence, that Japan wanted to be recognized as a power of the first rank. Taft and T. R. agreed, and in return, Katsura assured Taft that Hawaii and the Philippines would not be "menaced" by Japan. The framework T. R. had been waiting for was now in place. As he wrote to his son Kermit:

> I have been carrying on negotiations with both Russia and Japan, together with side negotiations with Germany, France and England to try to get the present war stopped. With infinite labor and by the exercise of a good deal of tact and judgment—if I do say it myself—I have finally gotten the Japanese and Russians to agree to meet to discuss the terms of peace. Whether they will be able to come to an agreement or not, I can't say. But it is worthwhile to have obtained the chance. . . . Of course Japan will want to ask more than she ought to ask, and Russia to give less than she ought to give.

While her father was pulling off this sleight of hand, weaving complicated issues into a possible treaty, Alice herself had simpler motives: to get Nick to propose. While reporters rushed after her, Taft secretly met with the negotiators of the warring nations. And as the ship moved from country to country, Alice danced on board with Nick and revealed the turmoil of her heart to her diary: "Oh my heart my heart. I can't bear it. I don't know what's the matter with me . . . He will go off and do something with some horrible woman and it will kill me off. Oh my blessed beloved one, my Nick."

In the classic example of what psychoanalysts call "reaction formation"—saying the opposite of what one thinks—Alice tapped a dinner partner on the shoulder, pointed to Nick, and nonchalantly asked, "Do you see that old, bald-headed man scratching his ear over there? Can you imagine any young girl marrying a fellow like that?" Her partner responded, "Why Alice, you couldn't find anybody nicer."

She didn't need the answer, though. Her mind was made up. She would have him. She didn't care what anyone said. She just needed to make him propose.

She was twenty-one, harboring childish traits, destined never to outgrow them, arrested in her longing for what she felt she had never had. Stuck. Stuck craving attention. Stuck in silliness. Stuck in grievances. She knew her parents had given Taft the task to watch over her during this important trip, but it was easy to get around him. She resented when Taft pleaded with photographers, which T. R. called "Kodak creatures," not to take pictures of her in her bathing suit. She felt he was monitoring her. She felt his fear of her behavior when the ship docked, crowds rushing forward, brass bands playing, and flowers offered. When she and Nick got left behind, too late to board the ship as it started sailing to their next destination, and had to be rushed in a launch beyond the tides, Taft exhaled in relief. He didn't want to go down in history as the one who lost Princess Alice.

She never gave up displaying the wildness the public craved. Crowds followed her and Nick everywhere. In Hawaii she learned to hula. With greedy delight she accepted the gifts she received at every stop, admitting, "I did so love my loot." Sitting on the floor at the low Japanese tables, she drank sake like a seasoned Japanese reveler. When, at a formal dinner, she discovered ants, she childishly laid a trail of crumbs to the table, thinking it would be funny when the ants came marching in. Taft saw what she was doing and told her to stop, explaining to her that her plan would embarrass and hurt their host's feelings.

Every once in a while, Taft would say, "Alice, I think I ought to know if you are engaged to Nick." To which Alice always replied, "More or less, Mr. Secretary, more or less." Which concerned Taft. He thought Nick dominated Alice's emotions in an unhealthy way. Their tiffs and makeups went on like the chorus of a love song. Their relationship was dramatic, passive-aggressive, and marked by accusations of neglect, detailed in a flurry of letters. As Nick wrote to her near the end of the tour, "Your losing your temper and getting these uncontrollable dislikes for me has got to stop. You say that it is because I get on your nerves by doing and saying foolish and rather conspicuously common things. . . . It is very decidedly the pot calling the kettle black, for no one could accuse you of over-refinement." Soon enough, however, she and Nick were back dancing on deck, teasing each other physically as well as in quick-witted exchanges.

To what lengths did she go to win and keep Nick? Did she compromise her heart, her integrity, even her body? It is hard at this distance to say. At the time, she was careful not to let anyone see her confused emotions. And in the spotlight, she and Nick presented a united front.

Bamie thought that Alice's behavior on the Asian tour was magnificent. "My little Alice that was really mine for four years," she wrote. "How perfect, how dear you are to the old aunt." Bamie did not share Edith's misgivings about Nick. No doubt by this time, Alice had exhausted every member of her family with her wild independence. When the tour was over, Alice and Nick decided that their engagement should be made public. Wishing to tell Edith first, she sought out her stepmother while she was in the bathroom, brushing her teeth, so Edith could not immediately respond. At the same time, Nick met with T. R. in his study to ask for Alice's hand. T. R. consented. Edith was resigned to Alice's ending up with Nick, stating she was "well satisfied." Nick's drinking and age difference were outweighed by his inheritance, intelligence, and pronounced desire to stay in politics. From Alice's perspective, he might also be the one to keep her in the White House, if not forever at least long enough for her to get her fill of being the nation's obsession. And at least as long as Nick could keep winning elections.

The engagement was publicly announced in December 1905. They would be wed in the White House at noon on Saturday, February 17. Invitations to the affair were more coveted than any Super Bowl ticket would be. Not just America but the world tittered in a manic state of anticipation. In New York and Washington, people surrounded the couple on the sidewalk, rubbernecking to catch any glimpse. When a reporter asked Nick if he popped the question on the Asian tour, he said, "I did not know officially that I was engaged until the announcement. I've been in what you might call a trance for so long that I am somewhat mixed as to dates."

Maybe Alice merely assumed there had been a spoken proposal because she wanted one. In any case, she had succeeded in corralling him. Americans expected a perfect marriage for Alice and Nick, and she was set on giving them one. To be severed from her childhood by the rite-of-passage of a wedding, she was setting off with a backpack full to the brim of childhood hurts, abnormal attention, and an exceptional tutorial in the art of politics. For nearly twenty-two years she had lived history without really knowing it. She understood how politics worked, whether or not she wanted to. Soon she would realize that while the world expected her wild antics, those physical outrages would not be appropriate in the married, adult world. Eventually, she would exercise her power verbally rather than in her behavior.

Her grandfather Lee wrote her: "I was not surprised in the least as I had read of [your engagement] for at least 365 days in the newspapers . . . Good! I hope [Nick] has a kind disposition, but with sufficient strength of character to make you:

> 1. Get up in the morning and breathe the fresh air.
> 2. Make your breakfast of something besides lemon juice.
> 3. Leave off cigarettes, cigars and cocktails.
> 4. When traveling leave at home the dog and snakes.
> 5. Conduct yourself so as to be happy and make him happy too.
>
> But you are all right and I congratulate [you] again and feel that you have done the right thing. [I hear] Nick is a first-rate fellow. So that point is settled."

Only Edith knew what Alice was in for. And Edith was too tired to care.

Twenty-two

The Most Valuable Present

DECIDING SHE WANTED NO BRIDESMAIDS, that *she* would be front and center, Alice spent the months between the announcement of her marriage and the actual day wallowing in the attention. Gifts flowed in to be displayed in the library over the Blue Room. When her father put a stop to receiving presents from other countries, Bamie said that at least he "didn't issue his awful ban before the string of pearls from Cuba arrived." Indeed, the pearls were stunning and immediately became Alice's favorite present. The government of Cuba had bought them in Paris for twenty-five thousand dollars as a reflection of the young nation's appreciation of what her father did to secure its independence. They were the perfect traditional gift for a bride, conveying warmth and eternal love with their silvery, satin texture. But they were also a metaphor for something rare, admirable, and valuable—something of what she was to her father: a gem born from an irritant, fine and lasting, never to be erased.

To Alice, those pearls could be more than a gift of statesmanship. They represented a private link, a connection fraught with significance. They were anointed with a meaning beyond mere jewelry. Wearing them aligned her to what her father called the greatest day of his life, his crowded hour: his military triumph in Cuba. Ordinarily, when a man is asked what is his most prized moment, he will answer the birth of his child. But not T. R. While he adored his children beyond measure, his most prized moment was the battle victory in Cuba. Now, every time Alice wore the wedding-gift pearls from Cuba, she might have felt her birth linked to the greatest day of his life. In any case, she wore them almost all the time. The "crowded hour" pearls were cherished.

We are left to wonder how much that simple symbolism could have healed both of them.

During the days before the wedding, Alice drove Nick to work, clopping through the streets in a high trap that her father gave her the year before, holding the reins and wielding the whip expertly, then stopping to let Nick get out at the Capitol. Letters between them flew back and forth like hands trying to catch hold of each other: "I ought to know it is too wonderful to last. Don't lose your head about anyone please don't, Nick. Think of me. I love you so very much, I am so jealous, my darling please."

"I don't like anybody here," he wrote from Ohio, where he had gone to touch base with his constituents. "It's simply because a foolish little person called Baby Lee has wound herself into the very inmost convolutions of my soul and I can't get rid of her for a moment, even if I wanted to. You are just a part of my life that nothing and nobody else can fill. . . . I love you all the more for taking an interest [in the politics of holding my seat and] I will talk more about politics with you next month, and I would honestly rather have your advice about people and things than anybody I know."

"My own beloved Nick, today has been very dull and tiresome because I haven't seen you once. And I haven't been able to think of anything else."

"My darling little girl, it's no use. I simply can't stay away from you any longer. . . . I shall be in Washington at 12:30 on the B&O on Sunday. We'll never be away from each other so long again. I can't stand it so you will have to make up your mind to be right by my side from now until I become a senile and decrepit old man. With wholly absorbing love."

Tourists to the House of Representatives caught sight of Nick in the chamber and identified him as the man who was going to be Alice's husband. Edith released the wedding program to the newspapers February 14, twenty-two years to the day since Alice Hathaway Lee had died. Did the wedding itself echo T. R.'s own wedding twenty-six years before? Did it remind him of a loss that had driven him to write, "Black care [depression] rarely sits behind a rider who is going fast enough"?

The wedding day dawned sunny and bright. At a little before 11:00, Alice put on her wedding dress as the thousand guests filed in, including both families, Supreme Court justices, congressmen, the diplomatic corps, and even Nellie Grant, President Grant's daughter, who had also been married in the White House. Franklin Roosevelt sat with his mother, Sara Delano, as Eleanor was at home, pregnant. Edith, assessing it was time to give Alice the customary mother-daughter talk, came to her and said, "Before you were born, your mother had to have a little something done in order to have you, so if you need anything let me know." Alice, understandably confused, stayed mum, unsettled about what "a little something" meant but determined not to let her emotions show.

Her white satin dress was trimmed with the lace saved from her mother's wedding dress. She fastened the necklace Nick had given her, pearls with diamonds, around her neck. The pearls aligned to her father's "crowded hour" would be her favorite, but Nick's pearls were what counted on this day.

As the music played, Ted Jr. walked Edith to her seat. At 11:30 Alice joined her father in the upstairs hall, and together they went down in the elevator to walk from the door of the state dining room to the altar built in the East Room. The Marine band played the wedding march while they slowly made their way to the platform decorated with white lilies. Holding her white-orchid bouquet, Alice released her father's arm to stand beside Nick. The Episcopal bishop of Washington conducted the fifteen-minute ceremony, and then official photographers came in. As Alice, Nick, and her father posed, Franklin Roosevelt got up to straighten Alice's veil. Franklin's mother, Sara, remarked that "Alice looked remarkably pretty and her manner was very charming."

But that photograph has yielded a fascinating interpretation. Edmund Morris, T. R.'s biographer, noted that T. R. stood with "notable stiffness, leaning away from Alice with his face devoid of expression," because he was struggling with the pain of seeing the lace covering his daughter's shoulder, the lace from Alice Lee's dress on the day he married her. The photograph certainly carries all the rigidity of the Victorian age, with social rules that Alice had been chipping away. But it also seems to carry this very personal message, as if the past in the picture appears ripe for infecting the future.

At the wedding breakfast Alice began cutting the wedding cake, but when the knife seemed too dull to do the deed, she borrowed the saber from a military officer and sliced a piece. Nick had been in the Harvard Porcellian Club, and since it was customary for members to attend a brother's wedding, a big group of them were there. They brought with them an African American steward whose father and grandfather had been the club's stewards before him. When the White House staff were confused as to why Louis was there and asked T. R. what should be done with him, T. R. replied in his inflected voice that "Louis should roam at will throughout the house and, moreover, have complete charge of the champagne." The fact he said this with respect, warmth, and irritation that anyone should question accepting Louis as an equal is significant, given that only six months later T. R. would make the most disastrous decision in his presidency, prodded by a racial tragedy in Texas—a decision that would vibrate in history, affecting even the alignment of the political parties today.

After the wedding breakfast, Alice went upstairs to put on her beige traveling dress. As she said good-bye to the family, she told Edith, with her usual sardonic wit, "Mother, this has been quite the nicest wedding I'll ever have. I've never had so much fun." Edith kissed her and said in return, not entirely jokingly, "I want you to know that I'm glad to see you leave. You have never been anything else but trouble." Too stunned to reply, Alice rushed to Nick and they climbed out the Red Room window and sped off in a car, the better to avoid reporters.

Interestingly, they honeymooned in Cuba. Alice not only planned to thank the president of Cuba in person for the exquisite necklace, she was also eager to see the place of her father's most valued moment. At the village of Daiquiri, she and Nick mounted horses to ride the Rough Rider trail. And as they did, Alice bitingly noted that "the hills were mildly sloping, on as small a scale as the war itself had been." Her bitterness may have been a way to belittle her father's "crowded hour" in their ongoing joust to outdo one another, but also she had received an anonymous letter soon after they headed off on their honeymoon, from a woman who told her, "I do not believe that Nick told you before he led you to the altar that he is the father of a beautiful child, our child. My child."

Whether or not that particular accusation was true, it was entirely believable that Nick had fathered children. No doubt the letter led to a great quarrel. We can only speculate about the depth of hollowness Alice felt. Later, she found Nick "drunk on the floor" and was revolted. For the first time she thought with seriousness of Edith's warning. But in public, she and Nick painted it over. When asked about the honeymoon, Nick said that it was the most delightful trip he had ever had, one of endless delight. Alice only smiled her approval. Journalists referred to her as Mrs. Longworth, and Nick called her "my wife." They began a curious silence when together. In tune with the expected position of a wife, Alice stood in Nick's shadow. One journalist considered whether "society is to have a princess royal" or whether "Mrs. Nicholas Longworth intends to conform to the etiquette which applies to the wife of a junior member of Congress?"

Not long after the couple returned to take up residence in Washington, Alice discovered how very much she missed her family. "Having become removed from them by marriage," she became aware of how delightful families are, of what good times they can have together. Late every afternoon, she went over to see them between tea and dinner. Kermit remarked, "I can't imagine Sister as a stately married lady." T. R. said, "I think Sister is much improved by her marriage." Bamie thought so also and contacted her British friends to tell them that Nick and Alice were making a wedding trip to see them, including the king.

And so it began. For over twenty years, Alice would keep up the charade of being happily married. The irony is that what nailed it in place was her craving for celebrity. That summer, she was the wife of a congressman running for reelection. The intertwining political lives of Alice and her father built up steam. Bamie was stepping back. She felt Theodore needed her less now, and Mr. Bearo needed her more. He was on track to become an admiral, and with Bamie's help he was awarded the title. However, when Bamie felt Theodore was threatened in any way, she could still become known. She helped him maneuver the Hepburn Bill through Congress, a historic precedent for government regulation of business in the public interest. Though more conservative than her brother, Bamie did feel frustration with big business interests—what she called "members of the plutocracy." Some plutocrats themselves began spouting what an Irish policeman had once said about T. R.: "He's a darlin' man. But he's so distressin.'"

In September 1906 Alice went to Columbus, Ohio, with Nick to unveil a statue of William McKinley. Her presence swelled the size of a crowd to some fifty thousand, who rushed forward hysterically to grab the streamers as Alice pulled them to reveal the statue. The crowd became so unruly that she and Nick had to climb through a window into the governor's office until the police could escort them out. Alice said she was terrified, yet described the moment as the "most exciting of her life."

Wanting to prove to Nick that she was a good campaigner, she sat patiently on platforms while he spoke. She hired a spiritualist to provide her with an "occult formula" to make sure Nick would win. The press noted: "Mrs. Longworth is the great issue in her husband's campaign. She accompanies him to his political meetings and probably makes more votes by her presence than he does by his oratory."

T. R. was worried that if Nick lost his congressional seat, it could unsettle Alice's marriage. Everything came to T. R. through his political lens. And that summer he was under unusual stress, a period Edith called "a suffering time." The terrible earthquake in San Francisco had to be handled through telegrams since no cross-country telephone existed. And the process was agonizingly slow. When he rushed out medical supplies and then learned that the Red Cross refused to help the Chinese population, he felt his "blood boil." As if his words became his body's own troubles, he suffered from a case of boils so troublesome, he had to go to bed for several days. Increasing the household's tension, Edith was distraught over Quentin's bad grades. Archie was suffering from severe headaches. Cubans were rebelling over a "lack of democracy," unhinging American investors. T. R. sent warships and troops to restore order, ranting, "I am so angry with the infernal little Cuban republic that I would like to wipe its people off the face of the earth." No, it seemed he had no patience left for anything. And then he got word on August 13 of what would be called the Brownsville affair.

After a nighttime scuffle in Brownsville, Texas, in which a bartender was killed, the townspeople found spent bullet shells at the scene and blamed members of the African American 25th Infantry Regiment, who were stationed at nearby Fort Brown. In spite of evidence that the shells had been planted, investigators accepted the statements of the white townspeople and mayor. When a Texas court found no soldier guilty, T. R. issued an ultimatum: If no man confessed or informed, all would be adjudged guilty. All soldiers denied any knowledge of the raid, yet T. R. accepted the townspeople's assumptions and decided to dishonorably discharge all 127 Black soldiers. Yet he didn't want his decision to affect Nick's election only a week away.

T. R. summoned Booker T. Washington to the White House for advice, but mostly to see how his decision would affect the Black vote—in effect, how he could *keep* the Black vote. Even though Washington implored T. R. to rethink his decision, he refused to revise it. In a display of stubborn arrogance, he waited thirty-six hours until voters had gone to the polls in Ohio, reelecting Nick, before discharging the soldiers and denying them pensions. Among them were six Medal of Honor recipients, including Charles Frazier, who had fought with T. R. in Cuba.

Some members of Congress wanted a follow-up investigation, but T. R. raged, saying, "It is my business. . . . It is not the business of Congress. If they pass a resolution to reinstate these men, I will veto it. I welcome impeachment." The Senate ultimately upheld T. R.'s decision, and the soldiers would not be exonerated until 1972, when all but one of them were dead.

T. R.'s record on race had always been mixed. His friendship with Booker T. had caused a sensation at the very beginning of his administration, and later he had invited several African American federal officeholders and their wives to a White House reception; when the invitees arrived, some congressmen rushed to the exits. No Black woman had ever been entertained at a private event at the White House. Southern newspapers again expressed their outrage. Yet T. R.'s blunder over the Brownsville affair would change American political history. It was one of the factors in African American voters leaving the party of Lincoln and becoming Democrats, a shocking reversal since the Democratic party in the South had been traditionally the party of slaveholders.

In his autobiography T. R. never mentioned Brownsville. He knew it was a mistake but he buried it in silence, just as he had buried the pain of losing Alice Hathaway Lee. His most arrogant, hasty, despicable moment could not be discussed. His instincts as a shrewd politician blocked his humanity, releasing his ruthless side. As his biographer Edmund Morris noted, with the Brownsville affair T. R. displayed what he knew so well but could not quite avoid in himself—the famous dictum that "power tends to corrupt, and absolute power corrupts absolutely."

Yet his instinct for power and pragmatism had helped Nick win in Ohio. "Let me congratulate you and Nick with all my heart upon the successful way in which both of you have run your campaign," he wrote to Alice. "I tell you I felt mighty pleased with my daughter and her husband." That note must have satisfied Alice's craving for his approval. When Congress assembled on December 3, Alice sat in the executive gallery, watching Nick greeting his colleagues. That night, at the annual diplomatic reception in the White House, she received them alongside Edith. As talk in political circles and in the newspapers revved up, pressing T. R. to run for a third term, he opined, "They are sick of looking at my grin and they are sick of hearing what Alice had for breakfast."

As T. R.'s presidency drew to a close, Alice spent as much time with her father as she could. In evenings at Sagamore Hill, she watched him come downstairs before dinner to view the sun setting across Long Island Sound. He would stand on the piazza and look and look, start to go in, then go back for another look "to see," he said, "the tall river steamer lights blazing up the Sound." He put cologne on his handkerchief to hold under Alice's nose for a whiff. Other times he would put a spray of crisp flowers in his buttonhole to bury his nose in them. It was as if he were cuddling the dwindling moments of his life.

As for Alice, there would not be a short last chapter for her. She would not exactly break Aristotle's rule that a drama should build toward a crisis to be released in a denouement, giving the audience a delightful sensation, unexpected but prepared for. It was just that she took her own sweet time getting there. For many decades, she would continue partying, laughing, teasing, and tantalizing. But history has given us a considerable irony: the same election that sent Nick back to Congress also sent to the Senate the man who would become the father of her child.

Twenty-three

"Don't Hurt Him; I Want to Look at Him"

It was expected that Alice would be pregnant by the summer. After all, her father always praised large families, and when she was living in the White House she liked to tease him at dinner parties by singing: "Teddy, Teddy, Rough and Ready, Hear his battle cry! Get the habit, Be a rabbit, Mul – ti – ply!"

So when Alice failed to announce a pregnancy, her father—and the nation—were disappointed. The disappointment was compounded by the fact that Eleanor had had a baby girl in May. Though Eleanor had married FDR almost a year earlier than Alice married Nick, Eleanor was eight months younger, and the cousins were always being compared. T. R. boasted to reporters that he was "delighted" to learn of the birth of his niece, and his comment must have hurt Alice.

So why wasn't she pregnant? Was it Nick's drinking? His mistresses? Journalists tattled that whenever they saw the couple alone, Nick was "in a silent mood [and] Mrs. Longworth looked tired and even angry." And Nick continued to feed his prior reputation. When a fellow congressman ran his hand over Nick's bald head and quipped, "Nice and smooth. Feels just like my wife's bottom." Nick rubbed his own head and said, "So it does."

His public profile continued to climb. In Ohio, a movement began to push Nick for the governorship—not a position Alice would welcome. She expected him to get her back to the White

House. Her father's presidency was judged a great success, but it was coming to an end. More and more, T. R. was already looking back at his accomplishments rather than looking forward: his sending of the US fleet, composed now of sixteen sleek battleships, around the world for sixteen months as a statement of the country's strength; his creation of the Food and Drug Administration and passage of the Pure Food and Drug Act (actions taken after he read Upton Sinclair's *The Jungle*); his executive order placing 230 million acres in federal preserves, bypassing Congress's reluctance to protect federal lands. As the 1908 election approached, he chose his successor, William Howard Taft, whom he expected to turn executive orders into laws as well as continue his agenda to regulate capitalism to provide a "square deal" for all Americans.

With T. R.'s support, Taft won the presidential election handily. T. R. participated in the inauguration, then left with his family for Sagamore Hill from Washington's Union Station, where he was seen off by three thousand well-wishers. With Bamie, Alice, and Edith—all in tears—he boarded the train, and as it pulled out of the station, he stood with Edith on the rear platform waving his shiny black topper as he listened to the people wishing him good-bye and good luck.

The presidency was the high point of T. R.'s life, and so it would prove to be for Alice. She was only twenty-five when Taft assumed office, but the road ahead for her would be distinctly rocky. Her father would grow disappointed with the performance of his protégé, and when Taft ran for reelection in 1912, T. R. tried to make a comeback with his own Bull Moose Party. The campaign split the Republican Party and also split Alice's already shaky marriage. Nick supported Taft and Alice her father, and she worked closely with T. R., reviewing his speeches and campaigning for him. Just days before the election, she confided to her diary about her and Nick: "We are surely drifting decidedly apart. It is so sad." She told her family that she wanted a divorce, and as she would describe much later, "They didn't quite lock me up, [but] they exercised considerable pressure to get me to reconsider. Told me to think it over very carefully indeed. The whole thing would have caused too much of a hullabaloo. . . . In those days people just didn't go around divorcing one another. Not done, they said. Emphatically."

During T. R.'s Bull Moose campaign, Edith's worst fear became reality. T. R. was in Milwaukee to give a campaign speech when a deranged former New York saloon keeper—from T. R.'s police commissioner days—came within a few feet of him and fired a bullet into his chest. As bystanders grappled with the shooter, T. R. yelled out, "Don't hurt him. I want to look at him."

Taking a few minutes to glare at the shooter as if looking death straight in the eye, T. R. turned silently away and gave a one-and-a-half-hour speech while bleeding through his shirt. The bullet had been slowed by T. R.'s glasses case and the thick pages of his speech. Edith rushed to be with him in the hospital and took over. Alice went too, and when she was allowed to see her father for a few minutes, she thought he looked surprisingly well, though uncomfortable. The surgeons decided to leave the bullet in; it was so near his heart. T. R. told Alice it had been an interesting experience and quoted an old Rough Rider saying: "How'd he do it? With a .38 on a .45 frame."

T. R.'s Bull Moose comeback bid for the White House split the party to the extent that the Democrat Woodrow Wilson won the presidency. Alice's choice to support her father rather than her husband's campaign to keep his congressional seat was the final damage to her marriage. Nick lost his election and blamed her. Though she continued to keep up the charade of her and Nick's marriage, she became disgusted at his drinking and amorous indiscretions and his lack of backbone.

And her father was fading. After the United States entered World War I, T. R. came to stay with Nick and Alice in Washington to try to secure a military appointment. Franklin Roosevelt, as assistant secretary of the navy, opened the door for his cousin. Alice went to the White House with them, watching as her father asked the president to allow him to raise a division and lead it abroad. The president turned him down, saying there was no policy for supplementary volunteer forces. "It was the bitterest sort of blow for Father," she said.

Also, his health was deteriorating. A two-year expedition through the Amazon he'd led nearly killed him, and lingering effects of the diseases he suffered put him in the hospital for forty-four days in 1918. That summer his son Quentin, a pursuit pilot in the US Army Air Service, had been killed in aerial combat over France. After Christmas, T. R. lay on the sofa in his library, reading and dictating letters. Edith took him out for drives in the car, but he was feeling less well by New Year's Day. The official citation of Quentin's death arrived on December 31, and T. R. died less than a week later, on January 6. He was sixty years old.

Archie cabled his brothers, Kermit and Ted, who were serving in Germany: "THE OLD LION IS DEAD." Alice thought of lines from the book of Job: "The old lion perishes for lack of prey, and the stout lion's whelps are scattered abroad." In their grief, Edith and Corrine walked together over the grounds of Sagamore Hill, past the pet cemetery where their numerous beloved animals, including T. R.'s Rough Rider horse, Little Texas, were buried. As they did, they heard the unfamiliar sound of small aircraft overhead. Pilots from the field where Quentin had trained were dropping laurel wreaths onto the lawn.

It was customary for widows to stay at home, reading the funeral service instead of being at the church and grave site. While some five hundred villagers and dignitaries attended the simple ceremony at Christ Church, Oyster Bay, Edith stayed at Sagamore Hill. No music, no eulogy. Apparently Alice stayed away too. A small group of political friends and enemies followed to Youngs Memorial Cemetery. Afterward as mourners waited at the train station to go back to town, one said, "It would be foolish to think that he could ever *really* die." Bamie stayed at Oldgate, relying on a wheelchair now from the arthritis that had benched her. But her spicy intellect was still roaming. Unable to travel to Sagamore Hill, she was turning her attention now to the career of her friend Sara Delano's son, Franklin.

It is tempting to assume that her father's death would usher in a liberating time for Alice, but it was not to be. Her longing for his approval, to catch his notice, swelled into a need to guard his legacy and his every political act. Most often, this meant she attacked critics with a sense of revenge. She wore a ring with his hair in it, and as often as possible wore the "crowded hour" pearls. Over the years, her own views would slide to the right, but in the immediate aftermath of his death she supported the progressive issues he championed. When the Senate debated the Treaty of Versailles and Wilson's concept of a global peacekeeping organization—which her father had at one time suggested—Alice sat in the gallery. She was following the politics, certainly, but she was also entranced by the oratory of Senator William Borah of Idaho.

She had known him since his arrival in Washington in 1907. Described as "an Apollo in appearance," Borah had a leonine head with a thick shock of hair. Born in Illinois but clearly a westerner, he had the pluck and swagger of T. R. When he met Alice he was forty-two years old and had been married for twelve years. He and Alice fell in love and had a long-lasting affair. He told her he believed that she was made in her father's image and was proud to claim T. R.'s wonderful daughter as a dear friend "of long years." He accepted her as his intellectual equal. One of Borah's friends even said that his one great desire was to be the successor of Theodore Roosevelt.

There were nineteen years between them, but they were a perfect match. They both loved horse racing and reading literature. His colleagues described him as "melancholy, pessimistic, moody, emotional, impulsive, a loner wrapped in an elusive charm, and could be imagined as a university professor, a moral crusader, even a poet."

In the late spring of 1924, Alice was stunned to discover she was pregnant. She was forty years old. Yet she embraced the thought of having her own child, especially since her father had so valued children, and she had not forgotten his tendency to compare her with Eleanor, who had six children in the first ten years of marriage to Franklin. For whatever reason, Nick seemed to be infertile. Mary Borah, too, had been unable to have children. But the obvious conclusion—that Alice's child was Bill Borah's—was not mentioned. The best thing, it was tacitly decided, was for all parties involved to let it be—let it seem that the child was Nick's and that their marriage was as solid as Nick and Alice pretended it to be.

When the news broke, Alice's star power reignited. The *New Yorker* wrote: "She is still the Princess Alice. . . . She does no official entertaining, gives no large parties, returns no calls. She breaks every rule in the book, and in Washington the rules count. Yet an invitation to the Longworths' is more prized by the discriminating than an invitation to the White House. If she does not feel like dressing, Alice—not the butler—may receive her guests at the door in a Chinese silk outfit something like a swell set of pajamas. She will sit on her feet on a tiger skin before the fire and smoke while Nick, after a wearing day on the floor of the House, fiddles with complete abstraction."

Nick would be fifty-six when the child arrived. Bill Borah would be sixty. This was Alice's crowded hour, the moment in her life when the child's birth would focus complete attention on her as well as provide a delicious secret to maintain. Silence about the truth was crucial, as it would threaten any presidential plans Bill Borah harbored. He couldn't take the chance that the scandal of being the father to Alice's child would be found out.

In November Alice went to Sagamore Hill to tell Edith she was pregnant. Only five days before, Henry Cabot Lodge had died of a cerebral hemorrhage at age seventy-four. *Bouleverse*, the French word meaning *distressed*, is what Edith wrote in her diary. The entry left it vague as what was the more distressing, Cabot Lodge's death or Alice's news. It would never be known if Edith was privy to the rumors swirling around Washington that Nick was not the father. In a letter to Bamie, Edith wrote, "Alice's news was rather a blow, and I dare say a few days at sea (on a trip to Cuba) are good for me."

Alice went into labor on February 14, in Chicago. Edith rushed to be with her. The fact that it was Valentine's Day, the day of Alice Lee's death, made them all jumpy, but the baby arrived in good health and Alice was fine, too, described by Edith as "looking younger than she had for years." Anxiety flipped into celebration. Edith hoped Alice would call her baby Alice, too, but the Longworths chose the name Paulina after a favorite apostle.

Alice told Nick that she thought of calling the baby Deborah with emphasis on *Borah*. Nick was not amused. "With all the gossip going around," he said, "why would you want to name her De-Borah?" Perhaps he knew the truth and didn't care. He met the baby the day after she was born and told reporters he was "a little bit jealous . . . because she looks so much more like a Roosevelt than a Longworth, but she's young yet." One paper printed, "She is a true descendant of her famous granddaddy." Borah wrote to Alice, "Good—like our Roosevelt."

As Paulina grew, Nick loved having photographs taken of her sitting on his lap in the chamber of the House. It was said that from the time he took one look at her, he fell head over heels in love. Newspapers suggested she was "the real speaker of the house." She and Nick became inseparable. Before her first birthday, he was elected Speaker of the House, and Paulina became the nation's most famous baby. Indeed, the whole country was wild about "the Valentine Baby."

By 1926 pundits were speculating that Nick would run for president. "Every move he makes is colored Alice blue. . . . [His wife] has the finesse of a fencer, a boxer, a bridge player with tact." But Alice did not take motherhood seriously. Its greatest value to her was promotional, helping her become even more conspicuous in the nation's politics. In February 1927 she was on the cover of *Time* magazine, which described her as "the most popular lady in the land." She was paid $5,000 (equal to $68,000 today) for appearing in a Pond's Cold Cream ad. Her appendix, which had been removed in 1907, was preserved in a government bottle of alcohol! For every move Nick made, Alice's star power eclipsed him. As discussions of his presidential chances were bandied about, people wondered how Alice would behave as First Lady. Would Paulina be as mischievous as Alice had been as the White House "wild child"? When Nick announced he would not run, headlines screamed: ALICE RULES NICK OUT.

Paulina grew up smothered by the attention her mother craved. She never had a chance to discover herself. Fame had landed on Alice at the age of seventeen, when her father became president. But Paulina was smothered by fame from the moment she took her first breath. It was her mother's fame, not hers—unearned, not sought. Fame was telling Paulina who she was before she had a chance to find out for herself.

She was never to feel that her mother sacrificed one moment of her own desires for her. It was Paulina's father whose face lit up the moment he saw her. Paulina brought out an unexpected side of him. Nick let her make fantasy pies on top of his bald head. He took her to the Capitol on Saturday afternoons to let a whole phalanx of congressmen join him in spoiling her. He took her to French and piano lessons and stayed with her.

Nick wanted to take Paulina onto the floor of the House; Alice thought that would be exploiting her. But he allowed photographers to snap pictures of him with his daughter. There was little Paulina at the zoo. On the streets of Washington. Nick gave her the nickname "Kitz" and watched Paulina learn to love the attention. She and her mother shared that love anyhow—they were all over the place all the time, talking vivaciously to newspapermen who poked their heads in the door. When Kermit saw Alice and Paulina together, he wrote his sister Ethel, "I saw sister in Washington, as much wrapped up in Paulina as ever. [Paulina] is more advanced, indeed does not seem like a baby at all."

But just as Eleanor lost her father at age nine, Paulina would lose Nick at age five. In March 1931 Nick was stricken with pneumonia while visiting a friend in North Carolina. Weakened by alcoholism, he quickly grew worse. On April 8 Alice arrived from Washington; Nick died the next day. Alice arranged a special train to take Nick's body back to Ohio and even invited his two mistresses to join her. Paulina stayed with her nanny at Nick's family home during the funeral. The outpouring of grief was significant; Nick had been an exemplary Speaker, amiable and insightful. He led by persuasion and was always elegant, often wearing spats and carrying a gold-knobbed cane. When three women were elected to the House, he provided a female restroom, which the Supreme Court would not do for another half century.

After Nick's funeral, there was a push for Alice to run for Nick's seat in the next campaign. Alice claimed that she was too shy to campaign; furthermore, she did not want to be seen as one of those women who "used their husbands' coffins for a springboard." She made it seem that uppermost in her mind was Paulina and how much she would miss her father.

Borah, meanwhile, was sliding into old age and depression. He apparently never had a relationship with Paulina, and the scandal of his and Alice's love affair died in the silence. With neither Nick nor Borah in her life, Alice soared, always in motion, renowned for her salon, always pushing her daughter to enjoy the limelight with her. But Paulina was genuinely shy, overwhelmed by what her mother expected of her. Alice never let her finish a sentence, feeding her lines to say in front of people to the point that Paulina developed a stammer. Alice wanted Paulina to learn repartee like that of her father and Bamie.

Perhaps Alice should have turned to Bamie for help in mothering, but she couldn't. Bamie was facing her own struggles. Her ankles had become so swollen with arthritis, she relied on her wheelchair. She continued to hold court at Oldgate, becoming an adviser to Eleanor and Franklin as his career soared. When Franklin, urged by Eleanor and Louis Howe, decided to take up his career in politics after his attack of polio, he went to Auntie Bye in his wheelchair to get her advice. What Bamie said to him has not been recorded, but no doubt it had the ring of Bamie's old magic to give him the courage to do what he did. In August 1931, just days before Bamie died at the age of seventy-six, Franklin's mother, Sara, went to visit her. Knowing she was dying, Bamie patted Sara's hand and said, "It's all right."

Twenty-four

Uncrowded Hours

As the Great Depression descended in the early thirties, Alice's life was profoundly different. Her father was dead. Her husband was dead. She had a seven-year-old daughter. Though she would be a Washington denizen for another fifty years, caustically commenting on eight different presidents and countless politicians, she would never be the center of attention as she had been when her father was president and her husband Speaker of the House. Her life was far from over, but the coming decades were distinctly anticlimactic.

She wrote a memoir, *Crowded Hours*, for Scribner's, with the famed editor Maxwell Perkins to guide her. But she found the writing boring. She mentioned neither her father's death nor her daughter's birth. Though the memoir was a bestseller, it revealed nothing of her personal life, only a list of all she had done as first daughter, and gratuitously listing the "loot" she had garnered on the Asian junket. She did admit she had been spoiled, mostly by herself, and she avoided blaming for the clumsy way her mother's death was handled in her life. The book came out in 1933, the year Franklin was inaugurated president, a deed for which she never forgave him. The presidency was supposed to belong to her brother Ted. One man or another was supposed to have been her sliding board back into the White House.

Paulina went to elementary school in Cincinnati, living at Nick's family home, then attended the Madeira School in Virginia. By the time Paulina was fifteen, Alice was using her as a stunt at her dinners, where politics was the main course. When Paulina was training a fox terrier puppy to do its business on a newspaper, Alice thought it was cute to have Paulina put a magazine on the floor with FDR's photograph on the cover and have the puppy pee on it. Dinner guests were appalled. Alice took no mind, but Paulina must have picked up the vibrations in the room. Being used by her mother for a mean joke must have been consistently distressing.

Alice developed a renowned imitation of Eleanor, complete with buckteeth and high-register voice. She performed it at dinner parties or anywhere else as a source of laughter. Though Franklin's New Deal program had its origins in her father's Square Deal, she excoriated it, saying—in print—that it paralyzed the country as illness had paralyzed FDR. Her grudges fueled her wit, pushing what she intended to be "good clean fun" into vitriol.

Paulina, however, struggled more and more as she grew older. When she left home to attend Vassar, her mental health quickly deteriorated. After a year the college expelled her for taking an overdose of sleeping pills, which Paulina later admitted to Kermit had been an attempt to kill herself. When she was nineteen, Paulina attended her first national Republican convention, which Alice hoped might revive her interest in life. In an interview at the convention, Paulina said, "It's the greatest thrill of my life. I never dreamed it would be this much fun, something happening every minute. . . . This is something I will never forget." But when the reporter asked her who would be her pick for president, she was silent, then said, "Mother's judgment is worth a lot more than mine. Ask her."

Politics would not help Paulina. She saw marriage as a means of escape and became engaged to Alex Sturm, a polo-playing Yale graduate from a wealthy Connecticut family, when she was nineteen. He was tall, handsome, and talented. He had published and illustrated a children's book. He was also ambitious. With fifty thousand dollars of Paulina's money, he cofounded a manufacturer of high-end firearms. But Alice didn't like him, perhaps because he was eccentric, wore a beret, and affected a British accent. He was also a troublesome drinker, but most of all he challenged Alice's control over Paulina.

Alice did not invite Franklin and Eleanor to Paulina's wedding. Alice's brother Ted had died in France just weeks before, and the celebration was muted. Paulina walked down the aisle on the arm of Ted's son Cornelius, wearing a gown featuring lace from Russia from Alice's days of collecting loot. Paulina also wore the Crowded Hour pearls that her mother so cherished.

But the promise of the wedding would not last. Two years after marrying, Paulina's daughter, Joanna, was born. Since Alice's relationship with Paulina and Alex was strained, she didn't see much of her granddaughter. When Joanna was five, her father, only twenty-eight, died of drinking-related hepatitis. Widowed at twenty-six, Paulina was unable to cope. She moved into a Manhattan hotel apartment, where a maid found her unconscious. She and Joanna then moved to a house about a mile from Alice in Georgetown. Alice knew Paulina needed help but didn't know how to provide it. In her usual tone, she told a friend that "Paulina was coming to live in Washington, but of course she couldn't live with *her*."

Converting to Catholicism, Paulina found temporary comfort in ritual and prayer. She volunteered at Catholic hospitals and worked with the progressive Catholic Workers movement, which some thought was a way to stick her finger in her mother's eye, since Alice always equated being "frightfully good" with being "frightfully boring." Yet Paulina's troubles continued, and in January 1957 ten-year-old Joanna found her mother unconscious on the couch. A neighbor called an ambulance, but Paulina died on the way to the hospital. The coroner's report called the cause of her death heart failure from a combination of prescription drugs and alcohol.

It took Alice five months to answer Eleanor's note of condolence:

> For months after Paulina died whenever I tried to write I simply crumpled. I do hope you understand because I want you to know how touched I was by your thoughts, your telegram, the spring blossoms on your letter. Joanna is with me now. We leave in a few days for a couple of months on a ranch in Wyoming. Perhaps some time when you are in town you would let me know and we could have a "family" moment together. I should so much like to have Joanna know you, and for me it would be a pleasure, as it was to have a glimpse of you at the Meyers' party.
>
> Affectionately, Alice

One of Alice's friends said, "It nearly killed her. It really did. If she didn't exactly blame herself for her daughter's years of unhappiness, she was more aware than ever that her own conspicuous persona—the bride at every wedding, the corpse at every funeral temperament she inherited from her father—had not served shy, sweet Paulina well."

Alice gained custody of Joanna. She went slowly with her, thoughtfully, carefully, awake to her missteps with Paulina and now open to learning the ways of mothering. To put someone else first, to shelve her own longing to be front and center, would somehow cure her of what she described as "feeling like an extra piece of baggage in relation to the family"—her family, the Roosevelts, the most remarkable American family of the first half of the twentieth century. The need for attention and spectacle was still there (for Joanna's thirteenth birthday, Alice invited Vice President Richard Nixon and FBI director J. Edgar Hoover), but by then Alice knew her shortcomings and tried harder to create a child-centered lifestyle for Joanna. And it helped that she and Joanna shared a love of horses and riding.

Alice found a place for Joanna to ride near Washington, and Joanna spent most afternoons at the horse farm, riding, growing, becoming confident from what the sport taught her. Alice took her every year to a ranch in Wyoming, a trip they never missed, even after Alice was thrown from her horse and broke her foot. She did not smother Joanna with politics or her expectations. She turned herself into the mother she should have been to Paulina. "I should have been a grandmother, not a mother," she said. She did not expect Joanna to display T. R.'s larger-than-life personality. Whatever of the Roosevelt genes that trickled down to Joanna was fine, but exalting them was off the menu. When Joanna laughed, Alice said it was "one of the pleasantest sounds I've ever heard."

Weakened by pneumonia, on February 20, 1980, Alice lay dying with her cat on her bed, Joanna beside her. With tons of books stacked all around her room, she also kept the dollhouse her grandfather made her to replace the one her mother had. At night, when she couldn't sleep, she would play with it, rearranging its furnishings, no doubt retreating in her mind to the childhood she could never quite move past. It is said that her last act was to stick out her tongue. But the most telling fact is that when she died, she was wearing the Crowded Hour pearls.

Epilogue

Her aunt Gracie left Alice a written description of the day she was born. As Alice described it, "It wasn't very illuminating but perhaps there was little to illumine. My mother apparently said something about how pleased she was that I was a girl, then sank back into a coma. The doctors huddled in corners. There was doubtless a lot of wringing of hands and deathbed watching. My father never told me anything about this . . . not that I even *had* a different mother. He was so self-conscious about it. He never mentioned her name to *anyone*. It was most curious. . . . awfully bad psychologically. And my maternal grandparents never mentioned her either. Nor my aunts, her mother's sisters."

This was part of her father's legacy, a legacy of silence that was a huge part of how her life was defined. Shortly before he died, T. R. worked on a book entitled *Theodore Roosevelt's Letters to His Children*, saying, "I would rather have this book published than anything that has ever been written about me." Despite the fact that he wrote Alice many letters over his lifetime, he did not include any of his letters to her in this collection, each of which is addressed to Blessed Ted, Dearest Archie, Darling Ethel, Blessed Archie-kins, and Blessed Quenty-Quee.

A strange and mysterious omission that says so much about Alice, his wild child.

Acknowledgments

AS I MENTIONED IN MY NOTE TO READERS, my fascination with Theodore Roosevelt and his daughter Alice began in the midst of writing *Borrowing Life*, a narrative history of the first successful kidney transplant. When I discovered that kidney failure, known as Bright's disease, was braided through the lives of various historical figures, as well as the lives of characters in literature, especially in Dickens, I was riveted by the fact that Alice Lee died of it, leaving her daughter Alice to muddle through the effects of her father's grief. At that point, all I knew about Alice was what we all knew—that she had traipsed through our culture for generations recognized by her antics. But when I realized how compelling she really was, not just as a noted personality in history but as a complicated person who clearly suffered from her own form of grief, well . . . it seemed that I should write what was not yet fully explored: the effects of a father on a daughter.

As my research took off from wonderful secondary sources, such as the definitive biography of Alice by Stacy Cordery, I saw that putting Alice's life on the canvas of her father's presidency would be an education for all of us, especially since the art of politics is much like an iceberg with most of it invisible below the surface. In finding facts I was chilled, exhilarated, or disgusted by them, and in the process I became so excited to share them with my readers, the work of writing ascended to an obsession. I ate with the Roosevelts. I traveled with them. I napped with them, their every living minute greatly on my mind. In editing, my wonderful editor, Kevin Stevens, kept reminding me, "Get back to Alice."

As the life stories unfolded, I found myself wanting to warn them like the child I once was in a movie theater, eager to cry out to the hero on the screen as trouble sneaked up: "Don't you see that coming!" Thank goodness the energy of imagination brightens our connection with every living thing on this earth.

Even though Theodore Roosevelt became president in 1901, look at how the issues he dealt with echo in our nation today!

When my agent, Mark Gottlieb, saw the value of this history too, this project took off. Again, editor Kevin Stevens was the key, for I had been lucky enough to work with him on *Borrowing Life* and instantly trusted his guidance when he saw what Alice meant to women's history, American history, and all things important to growing up.

My husband, Parker, was supportive, as always, especially when I immersed myself in a plethora of sources to root out the facts that added up to Alice's life; and every morning, during our coffee time as I babbled, sorting out dates and connections with enough obsession to make any listener's eyes roll, he suffered in silence. For nearly two years, my best friends and mentors through our horrendous 2020 pandemic were Bamie, Alice, Edith, and T. R. himself. My Monday coffee klatch of Jeanne, Vandy, and Celia gave more unconditional support as the pages kept coming, as did Scott and Beverly Griseck, who tacked up and pitched me up onto Tulip for a trot around the field while my mind sorted out how to structure this book. Listening to Shelby Foote on video explaining how his writing narrative history relied on his knowledge of structuring a novel was a special comfort—as was simply knowing of Bamie, finding in a rare-bookstore the memoir that Lillian Rixey produced from Bamie's letters. What a great feeling to think that I was bringing Bamie back into today for everyone to be as inspired by her as I am.

Finally, the key to my understanding the Roosevelts while I wrote was, simply, that I found my traits in all of them. As they became me, and I them, we seemed to form an imaginary team bound in the mission to write this book to enlighten all of us to the power, the majesty, and the worthwhile danger of love.

Bibliography

Books

Berfield, Susan. *The Hour of Fate: Theodore Roosevelt, J. P. Morgan, and the Battle to Transform American Capitalism*. New York: Bloomsbury Publishing, 2020.

Campbell, Joseph. *Myths to Live By*. New York: Viking Press, 1972.

Caroli, Betty Boyd. *The Roosevelt Women*. New York: Basic Books, 1998.

Cordery, Stacy A. *Alice: Alice Roosevelt Longworth, from White House Princess to Washington Power Broker*. Viking, New York, 2007.

Dalton, Kathleen. *Theodore Roosevelt, A Strenuous Life*. New York: Random House, 2004.

Davis, Deborah. *Guest of Honor: Booker T. Washington, Theodore Roosevelt and the White House Dinner that Shocked a Nation*. New York: Atria, 2012.

Fass, Paula S., and Mary Ann Mason, eds. *Childhood in America*. New York: New York University Press, 2000.

Gilbert, Allison. *Passed and Present: Keeping Memories of Loved Ones Alive*. Berkeley, California: Seal Press, 2016.

Harbaugh, William H. *Power and Responsibility: The Life and Times of Theodore Roosevelt*. Newtown, Connecticut: American Political Biography Press, 1961.

Longworth, Alice Roosevelt. *Crowded Hours: Reminiscences of Alice Roosevelt Longworth.* New York: Scribner's, 1933.

Marrin, Alfred. *The Great Adventure: Theodore Roosevelt and the Rise of Modern America.* New York: Dutton Children's Books, 2007.

McCullough, David, *Mornings on Horseback.* New York: Simon and Schuster, 1981.

Morris, Edmund. *The Rise of Theodore Roosevelt.* New York: Random House, 1979.

Morris, Edmund. *Theodore Rex.* New York: Random House, 2001.

Morris, Sylvia. *Edith Kermit Roosevelt: Portrait of a First Lady.* New York: Modern Library, 1980.

Morrison, Toni. *The Source of Self-Regard: Selected Essays, Speeches, and Meditations.* New York: Random House, 2019.

Peyser, Marc, and Timothy Dwyer. *Hissing Cousins: The Lifelong Rivalry of Eleanor Roosevelt and Alice Roosevelt Longworth.* Washington, DC: Anchor Books, 2015.

Renehan, J. Edward, Jr. *The Lion's Pride: Theodore Roosevelt and His Family in Peace and War.* New York: Oxford University Press, 1998.

Rixey, Lillian. *Bamie: Theodore Roosevelt's Remarkable Sister.* New York: David McKay Company, 1963.

Roosevelt, Theodore. *The Autobiography of Theodore Roosevelt.* Digreads.com Publishing, 1913, 2019.

Roosevelt, Theodore. *Letters to His Children*, New York: Scribner's, 1919.

Sarnoff, Charles. *Latency.* Lanham, Maryland: Jason Aronson Inc., 1989.

Saxton, Martha. *Being Good: Women's Moral Values in Early America.* New York: Hill and Wang, 2003.

Teague, Michael. *Mrs. L: Conversations with Alice Roosevelt Longworth.* New York: Doubleday & Company, 1981.

Teichmann, Howard. *The Life and Times of Alice Roosevelt Longworth*. Englewood Cliffs, New Jersey: Prentice Hall, 1979.

Articles

Boffery, Phillip M. "Theodore Roosevelt at Harvard." *Harvard Crimson*, December 12, 1957.

Dalton, Kathleen. "The Self-Made Man." Printed in the publication accompanying the documentary *The Roosevelts: An Intimate History*, by Ken Burns.

"Elkhorn Ranch." US National Park Service. www. nprs.gove/thro/historyculture/elkhorn-ranch, htm.

Pringle, Henry F. "Especially Pretty Alice." *American Heritage*, Vol. 9, Issue 2 (February 1958).

Sally Quinn. Interview with Alice Roosevelt Longworth. *Washington Post*, February 12, 1974.

Weatherford, Doris. "The Evolution of Nursing." National Women's History Museum. http://www.womenshistory.org/articles/evolution-nursing.

Zacks, Richard. "The Police Commish." Printed in the publication accompanying the documentary *The Roosevelts: An Intimate History*, by Ken Burns.

Endnotes

All author citations in the endnotes refer to books and articles listed in the bibliography.

Introduction

(The reporter in the introduction is not a specific reporter but represents the many who went to Alice for interviews. The descriptions and dialog, however, are accurate from documented sources.)

"they ring for me": Teichmann, p. 251.
For nearly twenty years: Teague, p. xii.
dumbwaiter: Ibid, p. xv.
"weaned on a pickle"; "thank god it wasn't his prostate"; "it just became him"
"in his head like scrabble": Teichmann, p. 251.
"what an extraordinary upbringing": Ibid., p. 202.
"Jerry Fords by the bale": Ibid., p. 226.
Dutch upstarts who made a couple of bucks: Ibid., p. 247.
Everyone has to do it his or her way: Ibid., pp. 233–234.
father's cartoon toothy grin: Teichmann, pp. 34–35.
"Scarlett O'Hara and Whistler's Mother": Ibid., p. 243.
"call me Mrs. Longworth": Ibid., p. 157.
"you white son of a bitch": Ibid., p. 198.
"I think it is excellent": Teichmann, pp. 208–209.
"I simply crumpled": Ibid., p. 199.
"she would have been president": Rixey, p. 292.

Part I: T. R. and Bamie

Chapter One

it was suicide weather: McCullough, p. 283.
an eight-pound, twelve-ounce baby girl; "only fairly well": Rixey, p. 49.
on Lincoln's birthday: Harbaugh, p. 51.
"he did not allow it to worry him": Sylvia Morris, e-book location 1126.

"Oh don't let my baby take cold": Cordery, p. 15.
in particular bugs and plants: Pringle, "Especially Pretty Alice."
associated spectacles with moral decay: Roosevelt, *Autobiography*, p 31.
"I had no idea how beautiful the world was": Ibid., pp. 17–18.
"sweet Motherling": McCullough, p. 224.
father's vigor for life: Rixey, p. 8.
recall in detail what he had read: Ken Burns, *The Roosevelts: An Intimate History*, DVD.
knew more about state politics, Burns, *The Roosevelts: An Intimate History*, periodical accompanying the DVD, p. 258.
"see changes that had taken place": Ibid.
"my voice is not as powerful as it ought to be"; defect of some "odd kind": Ibid., p. 256.
"Mr. Spee-kar!": McCullough, p. 257.
interrupt meetings to ask questions: Rixey, p. 36.
"formed an opinion on everything": McCullough, p. 257.
yellow rose in his buttonhole: Morris, *Theodore Rex*, p. 46.
"cling to the fixed and the venerable": McCullough, p. 39.
"got a greater joy of living": Roosevelt, *Autobiography*, p. 11.
"I should almost perish": Harbaugh, p. 16.
"you are more like him"; "no one but my wife": Rixey, p. 28.
"See that girl?": Harbaugh, p. 24.
clearly athletic enough: Cordery, p. 6.
more than the salary: Ibid., p. 5.
Alice Lee's home in Chestnut Hill: Teague, p. 7.
"guard her from every trial": McCullough, p. 223.

Chapter Two

"fearlessness when he does not feel it": Roosevelt, *Autobiography*, p. 42.
"every moment as it passed": Cordery, p. 368.
"locomotive in pants": Boffery, "Theodore Roosevelt at Harvard."
"extraordinary vitality": McCullough, p. 143.
"mouse leapt out": Sylvia Morris, e-book location 376.
frogs landed at her feet: Theodore Roosevelt, *Autobiography*, p. 17.
experienced knowing; he described himself as "grubby": Ibid., p. 19.
"Hush! He didn't hear": Harbaugh, p. 224.
enthralled Alice Lee's five-year-old brother; Feeling that everything was black; He meant to break it: Henry F. Pringle, "Especially Pretty Alice."
"I can tell Alice everything": Harbaugh, p. 24.
"a man loved a woman more than I love her"; "to retain his love": McCullough, pp. 223–224.
"tender as she can be": Harbaugh, p. 21.
would do exactly the opposite: McCullough, p. 229.
"never happier than when I am with you": Cordery, p. 10.

Chapter Three

"too sacred to be written about": Cordery, p. 163.
to hold his own in among them: Roosevelt, *Autobiography*.
"sucking the nob of an ivory cane": Morris, *The Rise of Theodore Roosevelt*, p. 178.
"simple but plentiful, heavy on the plate": McCullough, p. 281.

"happiest of all little mothers": Ibid., p. 282.
"I wish I could have my little new baby soon": Cordery, p. 15.
"and Alice is dying too": Harbaugh, p. 283.
gravity of her illness; where Bamie stayed by her mother's side: Rixey, p. 49.
Only blank pages would follow: McCullough, p, 287.
since it was a job that was well paid: Weatherford, "The Evolution of Nursing."
voted to adjourn until the following Monday: McCullough, p. 284.
Presbyterian church at Fifty-Fifth St.: Rixey, p. 50.
buried next to Greatheart and Mittie's mother: McCullough, p. 284.
roses tumbled down her christening robe: Teague, p. 18.
Roosevelt heirloom silver bowl: Cordery, p. 17.
"died in his arms": McCullough, p. 288.
"He did not want anybody to sympathize with him": Ibid., p. 286.
simply called "Baby"; "there was a sadness about his face"; "who have gone before me"; "the more we work, the better I like it"; when he sent her a telegram: Rixey p. 50.
"Bringing Cabot Lodge for a few days": Ibid., p. 52.

Chapter Four

"a little feminine Atlas": Rixey, p. 3.
"the Major Generaless": McCullough, p. 161.
waving "bye": Rixey, p. v.
"stooping gait": Sylvia Morris, e-book location 362.
"saved her from being a helpless, distorted cripple": Rixey, p. 6.
tuberculosis of the spine: McCullough, p. 33.
spine had been injured: Rixey, p. 4.
facedown on the sofa all day: McCullough, p. 33.
which some consider her memoir: Rixey, vii.
"she gave out a light and animation": Ibid., p. 100.
one of the richest women in America: Rixey, p. 32.
"shrugged at life": Ibid., p. 29.
new and undescribed species: Rixey, p. vi.
"if Auntie Bye had been born a man": Sylvia Morris, p. 107.
"the driving wheel of destiny": Rixey, p. vii.

Chapter Five

"What I will do after that, I cannot tell you": Morris, *The Rise of Theodore Roosevelt*, p. 259.
had they made a mutual home: Rixey, p. 58.
"far off from all mankind": Roosevelt, *Autobiography*, pp.70–95.
"the light went out from my life for ever": Harbaugh, p. 53.
lift logs from the cellar to them: Sylvia Morris, p. 79.
play with Elliott's daughter Eleanor: Peyser and Dwyer, p. 14.
"ancient wounded animal": Rixey, p. 53.
too empty to contemplate: Harbaugh, p. 52.
"a rider whose pace is fast enough": McCullough, p. 332.
"She would be just as well off without me"; "inhumane discipline that some said approached cruelty": Harbaugh, p. 54.

"match applied to a slow-burning fuse"; "I may be in Dakota on Election Day"; "At last I have been able to sleep well at night"; "soon get as restless with this life as with the life at home": Rixey, p. 55.
laughed until her sides shook: Cordery, p. 20.
"in so important and exciting a struggle": Rixey, p. 56.
"be likely to come back into political life"; "ready to be commanded for any movement": Ibid., p. 58.

Chapter Six

had fallen into alcoholism: Ibid., p. 59.
"longing for the past which will come again never": Sylvia Morris, p. 23.
"Theodore had not been nice": Ibid., p. 59.
hosted a party for the newlyweds: Cordery, p. 21.
Edith was twenty-five, T. R. twenty-seven: Sylvia Morris, p. 79.
"I have a feeling for Edith": Ibid., p. 39.
down the stairs toward him: Ibid., p. 79.
"no longer the moody teenage girl": Ibid., p. 80.
fell back into love: Rixey, p. 59, and Sylvia Morris, p. 79.
he would mention neither Alice Lee nor his father's avoiding military service: Morris, *The Rise of Theodore Roosevelt*, p. 10.
"If I am going to do anything at all": Rixey, p. 61.
"Theodore has insisted on my keeping baby": Ibid., p. 62.

Chapter Seven

left Baby Lee in New York under the care of Corrine: Rixey, p. 63.
asked him to be his best man: Sylvia Morris, p. 99.
Alice Lee would have bored Theodore to death: Caroli, p. 192.
rejoicing in his lively conversation: Sylvia Morris, p. 111.
"rather eccentric": Rixey, p. 65.
eye-popping gloves: Sylvia Morris, pp. 99–100.
kisses to Baby Lee: Rixey, p. 66–67.
little attention to money: Edmund Morris, *The Rise of Theodore Roosevelt*, p. 306, and Sylvia Morris, p. 139.
"going to the ranch for year or two": Sylvia Morris, p. 102.
"I have not the slightest belief in my having any political future": Rixey, p. 67.
soldiers marching past, singing: Alice Roosevelt Longworth, p. 20.
proposal that Alice "stay on with her"; best love to the darling; and many kisses: Rixey, p. 66.
please to not blame Edith: Cordery, p. 22.
She would not have it: Sylvia Morris, p. 103.
"I am an American through to the backbone": Ibid., p. 105.
"tackle some more ambitious historical work": Ibid., p. 104.

Part II: Alice

Chapter Eight

"These are for your new mother": Alice Roosevelt Longworth, p. 9.
"wonderful silky private part of woman": Caroli, p. 193.
Was Edith "papa's sister?": Cordery, p. 26.

"my mother who is in heaven": Alice Roosevelt Longworth, p. 8.
The three of them now sat together on the floor: Sylvia Morris, p. 109.
as a child of "another marriage": Ibid., p. 9.
"if you are very unhappy": Cordery, p. 23.
"like a little white penguin when she said good-bye": Ibid., p. 70.
for doing something silly: Sylvia Morris, p. 22.
a reason to think they were interfering: Rixey, p. 73.
"because Edith thinks she would like to ride her very much"; secretly hidden in her desk drawer; but could not hide it from each other; "We miss you dreadfully": Ibid., pp. 70–71.

Chapter Nine

left behind when her father remarries: Campbell, p. 221.
in a comfortable Victoria: Alice Roosevelt Longworth, p. 11.
to decorate the Civil War dead: Ibid., p. 12.
"like a couple of dusty, grimy beavers": Sylvia Morris, p. 109.
"do your bleeding in the bathroom": Peyser and Dwyer, p. 21.
"if she could be of real assistance: Rixey, p. 72.
"I do not think there is need of anyone else": Ibid.
but Edith was heavy and sickly now; "I am very glad our house has an heir at last": Sylvia Morris, p. 112.
She declared him "a howling polly parrot": Ibid., p. 113.
"Edie wants a pair of nursing corsets": Sylvia Morris, p. 113.
"lest someone should take baby brother away": Cordery, p. 26.

Chapter Ten

jump up and down on the sofa; "I ought to have been spanked": Alice Roosevelt Longworth, p. 12.
a lifelong disease of self-pity: Ibid., p. 13.
the household's tight budget: Cordery, p. 24.
her father's voice that she craved: Alice Roosevelt Longworth, p. 12.
get into their father's riding boots: Roosevelt, *Autobiography*, p. 11.
he was well into the research: Sylvia Morris, p. 113.
"two lines a day and is fatter than ever": Sylvia Morris, p. 116.
always aiming to match Parkman's epic vision: Morris, *The Rise of Theodore Roosevelt*, p. 393.
which T. R. called "fussy"; "Sister, go out and call for the carriage now": Teague, p. 42–43.
Alice found her a good playmate: Sylvia Morris, p. 136.
added another accent to her repertoire: Teague, p. 48.
especially astronomy and geology: Sylvia Morris, p. 32.
"make themselves felt in the neighborhood": Alice Roosevelt Longworth, p. 10.
they were routed out and sent home: Ibid., 10–11.
"plays more vigorously than any one I ever saw": Morris, *The Rise of Theodore Roosevelt*, p. 395.
"middle aged, fat, and lazy"; "Do not forget me or love me less": Sylvia Morris, p. 119.
"I hope to be home even before the 20th": Ibid., p. 120.
"oh that *dear* Bamie"; Edith soon made it homelike and comfortable: Ibid., p. 121.

Chapter Eleven

"I got Alice a beautiful dress": Sylvia Morris, p. 137.
planned to give birth to a monkey; recklessly on a pony named Grant: Ibid., p. 146.
she felt persecuted; "a horrid, savage noise that petrified us": Caroli, p. 395.
"She looks splendidly": Cordery, p. 30.
"That's the way the goat went": Teague, p. 49.
she felt she belonged: Ibid., p. 13.
The tendons were too short and turned her feet on the side: Sylvia Morris, p. 155.
she was very cautious: Alice Roosevelt Longworth, p. 18–19.
the doctor think she does not have enough cartilage": Cordery, p. 30.
She decided to be conspicuous: Sally Quinn interview with Alice Roosevelt Longworth, *Washington Post*, February 12, 1974.
"I do feel quite as sorry for the poor child": Cordery, p. 27.
Alice began to listen through keyholes: Teague, p. 151.
Edith described Eleanor in a letter; Edith would not allow Alice: Sylvia Morris, p. 137.
"As you know I never wished Alice": Peyser and Dwyer, p. 25.
T. R.'s eccentric habits: Sylvia Morris, p. 136.
to punish herself; "that is a dream never to be realized"; Elliott wrote charming lies: Sylvia Morris, p. 140–141.
"cried like a child for a long time": Ibid., p. 143.
a picture of his dead wife: Michael Teague, p. 151.
in one of his roundups: Alice Roosevelt Longworth, pp. 2–3.
"he had such berry tiny feet": Sylvia Morris, pp. 150–151.

Chapter Twelve

They couldn't afford to lose his secure salary: Rixey, p. 81.
"It was much worse than I imagined possible": Sylvia Morris, p. 153.
the ambassador's wife asked her: Rixey, p. 79.
They threw up in their shoe; "It was the one golden chance": Caroli, p. 67.
"I shall be myself again by Saturday when the darling gets back"; "afford to be identified with": Rixey, pp. 82–83.
From London, Bamie sent Alice and Eleanor: Peyser and Dwyer, p. 26.
She would never again squash Theodore's passion: Sylvia Morris, p. 152.
"I have a very strong feeling for the navy": Rixey p. 87.
"Aunty Bye won't love us as much now": Cordery p. 28.
"Father doesn't care for me": Morris, *Theodore Rex*, p. 251.

Chapter Thirteen

he told of dealing with criminals: Alice Roosevelt Longworth, p. 15.
She fed her appetite for thrills: Ibid., pp. 12–13.
cops took bribes; "for which I am sorry"; handing out awards to police officers for stopping runaway carriages: Zacks, "The Police Commish," pp. 26–29.
"He has that morbid *idée fixe*"; "when he has a breakdown": Rixey, p. 89.
"Though I have the constitution of a bull moose": Ibid., p. 98.
"for we don't want war": Ibid., p. 91.
who tried to endear themselves to Europeans: Rixey, p. 102.
"he seems to have recovered his tone entirely": Ibid., p. 94.
"A field of immeasurable usefulness": Zacks, "The Commish," p. 30.

"he would want to fight somebody at once": Rixey, p. 105.
projected isthmian canal: Roosevelt, *Autobiography*, p. 151.
"much better company than the American man": Sylvia Morris, p. 118.

Chapter Fourteen

"animal in a cage": Ibid., p. 162.
In 1897 she wrote her cousin Franklin: Cordery, p. 35.
"Oh, Franklin, I'd love to": Peyser and Dwyer, p. 27.
The two of them took a cab: Cordery, p. 35.
Alice Lee had been empty-headed and frivolous: Rixey, p. 114.
He called Alice a "guttersnipe": Cordery, p. 34.
Ted Jr. came down with ghastly headaches: Rixey, p. 112.
A crippling repression of their natural rambunctiousness: Ibid., p. 115.
her parents suddenly relented: Alice Roosevelt Longworth, p. 26.
"help Auntie about everything": Rixey, pp. 114–115.
she had no desire to return to Washington: Sylvia Morris, p. 171.
peppery high spirit: Alice Roosevelt Longworth, p. 19.
"Someone forgot to put a scarf on me": Rixey, pp. 119–120.
"I am sure she really does love Edith": Cordery, p. 36.
"Evidently you have done as much for Ted": Rixey, p. 116.
"this ends his political career for good": Sylvia Morris, p. 172.
"notch on the stick that stands as a measuring rod"; "my heart aches for him": Ibid., p. 173.
"he cannot help being a power": Rixey, p. 117.
"Come back safe darling 'pigeon'": Sylvia Morris, pp. 174–175.
Blessed Bunnies: Roosevelt, *Letters to His Children*, pp. 13–14.
"*Unleash the dogs of War!*"; training of nurses for the field: Rixey, p. 122.
learning to ride astride her father's saddle: Cordery, p. 37.
"the time of my life": Sylvia Morris, p. 181.
twenty-four-hour visit; "If I was in love with one Rough Rider": Alice Roosevelt Longworth, p. 24.
"Apparently, I am going to be nominated": Sylvia Morris, p. 185.

Chapter Fifteen

set to the tune of: Sylvia Morris, p. 188.
"certainly intelligent": Cordery, p. 38.
Alice in typical Alice-style: Cordery, p. 39.
"altruistic" meant "socialistic": Rixey, pp. 134–135.
"stop his nomination by this convention": Harbaugh, p. 133.
T. R. wrote Bamie,"The thing could not be helped": Rixey, p. 158.
Edith felt he had done a foolish thing: Rixey, p. 159.
not to talk to reporters: Alice Roosevelt Longworth, p. 34.
"keep the conversation rippling": Rixey, p. 174.
"see Theodore take the veil": Ibid., p. 159.

Chapter Sixteen

"Look out they don't get you, Mr. Vice President": Morris, *Theodore Rex*, p. 8.
"a young wild animal who had been put in good clothes": Davis, p. 171.
She was properly horrified but also fulfilled: Alice Roosevelt Longworth, pp. 39–42.

"come out at the Executive Mansion": Alice Roosevelt Longworth, p. 42.
her nonchalance at the change in their lives: Alice Roosevelt Longworth, p. 42.
he would just have to come get her himself: Davis, p. 173.
the Pullman car named "Olympia": Rixey, pp. 170–171.
"made her hurried trip unaccompanied by a maid": Sylvia Morris, p. 219.
"He's too good a man to win on a foul": Rixey, p. 171.
"that damned cowboy is president of the United States!": Morris, *Theodore Rex*, p. 30.
Theodore was trying to escape Secret Service surveillance: Rixey, p. 172.
"Poor Mrs. Theodore!": Ibid., p. 171.
"It will be a lot harder for you to be an ex-president than president": Ibid., pp. 175–176.
Edith's arrival: Davis, p. 161.
No Black person had ever been invited to dine with the president: Davis, p. 188.
An Associated Press reporter: Morris, *Theodore Rex*, pp. 54–55.
Another feature of Southern racist outrage: Morris, *Theodore Rex*, pp. 55–56.
the first time she saw her father as president: Alice Roosevelt Longworth, pp. 43–44.

Chapter Seventeen

Twain answered: Edmund Morris, *Theodore Rex*, p. 56.
"a tragic turn": McCullough, pp. 365–366.
gathered the press: Morris, *Theodore Rex*, p. 45.
"If the remains of his grandmother were discovered": Ibid., p. 82.
Her rude behavior: Cordery, p. 40.
filched tin trays from the pantry: Alice Roosevelt Longworth, p. 45.
"Haven't you a jail record?": Morris, *Theodore Rex*, p. 66.
Usually, presidents collated reports: Ibid., p. 68.
He wanted forest resources: Morris, *Theodore Rex*, p. 76.
"treetops so close to one another for many miles"; "fishes as big as two-year-old children": Marrin, p. 149.
The *Chicago Record-Herald* gushed: Morris, *Theodore Rex*, p. 77.
"rather be a full president for half a year": Rixey, p. 191.
curbing her husband's natural impetuousness: Rixey, pp. 179–180.
"Go to it, Pop!": Morris, *Theodore Rex*, p. 80.
the kitchen workers left from the McKinley White House; setting a precedent for every first lady thereafter: Davis, pp. 148–149.
Edith stood by her: Sylvia Morris, p. 230.
She made sure her cousin Eleanor had been invited: Peyser and Dwyer, p. 43.
"tomboyish-looking girl": Cordery, p. 50.
at Alice's suggestion: Peyser and Dwyer, p. 43.
Franklin called Alice's debut ball "glorious": Cordery, p. 51.
Alice would say afterward: Peyser and Dwyer, p. 39.

Chapter Eighteen

"I count on long misty moonlight evenings on the White House porch": Sylvia Morris, p. 233.
knew that the kaiser was "vain, coarse": Morris, *Theodore Rex*, p. 187.
"Miss Roosevelt was the most self-possessed person"; "It is only a few weeks since Miss Roosevelt has left the schoolroom": Cordery, p. 57.

Everyone wrote their names on the menus; "a princess of blood": Alice Roosevelt Longworth, p. 49.
lease land in Panama: Morris, *Theodore Rex*, p. 202.
"The family was always telling me": Cordery, p. 53.
"Several awfully nice Cuban men and girls": Ibid., p. 60.
"I feel that I want something": Morris, *Theodore Rex*, p. 344.
Rumors spread that she had been engaged: Cordery, p. 64.
"had a foolish temper fight": Peyser and Dwyer, p. 47.
wished he had come home from Kettle Hill with some sort of disfiguring scar: Burns, *The Roosevelts: An Intimate History*.
rather see them dead: Dalton, "The Self-Made Man."
what they called "singlesticks": Morris, *Theodore Rex*, p. 185.
"Well, Colonel, we broke about even!": Roosevelt, *Autobiography*, p. 93.
two black cigars: Cordery, p. 77.
Alice obeyed when told; As soon as the flowers began wilting; was installed at Sagamore Hill: Peyser and Dwyer, p. 49.
"looking well but crazier than ever"; She had long ago shrugged off sympathy: Ibid., p. 51.
He put her on a restricted allowance: Cordery, p. 80.

Chapter Nineteen

a young, ruddy-faced politician: Morris, *Theodore Rex*, p. 147.
"a prophet who is charged with a message to deliver": Dalton, *A Strenuous Life*, p. 221.
"I don't dislike him. I just don't want to live in the same world with him": Ibid., p. 220.
"without first discussing it with Auntie Bye": Rixey, pp. 181–182.
"Bye is as dear as ever and oversees the entire nation"; Bamie noticed that T. R. worked too long: Ibid., p. 182.
up to 20,000 people gathered to hear him: Morris, *Theodore Rex*, p. 137.
Bill was six foot three and as muscular as a bull: Ibid., p. 137.
"We are passing through a period of great commercial prosperity": Morris, *Theodore Rex*, p. 138.
much of his audience could wander off": Ibid., pp. 138–139.
"Poor Craig. How my children will feel"; "It takes more than a trolley accident to knock me out": Ibid., pp. 142–143.
Soon he was rolling around in a wheelchair: Ibid., pp. 148–149.
T. R. allowed himself to be semi-anesthetized with whiskey: Ibid., p. 150.
"father having a hard time"; "Have begun to get up for breakfast"; "Father very busy": Cordery, p. 66.
"I think it is time that the government should have something to say": Cordery, pp. 66–67.
"such a consequence as the world has never seen": Ibid., p. 67.
T. R. felt that he should not intervene: Morris, *Theodore Rex*, p. 133.
authorized state troopers to shoot to kill; "live the life of a human being": Ibid., p. 152.
"I would greatly like to see you on Friday next October 3": Berfield, p. 171.
Alice followed it all: Alice Roosevelt Longworth, pp: 54–55.
"What wouldn't I give to be a most marvelous belle": Cordery, p. 67.
The mine owners trusted him: Berfield, p. 183.
"May Heaven preserve me from ever again dealing with so wooden-headed a set": Rixey, p. 211.

"They were not in danger of dying of cold": Ibid., p. 209.
"Theodore has tied so many knots with his tongue": Ibid., p. 211.

Chapter Twenty

"I want more": Cordery, pp. 94–95.
Always aware when she had her father's attention: Ibid., p. 151.
"the Resolute Desk": Morris, *Theodore Rex*, p. 176.
When T. R. put some of his favorite things on it: Ibid., p. 257.
"No one paid very much attention to poor Alice": Cordery, p. 67.
found Emily on the roof: Alice Roosevelt Longworth, pp. 60–61.
"If you remark to him that God is Great": Morris, *Theodore Rex*, p. 319.
However, he only succeeded in acquiring bruises: Ibid., p. 320.
"Victory. Triumph. My father is elected": Ibid., p. 363.
he often went to the Washington Monument late at night: Dalton, *A Strenuous Life*, p. 173.
It was unlike any inauguration America had ever seen: Rixey, p. 259.
"Much has been given us"; "Well you do it. Why shouldn't I?": Peyser and Dwyer, p. 53.

Part III: Paulina and Joanna

Chapter Twenty-one

He knew how much Alice prized the value of money; "I cannot live without money": Cordery, p. 101.
"After supper we all sang and Nick played": Ibid., p. 97.
At the last minute, Alice and Maggie sent a telegram: Peyser and Dwyer, p. 50.
"Nick love me be kind to me": Cordery, p. 97.
"He turned to politics for diversion": Ibid., p. 105.
"My mother has been informed by many": Ibid., p. 106.
"Your friend from Ohio drinks too much": Cordery, p. 100, and Peyser and Dwyer, p. 55.
"spirits were high and she better not take any more": Alice Roosevelt Longworth, p. 61.
"Be careful; he's dangerous"; "The reporters were in a spin"; "Old nasty Maggie"; "Here's my answer": Peyser and Dwyer, p. 55.
together they smoked on the White House roof; he was schooled in the art of deception in relationships: Ibid., p. 56.
visiting prostitutes on K Street: Cordery, p. 106.
"he made violent love": Dalton, *A Strenuous Life*, p. 278.
"May I be permitted to call you 'Little Alice'"; "Oh, Nick I love you passionately.": Cordery, p. 111.
"You were more charming than ever here"; If her stepmother didn't approve of him, Bamie did: Ibid., p. 112.
"Father is making peace between Russia and Japan": Ibid., p. 114.
T. R. realized he needed Alice: Morris, *Theodore Rex*, p. 380.
"primed and ready"; ALICE IN WONDERLAND: Alice Roosevelt Longworth, p. 71.
"massive old fellow who looked a little like a Bismarck gone to seed": p. 74.
"Alice at present travelling in particular for her health": Alice Roosevelt Longworth, p. 81.
"*White House Dove of Peace*"; "Alice's Adventures in Wonderland": Morris,

Theodore Rex, p. 401.
Edith too sent letters with political views: Cordery, p. 132.
"intelligence of about eight guinea-pig power": Morris, *Theodore Rex*, p. 393.
Hawaii and the Philippines would not be "menaced": Morris, *Theodore Rex*, p. 399.
"I have been carrying on negotiations": Roosevelt, *Letters to His Children*, p. 133.
"Oh my heart my heart. I can't bear it": Cordery, p. 130.
"Can you imagine any young girl marrying a fellow like that?": Peyser and Dwyer, p. 60.
When she and Nick got left behind: Alice Roosevelt Longworth, p. 79.
"Alice, I think I ought to know if you are engaged to Nick": Alice Roosevelt Longworth, p. 88.
"Your losing your temper": Cordery, p. 131.
"My little Alice that was really mine": Ibid., p. 137.
T. R. consented and by then, Edith was resigned; "I did not know officially that I was engaged": Ibid., p. 134.
"I was not surprised in the least": Ibid., p. 142.

Chapter Twenty-two

"The most valuable present": Alice Roosevelt Longworth, p. 110.
"didn't issue his awful ban before the string of pearls from Cuba arrived": Rixey, p. 162.
bought them in Paris for twenty-five thousand: Cordery, p. 143.
"I ought to know it is too wonderful to last": Ibid., p. 154.
"I will talk more about politics with you next month": Ibid., p. 252.
"with wholly absorbing love": Ibid., p. 155.
"who's going to be Alice's husband": Ibid., p. 152.
"Before you were born": Ibid., p. 156.
lace saved from her mother's wedding dress: Ibid., p. 157.
As the music played: Alice Roosevelt Longworth, p. 113.
"Alice looked remarkably pretty and her manner was very charming": Cordery, p. 158.
"notable stiffness": Morris, *Theodore Rex*, p. 427.
"Louis should roam at will": Alice Roosevelt Longworth, p. 114.
"I want you to know that I'm glad to see you leave": Morris, *Theodore Rex*, p. 437.
climbed out the Red Room window: Cordery, p. 160.
"the hills were mildly sloping": Cordery, p. 167.
"I do not believe that Nick told you"; "I think Sister is much improved by her marriage": Ibid., 164.
when Bamie felt Theodore was threatened in any way": Rixey, p. 273.
"He's a darlin' man": Ibid., p. 276.
Alice said she was terrified: Cordery, p. 180.
She hired a spiritualist: Ibid., p. 187.
a period Edith called "a suffering time"; he felt his "blood boil"; "I am so angry with the infernal little Cuban republic": Dalton, *A Strenuous Life*, p. 320.
Among them were six Medal of Honor recipients: Ibid., p. 322.
No Black woman had ever been entertained: Morris, *Theodore Rex*, p. 203.
"power tends to corrupt": Ibid., p. 554.
"I tell you I felt mighty pleased with my daughter": Cordery p. 182.
"They are sick of looking at my grin": Ibid., p. 191.

Chapter Twenty-three

"Teddy, Teddy, Rough and Ready": Cordery, p. 469.
"Mrs. Longworth looked tired and even angry": Ibid., p. 178.
"We are surely drifting decidedly apart": Peyser and Dwyer, p. 83.
"They didn't quite lock me up": Teague, p. 158.
"Don't hurt him. I want to look at him": Sylvia Morris, p. 386.
T. R. told Alice what an interesting experience it had been: Alice Roosevelt Longworth, p. 217.
"It was the bitterest sort of blow for Father": Ibid., p. 226.
THE OLD LION IS DEAD: Renehan, pp. 221–222.
Pilots from the field where Quentin had trained: Ibid., p. 222.
"It would be foolish to think that he could ever *really* die": Sylvia Morris, p. 437.
"She is still the Princess Alice": Peyser and Dwyer, p. 157.
"Alice's news was rather a blow": Sylvia Morris, p. 462.
the Longworths chose the name Paulina: Ibid., p. 463.
"With all the gossip going around": Cordery. p. 321.
ALICE RULES NICK OUT: Peyser and Dwyer, p. 159.
"I saw sister in Washington": Cordery, p. 340.
Paulina developed a stammer: Ibid., p. 361.
he went to Auntie Bye in his wheelchair: Rixey, p. 290.

Chapter Twenty-four

later admitted to Kermit: Peyser and Dwyer, p. 229.
"It's the greatest thrill of my life"; Alice didn't like him: Ibid., p. 242.
"Paulina was coming to live in Washington": Ibid., p. 257.
"For months after Paulina died"; "It nearly killed her": Ibid., p. 260.
"feeling like an extra piece of baggage": Cordery, p. 476.
"I should have been a grandmother, not a mother": Peyser and Dwyer, p, 261.

Epilogue

Her aunt Gracie left Alice a written description of the day she was born: Teague, p. 4.

Photograph Credits

Grateful acknowledgment is made for permission to reproduce the following images:

Frontispiece: *Alice Roosevelt, 1888*, courtesy of Sagamore Hill National Historic Site, National Park Service, Oyster Bay, New York

Insert:

Alice Hathaway Lee, Getty/MPI

Alice as a baby, courtesy Sagamore Hill National Historic Site, National Park Service, Oyster Bay, New York

Studio portrait of Alice Roosevelt and her aunt Bye, courtesy of the National Park Service, Theodore Roosevelt Birthplace National Historic Site

Alice Lee Roosevelt, age six, courtesy of Sagamore Hill National Historic Site, National Park Service, Oyster Bay, New York

Alice with Theodore Roosevelt Jr., courtesy of Sagamore Hill National Historic Site, National Park Service, Oyster Bay, New York

Roosevelt children in fancy dress, photo by Barnett McFee Clinedinst, 1898, courtesy of Sagamore Hill National Historic Site, National Park Service, Oyster Bay, New York

The Roosevelt children with their pets, photo by Pirie MacDonald, 1900, courtesy of Sagamore Hill National Historic Site, National Park Service, Oyster Bay, New York

Edith Roosevelt, Getty/MPI

Roosevelt family portrait, 1903, courtesy of Sagamore Hill National Historic Site, National Park Service, Oyster Bay, New York

Alice in front of tree at the White House, photo by Frances Benjamin Johnston, courtesy of Sagamore Hill National Historic Site, National Park Service, Oyster Bay, New York

Alice Roosevelt's wedding: Getty/Hulton Archive

Alice Roosevelt Longworth wearing pearls, Getty/Corbis Historical

The Roosevelt family at the White House, courtesy of the National Park Service, Theodore Roosevelt Birthplace National Historic Site

Alice Roosevelt Longworth and two-year-old Paulina, Getty/Bettmann

Alice Roosevelt Longworth at eighty-five, Getty/Bettmann

Index

About the Author

Shelley Fraser Mickle fell in love with books when her grandmother read to her as a young child. Thinking of reading as the magic of silent language, she set her sights on being a writer. Her first novel, *The Queen of October*, was a 1989 New York Times notable book; her second novel, *Replacing Dad*, became a CBS movie; and her third, *The Turning Hour*, received a Florida Governor's Award as a suicide prevention tool in high schools. Her nonfiction books for children mark the beginning of her career in narrative history: *Barbaro*, a Bank Street Award winner, and *American Pharaoh: Triple Crown Champion*, named by the New York Public Library as one of the best books for children in 2017. Her first adult nonfiction book, *Borrowing Life*, was a Book Award finalist for the American Science Association. She is the mother of two grown children. Writing humorous essays about raising them led to her being invited by NPR in Washington to broadcast commentaries from 2000 to 2006. She lives with her husband on a farm in Gainesville, Florida, sharing life with a cast of animals.